On Mission

YOUR JOURNEY

TO AUTHENTIC

LEADERSHIP

On
Mission

JOHN BUFORD, Ph.D. & SEAN GEORGES, J.D., LL.M.

GREENLEAF
BOOK GROUP PRESS

For those who aspire to lead more authentically.

Published by Greenleaf Book Group Press
Austin, Texas
www.gbgpress.com

Distributed by Greenleaf Book Group

For ordering information or special discounts for bulk purchases, please
contact Greenleaf Book Group at PO Box 91869, Austin, TX 78709,
512.891.6100.

Design and composition by Greenleaf Book Group
Cover design by Greenleaf Book Group
Author photograph by Tarrah Georges

Publisher's Cataloging-in-Publication data is available.

Print ISBN: 978-1-62634-941-4

eBook ISBN: 978-1-62634-942-1

Part of the Tree Neutral® program, which offsets the number of trees
consumed in the production and printing of this book by taking proactive
steps, such as planting trees in direct proportion to the number of trees
used: www.treeneutral.com

TreeNeutral®

Printed in the United States of America on acid-free paper

22 23 24 25 26 27 28 29   10 9 8 7 6 5 4 3 2 1

First Edition

To all who gave us the precious opportunity to learn, the room to grow, and the privilege to lead in pursuit of many worthwhile missions: You have helped forge us into better leaders and more authentic human beings. We are deeply grateful.

Contents

Our Journey

We have written the book we wish we had during our own leadership journeys, which often felt as if they were more of an accidental trek through an unmapped wilderness. Had we been equipped with a foundational resource like this as we began to grapple with what it meant to lead and who we were as leaders, we would have been better prepared to lean into learning opportunities as they appeared, we could have avoided some wrong turns, and we could have moved forward with more speed, purpose, and confidence.

While understanding core leadership principles and developing a clear philosophy from which to lead matter a great deal, the nature of your learning journey is how you will progress; your life's experiences are the stuff of your education and the basis for your understanding. Our purpose in writing this book is to equip and support you on your unique journey to become a more authentic leader.

To help you understand who we are and where we've been, we'd like to share a brief summary of our own leadership journeys.

Since we first met at the age of eight, we have been best friends. The seeds of this book were planted as we stumbled through our youth in a small

Illinois farm town (there was no stoplight). Although we were barely aware of it at the time, we were beginning to learn important lessons about ourselves, human nature, teamwork, and leadership.

As high school athletes, we started to more fully appreciate the importance of leadership and teamwork. During our junior year, we endured a winless football season. While we don't enjoy reflecting on that season, it was a challenging experience that tried and developed our character. Despite that disappointment, we suited up again and played our senior year. The resulting winning season, in which we tied for the conference championship, profoundly shaped our understanding of loyalty, endurance, commitment, teamwork, and leadership. We learned what is possible when a group of individuals come together as a team and put their full faith and commitment toward accomplishing a mission they deem worthy.

Our individual family tragedies spurred us to look to a wide variety of men and women as role models: coaches, Boy Scout leaders, teachers, grandparents, and others. Along the way, we were exposed to diverse values and belief systems, character traits, and leadership styles. We began to pay close attention and learned to appreciate the many ways people influence one another and leaders practice their craft.

As we entered early adulthood and furthered our formal education—John in Marine Corps Basic Training and at a state university and Sean at the Naval Academy—we started to learn about leading and following in a more structured, comprehensive way. We both became Marine Corps officers, and after our military careers had run their courses, we continued our intentional leadership journeys in the fields of law, business, and postsecondary and outdoor education and through community service.

We learned to follow and lead real people in real situations with real consequences. At every step, we observed intently, read widely, and thought deeply about the nature of leadership and our opportunity to impact others. We mentored and were mentored. We coached and were coached. We taught, and we learned. To this day, we continue to be active students of leadership. Although we succeeded in many ways, we also experienced setbacks and failures and found failure to be nothing more than another learning opportunity. We traveled some different paths, but we've confirmed our fundamental agreement on our core beliefs about leadership, encapsulated in the following points:

- The essential concepts of authentic leadership are clear and universal, regardless of the nature of the mission.

- There is an inexcusable leadership vacuum in our society that is not being meaningfully addressed.

- No clear guide exists for those who want to embark on an intentional learning process to become a more authentic leader.

Rather than cursing the darkness, we committed to carrying our personal leadership responsibility to shine some light both on what it means to lead in an authentic way, and on the intentional learning journey each of us must take to lead well. As servant leaders, we are fully committed to leading authentically in our own lives and to developing leadership in others along the way. Equipping and supporting those who wish to lead is an important role that comes with being a leader. We created our own leadership development company to launch our initiative: appropriately named On Mission Leadership. We are now officially "on mission," working to equip and support leaders who have committed to their leadership development so they can lead more authentically and effectively in all areas of their lives.

Our society has failed to address leadership development in a meaningful way. Except for the military and a relatively few businesses and service organizations, little serious effort has been made to develop authentic leaders ready to serve in a wide range of missions. The organizations that truly embrace leadership development as a priority are rare. At the same time, no single program, however well designed, can effectively transform any human being into an authentic leader. Becoming a leader requires a personal commitment to a lifelong learning journey. Each of us must take personal responsibility for that learning journey, using the fabric of our own lives to develop our leadership capabilities. Becoming a real leader requires you to be intentional about your experiential learning. Open the books, watch the podcasts, and engage with your coach, while you also seek out and get real-world experience leading and following. Take charge of your learning journey; design it, create it, and live it.

Our hope is that the book you have in front of you will help illuminate what it means to lead as a servant and what it takes to more fully develop your ability to lead. This is our attempt to articulate what we know about leadership. Based on our combined eighty years of military and civilian leadership experience, we firmly believe it will light the way for you to begin—or to accelerate with renewed energy and focus—your own intentional leadership development journey.

Deepening Channels

I n our effort to shed light on the essential nature of leadership and the importance of a personal journey of development, we found inspiration in a passage from Robert Pirsig's *Zen and the Art of Motorcycle Maintenance*:

"I would like not to cut any new channels of consciousness but simply dig deeper into old ones that have become silted in with the debris of thoughts grown stale and platitudes too often repeated. 'What's new?' is an interesting and broadening eternal question, but one which, if pursued exclusively, results only in an endless parade of trivia and fashion, the silt of tomorrow. I would like, instead, to be concerned with the question, 'What is best?' a question which cuts deeply rather than broadly, a question whose answers tend to move the silt downstream . . . Some channel deepening seems called for."

Much ink has been spilled in the attempt to describe leadership and what it means to lead. We've read a great deal of it and have found much of it to be worth exploring. At the same time, we're often left feeling that much of what has been written is made up of "thoughts grown stale, and platitudes too often repeated," or "an endless parade of trivia and fashion" to quote Robert Pirsig. We challenged ourselves to dig deeper and focus on what really matters in leading so that we could provide you the fundamental understanding you will need to develop your ability to lead authentically.

There is nothing new under the sun when it comes to leading authentically, or in developing leadership competence and confidence. What unique value, then, do we bring to you? Our focus is on the practical. Rather than simply restating platitudes or advocating for what's new, we address the question of what is best. Our intent is to provide you with the clear insight and practical tools you will need to become a more authentic and effective leader. We crafted *On Mission* with one overarching goal in mind: To provide you with the solid foundation you'll need to successfully navigate your unique journey to authentic leadership. We will equip you to overcome both the real and perceived obstacles standing in the way of your leadership development as you meet the responsibility to lead in your own life. Our goal for you is ambitious, but if you pursue this path with intention and commitment, you can experience a deep transformation in the way you look at leadership and the way you lead in your life.

Our convictions about leadership were not shaped quickly or easily, nor were they derived from any single source or experience. In clarifying what is best, we mined our combined lifelong studies of academic research, professional literature, leadership and management texts, historical accounts, and case studies. We also tapped into our own rich experiences in a broad spectrum of fields with a range of missions, from the serious to the mundane, and from the perspective of the diverse cultures to which we've belonged, from the hypercompetitive to the benign. We reflected on our decades of teaching and learning, coaching and being coached, and leading and following adolescents, young adults, and adult professionals of many demographics and backgrounds. What we have learned and what we present to you is the product of these experiences.

Three important truths ground this book:

First, leadership is about people. People are inherently social beings who respond positively to authentic leadership and who perform at considerably higher levels as interdependent members of healthy teams with a clear mission focus.

Second, the leadership concepts that form the foundation for authentic leadership are clear, practical, and universal in their nature and application, regardless of the environment or the team's mission.

Third, each of us is on an individual learning journey with respect to our own leadership development. The intentionality and quality of that journey will determine how we develop as leaders. Deep learning requires deep experience; those experiences can yield wisdom; the application of that wisdom will enrich your life and your ability to serve the people around you as you move to accomplish your shared mission.

If you approach the information and exercises in this book with intentionality and commitment, you will shape a powerful, clear leadership perspective, which is that of a servant leader. Armed with this empowering servant leadership perspective, you will be better equipped to find the answers to the questions you develop along the way. We also offer time-tested tools and insights that will sustain your forward progress as you navigate your unique leadership journey. If you take this learning journey seriously, you will embark on an intensive and deeply personal developmental process that will continue for months, years, and ultimately a lifetime. We have never met an authentic leader who believed they had completed their learning journey.

To get to the whole truth of what it means for you to fully develop your own leadership capabilities, you've got to go beyond an intellectual understanding of concepts and principles. While understanding is an important starting point, you must internalize that understanding by working through the experiential side of your learning. Applying your understanding to your life's experiences is required. That's a key part of the "becoming" process. We will challenge you to seek out opportunities to experience both leading and following the lead of others. There is no substitute for these kinds of experiences, so roll up your sleeves and get at it! Your growth as a leader rests squarely on your own shoulders. The pace and progress of your leadership development will be determined by your level of commitment and effort.

The process of becoming a more authentic leader is invigorating, creative, and enriching. It will transform and expand both who you are and your capacity to engage constructively with those around you. Along the way, you will learn, relearn, evaluate, and reevaluate your beliefs, assumptions, principles, and practices. The wisdom you develop will form the basis for your conduct as a leader. Since you will never completely master the practice of leadership, it's important that you get to work immediately.

To lead more authentically, you will need to get comfortable moving beyond your comfort zone. Real learning and growth take place when you push the boundaries of your current set of habits, experiences, and understandings. That's where you are compelled to consider and adopt thoughtful ways of engaging with your teammates, understanding your team, its culture, and the environment it operates in. Along the way, you will strengthen your relationships and deepen your knowledge of yourself and your teammates. Get comfortable with pushing that envelope through committed action.

Your personal and professional comfort zone ends where your fear of failure or rejection now rests. You, and you alone, know precisely where that is. We can assure you that failure, rejection, and mistakes are rarely fatal. Learning, growth, wisdom, competence, and confidence await you and your teammates as you continue to expand the boundaries you've set up in your life and as your team moves beyond its current practices. Challenge yourself. Challenge your teammates. Get comfortable being uncomfortable.

One of the ways to push your current boundaries is to ask yourself some tough questions. Here are a few to consider as you gear up for your intentional journey:

- How would I engage with others to increase their commitment to our team's mission?

- How would I engage with my teammates to influence their actions consistent with our team's culture?

- How will I gain greater leadership competence and confidence?

- How will I know if I am leading more authentically?

- How will I help others develop their leadership capabilities?

When you get intentional about your leadership journey, you will begin to develop answers to these important questions as you develop the tools, skills, and confidence to navigate your own path to becoming more authentic as a human being and as a leader.

Clarifying expectations is an important leadership responsibility, so we want to be clear about what we expect of you: We expect you to commit fully to your developmental journey and, armed with that commitment, to move forward with resolve. Our personal choices and commitments directly influence the quality of our lives, the depth of the relationships we cultivate, and the people we become. You have choices to make and commitments to keep. If you take full personal responsibility for the opportunity now to become a more authentic leader, regardless of your background, experience, or the nature of your team's mission (personal, professional, community), you will accomplish remarkable things in your life.

As with every worthwhile accomplishment in life, the outcome derives from a decision to commit. Commit yourself and your resources (your time, your attention, your energy, and your discipline) to the journey ahead, and see it through as you move toward your destination. Starting right now—yes, we mean *today*—exercise your personal power of commitment to launch a powerful, intentional development process.

Leaders are also responsible for creating a clear, vivid vision of the way ahead. When this vision comes to life in the minds and hearts of your teammates, you can influence their behavior, actions, and commitment in powerful ways. Our vision—and the vision of On Mission Leadership—is simple: A community of authentic leaders committed and prepared to serve. If your leadership journey helps you to become a part of this broad community of servant leaders, we will have accomplished something significant. But first, let's do some groundwork.

REFLECTION

If you have not yet started a journal, do it now. Format doesn't matter, but make sure it is within reach throughout the day; you never know when an insight or a source of inspiration will present itself. And trust us, they can be fleeting. Start with a focus on leadership (you can expand later), and title your journal "My Leadership Journey." It is valuable to commit to an achievable discipline on when and how often you will write (each morning, at night before you go to bed, after you've had a chance to reflect on an important experience). Most importantly, though, get started. Start right now. We will give you some prompts along the way.

Part 1

Groundwork

CHAPTER 1

You Are Now Being Called to Lead

The ability to lead authentically, to *move* another human being to commit to and act in support of a shared mission, is one of the most valuable known to mankind. We are not talking about the narrow impact one can have on others using incentives, manipulation, threats, or fear. That is not leadership. We are focused on something far greater, far deeper, and much more profound: the deep influence which comes from serving those you share that mission with, whether they're at home, at work, or in your community.

You've undoubtedly heard the phrase *You need to lead!* at important turning points in your life. Whether it was whispered urgently in your ear by a parent or loved one or written in an e-mail by a friend or colleague, these words can hit hard. However, nothing will happen until you make a deliberate decision to take ownership of your responsibility to lead; until you finally hear, in your own voice, in your own mind, "I need to lead!"

When that occurs, you'll know it's time for you to step up and fill the leadership gaps in your life, at home, at work, and in your community. No other human being walking this Earth can step into your shoes, in the context of your life and your relationships, and lead from where you stand. But your failure to step into that gap will leave a dark, gaping hole for others to overcome. While that may sound a bit dramatic, it is the truth. Now is the time for you to shift from being a mere passenger on an unintentional, accidental journey to taking full responsibility for your intentional, deliberate learning journey. If you need a wakeup call, this is it! Your alarm clock is going off and your cell phone is ringing; the days of being a bystander are over. You need to lead—and lead authentically.

MIRROR CHECK

Learning to shoulder your leadership responsibilities by showing up as an authentic leader is one of the most important aspects of your life. But here's the problem: No one is going to materialize out of the blue and prepare you for leadership. You've got to do the work. It's up to you to invest your time, attention, and effort in shaping a deliberate leadership journey. Each of us has important responsibilities to provide leadership to our family members, our teammates, and our colleagues. Each of us has a responsibility to *serve* the people in our lives in bringing about important outcomes and accomplishing critical missions.

You've probably experienced what it is like to be a part of a team, or a group which calls itself a team. But real teams that function at a high level require authentic leadership. Without the influence of committed, authentic leaders, a team will inevitably fall short of operating at its true potential, and what could have been accomplished will never materialize.

There is a crucial question you need to answer as you begin your intentional leadership development journey: *Why should I develop my ability to lead?* We lead to bring greater purpose to our lives and value to others by joining our energy, experience, and passion with theirs. In that sense, leadership is a powerful creative force, creating a team where there was only a group of independent human beings, and creating results and outcomes out of hopes and dreams. Once you understand the purpose you wish to serve, you will find yourself operating at a higher level, one where your personal mission and that of your team is aligned. We call that a state of being *on mission*. When you are on mission, you can lead others in a powerful and authentic way, as a servant. It is then that you can most effectively tap into the best of those who share a team's mission.

There will be important points on your journey where you must pause and focus on the reflection in the mirror to get some clarity about the person looking back at you. Self-knowledge is needed on the path to authenticity as a human being and as a leader. Although you will continuously learn and evolve, you need to understand your motivations, values, ethics, and your core beliefs about the people around you. That is important inside work that no one other than you can accomplish.

Let's do some reflecting. Find a quiet space without interruptions. Consider what is driving your desire to grow and develop as a leader. Discovering what is behind your wish to become more authentic in how you lead will directly impact the depth of your commitment to this learning journey. Consider what is really driving you to lead:

- Am I simply curious about leadership?

- Do I want to bring about a constructive change in my personal relationships at home, work, and in the community?

- Do I think developing my leadership abilities will make me more valuable on the job and accelerate my next promotion?

- Does the act of serving others as a leader hold intrinsic value for me?

- Am I interested because no one else is stepping up?

There are no correct responses to these questions. Your answers are your answers. Your personal motivation may be simple or complex; it may be purely selfish or more selfless. We aren't judging. At this point, the important thing is that you begin to look inside your head and heart to identify and understand what moves you to learn and develop.

Your initial motivation for leading may very well transform into something deeper as your personal leadership journey unfolds. You may find yourself, on a sliding scale, moving from *purely selfish* to *purely selfless*. As you come to fully appreciate what it means to lead in an authentic way (serving your teammates in accomplishing a shared mission) and embrace what will be required of you to lead authentically (humility, love, trust, respect, attention, effort and commitment), your reason to lead may shift. Opening to that possibility is an important part of your journey.

After you've defined, with honesty, your current motivation to develop your leadership capabilities, you can begin to seek answers to some important questions around what leadership is and how you approach it:

- Why are you paying attention to the subject of leadership?

- How do you define leadership? What does it really mean to lead?

- What leadership examples (both good and bad) have you had in your life? What did you take away and internalize from those examples?

- How effectively do you lead now in the range of roles in your life?

- Why does *your* ability to lead matter—to you, and to others in your life?

- How might leading more authentically affect your relationship with and impact your teammates, your family, and your community?

These are good starting questions, and you've probably got more. That's great. Write your questions down in your journal if they feel important to you. Work through some answers to those questions and write those down. You can revisit these during your learning journey, and watch your answers develop.

We can't give you the answers to these questions, because they relate specifically to where you stand and how you view things *now*. You will explore and develop your answers. You may have to look back into your life's experiences and pull some insights and wisdom gained from the bag of memories you may have hidden in the attic. There may be some things you'd rather forget from your unintentional, fractured leadership journey thus far, but be assured, there is wisdom to be gathered, refined, and applied to your ongoing journey. This is what your journey is for. It won't always be easy going, but we will be with you as you set out to make sure you get a good start. We are going to share our insights, experiences, and learning with you. While we are certain these will help you find what you need, you alone must do the hard work required to nail down your responses as you set out on your learning journey.

LEADERSHIP MATTERS

We can tell you, conclusively, that *leadership matters*. We can also assure you that the quality of *your* leadership matters. It matters not only to you and to those you engage with in your personal and work life, but to all of us. In a larger sense, we are all connected like never before, and we now have a personal stake in how your leadership journey unfolds. When you lead in an authentic way, influencing others through acts of service in the context of real relationships, your impact will extend well beyond the people you are now engaged with. That influence will reverberate through them and their relationships, influencing people and events well beyond your current scope of relationships and responsibilities.

Consider, for a moment, the potential impact of your leading as a part of a team of leaders in accomplishing a meaningful shared mission. Oh, the things you could do as a member of a real team infused with authentic leadership! Let your mind play with this for a while. What could *we* (you and your family or your home team, you and your work team, you and your project team, you and your organization, you and your community) create if we operated as a real team, aligned with a clear and compelling mission, in service to one another? The possibilities are truly endless.

Now, think of the opposing scenario. If you chose *not* to lead in your life (it is a choice) and, instead, decided to maintain a limited role as an independent contributor with little or no responsibility for others, the outcome would be quite different. You would likely develop superficial personal and professional relationships; you would lose opportunities for personal and professional development and satisfaction; personal, professional, and team potential would go unrealized; problems would go unrecognized, and their solutions would not be developed; you would experience a profound level of frustration; and accomplishing your team's mission would become less likely. In short, a decision to avoid the leadership responsibilities that now exist in your life would create a much darker picture. We urge you to lean into and embrace the leadership responsibilities that now await. We need you to lead in your life. More importantly, you need you to lead in your life.

Here's another thing. The level of leadership on any team will shape the likelihood of a positive outcome for that team and for all involved. The quality of leadership on a team determines not only the level of a team's performance but, often, its very survival. James O'Toole, in *Leadership A to Z*, may have said it best: "All groups and organizations are capable of getting by without leadership. But all high-performing organizations have leadership."

A collection of individuals with a common goal or objective may be able to function at a maintenance level without real leadership. It *may*. But neither its individual members nor the group as a whole will be able to explore, develop, or reach their performance potential without leadership. Such a group will certainly not develop the capabilities and resilience necessary to weather adversity, identify and overcome obstacles, and successfully take on opportunities. Keep this in mind: A collection of individuals does not become a *team* simply because they call themselves one or wear the same uniform. Forming a team is a social transformation requiring leadership.

Without the impact and influence of an authentic leader, confusion will become the order of the day, goals and objectives will remain poorly defined, roles will quickly misalign with the group's mission, expectations will remain uncertain, resources will be squandered, individual interests will diverge, and responsibility gaps will appear and widen. At best, groups without leadership will struggle mightily to reach even a level of mediocrity in their execution and performance. At worst, such groups will collapse under the weight of internal and external pressures, often crumbling upon first contact with adversity. Without the elevating, aligning impact authentic leadership provides, the combined effort of even the most talented collection of individuals will soon grind to an unceremonious halt.

DRIVING A SHIP OR LEADING A CREW?

When I joined the faculty of a small liberal arts college, I was anxious to meet the president. My previous experiences had taught me the significant impact leaders can have on organizations, ranging from small teams on wilderness expeditions to complex bureaucracies deploying thousands of people over several continents. I wanted to find out what type of person was in a position of leadership for our organization.

During my first faculty meeting, the college president presented the state of our school and the plans for the upcoming academic year. The first thing I noticed was his executive presence—his impeccable dress and apparent command of the room. For twenty-five minutes, he spoke from his written notes with precision and conviction, laying out enrollment projections, financial metrics, plans for capital projects, and the like. He obviously knew the business side of higher education, and I felt we were in good hands.

But something didn't sit right with me. I noticed he referred to our college's community members as "the trustees," "the staff," "the faculty," "the student body." He even referred to our college as "the institution." His third person communication style was new to me and drew my attention.

Over the next few years, our college, like many small colleges at the time, experienced a contraction in enrollment and faced significant financial challenges. I had learned from experience that adversity requires unity of effort. But in various interactions with my colleagues, I began to sense their angst and distrust—an us versus them mentality with the administration as the adversary. I then began to understand the impact of the president's language: Rather than pulling his team together to achieve a common goal, the faculty and staff seemed to be looking over their shoulders to avoid some dangerous personal fate at his hands. This deep level of distrust and the cynicism it produced manifested in gross inefficiency and a downward spiral in team performance.

A few years later, our college found it necessary to hire a new president. What struck me from the beginning was that the new president spoke in the first person, in terms of ownership and shared responsibility. "The enrollment numbers" became "our student enrollment." "The board of trustees" became "our trustees." "The faculty, the staff, and the student body" became "us" and "we." Predictably, our college community began to pull together, and performance improved dramatically.

continued

> The contrast between these two leaders—in their words and deeds—was stark. When I interacted with the previous president, I felt I was a passenger on his ship, dependent on him to keep the ship afloat. When I interacted with the new president, I felt I was part of a crew, and my captain was counting on me and my teammates to help steer the ship to an exciting destination.
>
> —John

When authentic leadership is present and actively engaged, a group of individuals can transform into a team aligned with a common mission. Only then can these people begin to explore, align, and tap into their individual and collective performance potential. Leadership is not the responsibility of a single person; leadership is a shared set of responsibilities we have to one another. Leadership enables and supports human beings in the effort to accomplish a shared mission. In real teams, individuals transition from merely being (and seeing themselves as) independent contributors, to being interdependent teammates. As interdependent members of a team, people begin to commit to the shared mission and find the support they need to reach for higher levels of effectiveness. Authentic leadership helps to create an entirely different reality.

The quality, breadth, and depth of leadership within any team directly affects that team's ability to develop, execute, adapt, react, and respond to dynamic environmental pressures. This is especially true when rapid change is the order of the day, as it is for all of us. Authentic leadership is a critical ingredient in the success of any team-based human endeavor. Leaders work to develop and drive individual and collective energy, effort, creativity, and commitment, providing meaning and clarity where there would otherwise be darkness and confusion. In a competitive world, the presence of authentic leadership in any organization is a matter of existential concern.

AWARENESS

All of this begs the question: *How do I become a more authentic leader?* Warren Bennis, one of the most highly regarded leadership scholars and a modern pioneer in the field of leadership studies, captured an important truth about the process of becoming a leader: "The process of becoming a leader is much the same as the process of becoming an integrated human being. For the leader, as for any integrated person, it is life itself." There you go. Your life is where you go to learn leadership. Becoming a leader is the same process each of us goes through when we choose to actively and intentionally develop ourselves as mature, fully formed human beings. It is the context of your relationships within your home, your workplace, and your community (in the broadest sense of the word), that provides your best training ground. That's where your leadership journey takes place; where your experiences and learning will occur, if you will approach the process with energy, awareness, and intention. Open your eyes to what is happening within you and around you as you engage with the people in your life.

Your leadership journey has actually been underway for some time. It has most likely consisted of a patchwork of fragmented and often accidental experiences, which you've stitched together so that you can draw some lessons. Some of these experiences left a lasting impression while others went largely unnoticed. That is all about to change, if you will apply yourself with intention. We are now challenging you to become much more intentional, to increase your level of awareness a couple of octaves and take full ownership of the quality of your life's journey. Only then can you transform it into something powerful and practical.

Opportunities to learn and grow as a leader are all around you. Let's say you are following another's lead. Great! Your leadership school is now in session! You can learn important lessons about the leader–follower relationship while following. The military uses this method extremely effectively. When you are in a situation where you are following, you get direct experience in what works and what doesn't. Pay attention to what your positional leader is doing and saying to influence your thinking, to shape your actions, and to affect your level of commitment to the team's mission. Observe closely how their level of commitment and their behavior (words and deeds) impact your own behavior and commitment (for good or ill). Which of their behaviors affect you positively (if any)? Which are counterproductive? What is this person doing or not doing that moves you and resonates with you? What does this "leader" (whether this person is, in fact, *leading*, is an entirely separate question) do that has the effect of moving or inspiring you to contribute to the team's mission? At the same time, what are they doing to demotivate, deflate, or cause you to disconnect? You can glean much wisdom from your past and present experiences, even those in which you follow the lead of another in your family, at school, at work, or in your community.

When you are presented with the opportunity to lead—and you will—pay close attention to your thinking, your assumptions and beliefs, your communications, and your behavior. What impact do you have on others through what you say and do? How are you influencing their level of commitment, their performance, their relationships with you and your other teammates, and the team's performance overall? What is the quality of your impact when you choose to *serve* your teammates in how you lead?

Up to this point in your life, your leadership journey has likely been more akin to a random collection of fractured experiences. Let's change that. Starting right now, the way forward can be completely different. How will your learning journey transform? It's simple: Take full responsibility for the quality and nature of your journey. When you accept responsibility to shape it, you will create a set of learning experiences that are intentional and powerful rather than accidental and often disheartening. Start right now, where you are, with what you've got, and begin to shape your intentional journey. That is when the magic begins. As if awakened from a deep sleep, you will begin to uncover leadership principles, teachers, mentors and coaches, and resources all around you. Your own life is the best school of leadership development, so start there.

AUTHENTICITY

You will notice our frequent use of *authentic* to describe real leadership. There is nothing tricky or proprietary in our use of the word. When we refer to authentic leadership, we are simply talking about the genuine article—*real* leadership, as opposed to a pale reflection of leading. Authentic leaders find ways to *serve* their fellow teammates through real relationships founded on deep trust and mutual respect, in support of a shared mission. When you work to build those relationships, your teammates will respond in a sustained, committed, and often inspired manner; they will be disposed to permit you to influence their behavior and commitment. When you find ways through your actions and behavior to serve them with humility, and when you consistently make visible your commitment to them and to your team's mission, you are leading in an authentic way.

People do not respond in sustained, committed, or inspired ways to artificiality, posturing, threats, or manipulation. Most human beings have highly sensitive antennae when it comes to inauthentic attempts to influence their actions and behavior. We have a strong aversion to someone who is not being real about their motives or commitment, and when there is any doubt, we tend to keep them at arm's length until we can satisfy ourselves one way or another. Ralph Waldo Emerson said it best: "What you do speaks so loudly that I cannot hear what you say." You cannot deeply influence another person by merely *appearing* to be a leader (whatever that means), posturing, pulling rank, or hiding behind a desk or a title. Instead, focus on your consistent behavior and actions; focus on earning trust through your consistent engagement and genuine relationship built on respect. Seek to become the real thing: an *authentic* leader.

Authenticity is a key aspect of what it means to lead. Don't try to learn how to carry yourself, communicate, dress, or walk "like a leader" or like you think leaders should walk, talk, and speak. Instead, do the work to *become* a real leader. That requires some committed internal work with your mind and your heart, which is the reason for your learning journey. An authentic leader engages in human ways with the people they seek to influence, from a place of humility which places the focus on others rather than self. That's a servant leadership perspective. A leader then invests their time, attention, and effort in building that relationship, committing their energy, talents and abilities to their teammates so that the team can move toward mission accomplishment. If you hope to have real influence as a leader, engage constructively with your teammates as an authentic person. Authenticity is a key foundation for leadership.

WHAT IS LEADERSHIP?

Getting clear on what leadership is, and what it means to lead, is of paramount importance as you begin your intentional learning journey. Let's place some important definitions in your backpack before you head out. Although you can find numerous definitions online, we invite you to consider the definitions we've carefully crafted based on our combined eighty years of education, training, and experience. We'll develop them more fully later, but we want to get them in front of you now. They have served us well. Here you go:

> *Leadership is who you are and what you do to influence others to commit and act in alignment with the mission.*

> *A leader is one who carries a personal responsibility to serve others in support of a shared mission.*

> *You lead through relationship, in service to others, in pursuit of a shared mission.*

We encourage you to write these down in your journal and consider them thoughtfully as you move forward. They seem simple enough, don't you think? Can leadership be that simple? Yes, it *is* that simple! But it isn't always *easy* in its application in your life. Here's the rub: While understanding the definition is simple, learning how to lead in the context of your life requires an ongoing, never-ending journey of discovery. Gaining *competence* and *confidence* in leading requires you to embark on an intentional learning journey in which you explore and discover your best and highest role in service to your teammates, in alignment with your team's mission.

LEARNING TO LEAD ISN'T EASY, BUT NOTHING WORTHWHILE IS EVER EASY

First things first. Before you can start your intentional leadership journey in earnest, you must accept the reality that you now have important leadership responsibilities to and for the people in your life. Leadership is not a set of responsibilities limited to the workplace. That narrow workplace focus is a part of the problem with leadership development. Leading doesn't involve your taking on certain behaviors or perspectives during the workday, then setting them aside on your drive home. You don't drape a superhero cape over your shoulders as you arrive at work each day, then leave it on your chair as you finish your shift. Your responsibility to lead extends across the full spectrum of your life, in virtually all relationships. When you fully embrace that personal responsibility with humility, not as "the leader" but as "a leader" (a person capable of leading), your intentional learning journey can begin. Leading becomes authentic when you embrace it as a core aspect of who you are in relation to your world.

Many people fail to lead because they don't even recognize the leadership responsibilities in their lives. Make no mistake, you are being called to lead—and to lead *now*—at home, at work, and in your community. The real question is whether you will accept that call and show up as a person ready to carry those responsibilities. This is ultimately your choice, but we strongly encourage you to embrace it. When you do, a rich learning journey will begin, and a deep transformation will begin to unfold.

Your learning journey will accelerate when you permit yourself to be vulnerable, human, adaptive, humble, empathetic, and resilient. As you navigate through your leadership experiences as a servant leader, your level of self-awareness and your awareness of others will increase. Since you are focused on those you serve rather than yourself, you will become more deliberate in your approach to people and events, understanding that what you do and say, and what you don't do and don't say, has impact.

As we touched on earlier, your learning journey will require you to mine your past experiences for insights and wisdom to apply as you move forward. You will become more mindful as you engage in leading and following experiences along the way. When you combine your thoughtful reflections with ongoing reading, study, analysis, feedback, and coaching, your development will accelerate. When you lead as a servant with a mission focus, you will naturally open your mind and heart to others, out of a deeper sense of humility. With humility, which is required for you to serve in your leading, you will actively seek feedback and value input from those around you.

Let's talk about humility a bit more, because it can be a sticking point for many who think they want to lead. Humility is a quality necessary for anyone who wishes to lead as a servant, and it is critical to your learning journey. True humility can be difficult for some; pride, ego, fear, and insecurity can get in the way of real learning. But these are also choices. Exercise discipline. Choose not to let your sense of self-importance become an obstacle on your journey! Leading is about serving others in pursuit of a shared mission, which means leading isn't about *you*. You cannot lead authentically if you place your interests above those of your teammates. Leading is about *us*; it's about serving your teammates so you can advance together toward your team's mission. Get over yourself and get on with the privileged work of serving your teammates.

Personal growth and development can be uncomfortable because we don't always like what we see when we take a hard look at our motives and behaviors. During your intentional journey, you should get comfortable with—or accept the discomfort that comes from—looking closely at yourself in the mirror. Know this: You will fall short, and you will make mistakes. That comes with being human. Your primary responsibility in those situations is to learn: to feel the sting, reflect on the experience, and learn and adjust. Leading does not require you to be perfect; it requires you to be a thinking, feeling, authentic, committed human being. Along the course of your learning journey, the person in the mirror must continually be evaluated, held accountable, questioned, and challenged.

Yes, you will try and sometimes fail, but you will grow and learn the entire time. You will develop the discipline and habit of getting back on the horse after you've fallen; you will reflect on and evaluate the experience and try again. You will sometimes even make the same mistakes again, but your judgment will improve, you will recognize a better way more readily the next time, and you will more easily gather yourself and try again. It will be hard, but it will stretch you.

Depending on where you are right now, you may need to reevaluate the way you see yourself and the people around you. Your journey will require you to take a closer look at how you define both your relationships and the nature of your responsibilities to others. This journey won't be easy, but few worthwhile things ever are. The process of becoming an authentic leader will require your deep, committed attention, focus, and effort. You must try, fail, and try again. We can, however, assure you that the journey will be worthwhile.

CHAPTER 2

What Brings You Here?

Your leadership learning journey has been underway for some time, although you probably weren't aware of it. Some of the most important things you need to know about leading people will come from looking back, thoughtfully mining the life experiences you've *already* had. In those experiences, both the difficult and the happy, there is much to be learned about who you are, about human nature in general, and about how we influence one another. When you start exploring your past experiences from the perspective of an intentional learning journey, you will be better equipped to draw practical wisdom to apply as you move forward and lead. The key is your intentionality and your self-honesty. Start sifting through those experiences. This is a part of the challenging work required for you to lead authentically.

REFLECTION

- ✓ What are the three most important leadership lessons you've learned from your experiences leading and following others?
- ✓ What behaviors did you exhibit that were most significant in the three leadership lessons you chose?

Once you begin to understand the forces and conditions that influenced you up to this point, you can deliberately shape the journey ahead. Awareness and intentionality are sources of real personal power, and we urge you to wield that power. To become a more authentic leader, take responsibility for your leadership development journey by beginning to mine your past experiences, applying that learning in the present, and leaning into the future.

WHY LEAD, AND WHY NOW?

Leading authentically centers on the personal responsibility you carry to and for others. Since leading is about *us* in accomplishing a shared mission and not solely about you or your interests, it seems fair to ask why anyone would want to lead at all. What is your *why*? Your answer to that question matters. A clear, deeply held sense of purpose will provide fuel for your leadership journey, especially when it becomes difficult.

Perhaps you developed a sense of responsibility to and for others early in your life based on the influence of a family member or a teacher; maybe the call to lead came from a defining event that brought to light your need to lead, or to lead at a higher level. Reflect on the reason why you are moved to become a more authentic leader. Embrace it; it's an important part of your life story.

Understanding where you are right now will help you to clarify why you are moved to become a more authentic leader. Your interest may come from a more immediate situation, such as one of the following scenarios:

YOU'VE RECENTLY BEEN PROMOTED TO A POSITION THAT REQUIRES YOUR LEADERSHIP

Your contributions have been deservedly recognized, and you've recently been promoted to a leadership position. Here's the problem: It's no longer just about your performance. You now have leadership responsibilities to and for a team. The people around you are looking to you for leadership and support. Unfortunately, you've had little or no leadership preparation and precious little time or resources to develop your leadership capabilities on your own. You don't know who you are as a leader, you are unclear about your first step, and you don't know where to go from there. The game has changed. You need to lead. Now. You are asking yourself an important question: *How do I start?*

YOU HAVE NO FORMAL LEADERSHIP TITLE, BUT YOU SENSE YOU HAVE A RESPONSIBILITY TO LEAD

You are a solid teammate, and although you have no leadership title, you have a sense that you can contribute to your team's performance at a higher level, as a leader. But without a title or formal authority, you don't believe you can engage as a leader. You believe you can impact your teammates' performance by leading from within, but you are uncertain about how to lead your peers. You are asking yourself an important question: *Without formal authority or title, is it possible for me to lead others?*

YOU ARE IN A FORMAL POSITION OF AUTHORITY, BUT INDIVIDUAL AND TEAM PERFORMANCE IS LACKING

You've got a position with a title and a level authority. Some of your teammates are not performing at their potential, and their commitment is in question. The team's performance is subpar, and accomplishing the mission appears unachievable. Morale is low, communication is suffering, your teammates lack confidence in your ability to lead, and frustration is the order of the day. You know you need to lead more effectively, based on a simple evaluation of your team's performance. You sense that a dramatic shift in your behavior and actions needs to occur, but you lack the competence and confidence to lead effectively. You are asking yourself an important question: *How can I turn this team around?*

YOU CONSIDER YOURSELF TO BE A GOOD LEADER, BUT YOU ASPIRE TO BECOME AN OUTSTANDING LEADER

You have gained some level of leadership knowledge, experience, and competence. You've had a measure of success with people who believe you lead competently, but you know it's not enough. You want to lead more authentically and effectively in every aspect of your life. You are convinced you can have a greater impact on your family, your community, and your work if you do so. You've decided to commit to elevating your ability to lead. You're self-motivated to move in that direction, and you have the courage to venture outside your comfort zone where you know you can change and grow. You've already begun to ask yourself an important question: *How do I lead at a higher level?*

Do any of these scenarios describe your situation? If so, great! You are in a perfect place to start your intentional leadership development journey. If not, read on. Regardless of your circumstances, one thing is clear: You are here now because you want to become a more effective leader.

WHAT IS INEFFECTIVE LEADERSHIP?

When you are authentic in your leadership, you can serve at a higher level, and you can have a deeper impact on your teammates as you serve them, propelling the team to accomplish its mission. To more fully appreciate what it means to lead authentically, let's first briefly explore the other side of the coin.

Unfortunately, most people have observed or been subjected to ineffective or inauthentic leadership in their work and personal lives. While you can still learn a great deal about leading from those who led poorly or not at all, these can be hard experiences. We've gained wisdom not only from our own failed efforts to lead but from those who failed in their own effort. Some of our worst leadership experiences have motivated us to look deeper and work harder.

You may have attempted to lead others in ways that were, well, ineffective. If so, you are now in a judgment-free zone and a place of deep learning. Tease your learnings from those experiences. Perhaps you've observed or experienced others whose attempts to lead were inept or counterproductive. Reflect on those situations, answer these questions, and take note.

REFLECTION

Think of a situation in which you've observed or experienced ineffective leadership:

- ✓ What specific behaviors did the person attempting to lead exhibit?
- ✓ How did these behaviors impact you, other members of the team, and the team's performance?
- ✓ What impact did this have on both short- and long-term results or mission accomplishment?

A few thoughts about ineffective leaders are worth mentioning, although we won't stay here long. Ineffective leaders rarely come in the form of an evil villain from a Disney movie. They can be smart, capable, and passionate, but something is missing. *They lose sight of the people.* They sometimes lack humility, and ego can become a primary driver of actions and behavior; they may be uncertain, aloof, or distant, and more comfortable investing their time and energy in activities other than building authentic connections and relationships with their teammates; they may lack a servant leader perspective, and rather than serving their team in accomplishing the team's mission, they seek to have their own interests served by the team.

Ineffective leaders are not evil, they are *negligent.* That negligence is often born of ignorance. One of an authentic leader's primary responsibilities is to care for their people: the human beings who do the lion's share of the work required to accomplish the team's mission. Ineffective leaders fail to comprehend how important it is to create a supportive culture and build human relationships that align and drive individual and team performance. Ineffective leaders often fall back on management principles and processes. You cannot manage a group of people up a mountain. You can, however, lead a team to the summit. There is a world of difference between the two.

Ineffective leaders often have a difficult time building meaningful, healthy relationships with their teammates, or they simply don't see the real value in doing so. Rather than serving their teammates through leadership, ineffective leaders approach their leading with an "org chart" perspective, a top-down approach, managing people like a herd of cattle. Instead of exhibiting authentic leadership behaviors grounded in mutual trust and mutual respect, ineffective leaders hide behind a title or wield their power, office, or experience like a weapon. They attempt to control behavior to obtain compliance and desired results through policies, financial incentives, or threat of punishment.

Authentic leaders, on the other hand, choose to influence their teammates' behavior and commitment through real relationships based on commitment to people and the mission, fueled by love. In the end, the inability (or unwillingness) of ineffective leaders to form constructive relationships with their teammates leaves no foundation from which to serve, resulting in low levels of influence, low levels of commitment, and poor results.

A fully committed, mission-focused team will outperform an over-managed, tightly controlled group of individuals every day of the week. Compliance with performance standards may be relatively high with heavily managed groups (in those rare instances when expectations are made clear), but that performance can best be described as "merely compliant" rather than "fully committed." In heavily managed groups without authentic leadership, members focus on "full compliance" rather than "full commitment." While they may sometimes surpass designated expectations, acts of creativity, leadership, and initiative become rare; they are neither sought nor encouraged. Relationships among teammates are typically shallow, as people engage as prescribed in the org chart. Relationships with management are often strained if they exist at all, and they can easily become adversarial when the pressure is on. Individual and team development opportunities, which typically pay off only in the longer term, tend to be undervalued and are among the first to be cut when things get tough. Mission accomplishment usually follows the path of team relationships: As relationships fail to develop and deepen, the mission becomes more and more elusive.

The ugly truth is that most people haven't been properly prepared to shoulder their leadership responsibility. Much of what makes positional leaders ineffective is the result of ignorance rather than an intent to do harm. In fact, few with leadership titles have given serious consideration to what it *means* to lead another human being in the direction of a team's mission. This lack of meaningful leadership preparation typically results in a scenario resembling the following: When placed in leadership situations, the unprepared find themselves frozen in a state of flat-footed panic, unsure of how to take the first step. They then do one of two things: either avoid the responsibility entirely or fall back on what they have observed in others. Inaction can be fatal, but following the example of a dysfunctional or ineffective leader is malpractice. And once ineffective leadership establishes a toehold, it is often difficult to root out, as it spreads and begins to cement itself within a team's culture.

Aspiring leaders can fail for a variety of reasons, but ignorance is often at the heart of the matter. Some have yet to develop a healthy leadership philosophy. Others have only a weak understanding of what leadership is and how it operates. In virtually all cases of failed leadership, there is a common characteristic: The positional leader has not committed to their own leadership development journey; they have not gained the competence to lead. Competence precedes confidence. First you must develop a base level of *competence*, which comes from your journey, through intentional experiences leading and following (learning through success and failure) combined with focused education and training. You then begin transforming a degree of competence into a sense of *confidence*.

Don't fall into the management trap; you cannot meet your leadership responsibilities by applying management practices and processes (e.g., issuing written policy statements, establishing key performance indicators, developing project management spreadsheets, and micromanaging performance). These things may come in handy to meet your management responsibilities. However, leading real people in real situations with real consequences will require you to establish meaningful relationships, apply core leadership principles (which we will help you discover), and consistently exhibit authentic leadership behaviors (e.g., engaging in respectful, meaningful two-way communications with your teammates). Save your management skills for inanimate objects, or systems and processes. Lead people. Manage things.

A few words about popularity and leadership. Seeking popularity to gain influence with your teammates is a fool's errand for a leader. When you seek popularity, you seek something which is fleeting and fickle; you are one unpopular decision away from losing the foundation for your influence. Popularity is a feeling about you, an opinion often based solely on what you either have done or can do for that person. Popularity may serve as a foundation for your influence for a brief season, when all is well with the world and the sun is shining, but when the weather changes and adversity rears its ugly head, it will fade in a heartbeat. Popularity is not the equivalent of an authentic, trust-based relationship which is forged over time. Aspiring leaders who try to befriend their teammates as the foundation for their influence cling to the misguided hope that if everyone is happy and in harmony, the team will operate reasonably well. That's a mistake. If it were that easy, we would simply offer up cupcakes and balloons every afternoon (if that's what the people wanted).

Then there are those—and you know who they are—who, out of ignorance, cruelty, or plain laziness, resort to various forms of emotional or physical manipulation to get others to do what they think needs to be done. These aspiring leaders seek to shape and influence their teammates' behavior not through the power of example or leadership, but through the promise of reward or the threat of punishment. They use the blunt force of authority or sanctioned power as a weapon to force certain behavioral responses. Make no mistake about it: This approach is nothing more than manipulative, and manipulation has nothing to do with leading authentically as a servant.

Healthy relationships built on mutual respect and trust must be the foundation of your leadership influence. The problem isn't that those who fail to lead lack intelligence or drive; most of them are very intelligent and highly ambitious. But they haven't done the work required to shoulder the responsibility of leadership. Authentic leaders lean into that work, which includes gaining a clear understanding of who they are and honing their interpersonal skills. That's an important part of the learning journey required to reach a level of authenticity in your leadership. You've got to do that work so you can be authentic and build genuine human relationships with your teammates, the foundation for influence.

If you fear the idea of engaging with people on a deeper level, you will either engage superficially or avoid it entirely. Authentic leadership requires you to influence from a foundation based on love, respect, and trust, rather than fear and control. A fear-based belief that people are best kept at arm's length will render an aspiring leader wholly ineffective. Any attempt to carry out your leadership responsibility without the ability to form healthy relationships will ultimately fail. You cannot lead from that place.

WHAT IS AUTHENTIC LEADERSHIP?

Authentic leadership is simply *real* leadership: the genuine thing. Authentic leaders are mission-focused servant leaders. They serve their teammates through trust-based relationships in ways which influence their teammates' behavior and commitment to the team's mission. The positive impact of this leadership is profound, and mankind has not yet developed a reasonable substitute for it. When we lead from a place of service to our teammates, through real relationships where trust has been extended and earned, our personal example and our respectful engagement gives us a solid foundation for legitimate influence. Authentic leaders in support of a meaningful mission become a part of something greater than themselves: a valued member of a real team engaged in a collaborative, focused effort to accomplish something with purpose.

When authentic leadership is present within a team, leaders can create an environment which produces a valuable set of emotions. In servant-led teams, members feel *empowered* (because they have a voice and they share authority, responsibility, accountability, and leadership), *cared for* (because attention, energy, and resources are invested in their emotional and physical well-being), *elevated* (because much is expected of them and they are properly supported in meeting those expectations), *energized* (because energy is invested in them, and they are aligned with a meaningful purpose and surrounded by committed teammates), *challenged* (because they are asked to push beyond their present personal and professional comfort zones), *respected* (because they are treated with respect, given the opportunity to earn it, and required to extend that opportunity to their teammates), *trusted* (because they are extended the opportunity to earn trust and led by those committed to being worthy of trust), *valued* (because their individual and team contributions are important and are recognized), and *loved* (because they are loved; servant leaders lead with love).

When leaders successfully create such a culture and conditions, people perform individually and collectively at their highest levels; they become more collaborative and more committed; the team strengthens and becomes more resilient, enabling it to operate under the most adverse conditions.

These feelings arise naturally from real conditions promoted and protected by authentic leaders. These feeling grow and deepen over time, and the culture surrounding such teams strengthen and support everything the team does. But the foundation for such a culture must be real: common values, deep commitment, mutual trust, a shared sense of responsibility, a service orientation, and meaningful support.

Authentic leaders help their teammates develop their individual potential and their unique capabilities, including their own ability to lead. They help their teammates get the right things done in a team context and move them individually and collectively toward accomplishing the shared mission.

How do leaders accomplish such remarkable things? The concept is simple, although the work is hard: Authentic leaders serve their teammates through who they are and what they do, in the context of the team's mission. In serving, leaders *elevate* their teammates' individual performance and the team's ability to execute. Leaders establish healthy, genuine relationships with their teammates and find ways to influence through the power of their consistent example and the level of their commitment to the team's mission, and they positively impact others through their constructive influence, founded on these relationships.

Leaders keep the team's mission in their line of sight, which helps align their decisions and actions with the mission. Everything you do and don't do, and everything you say and don't say, in service to your team, is done in the interest of serving your teammates so that they are more capable of moving in the direction of the mission. Authentic leaders help their teammates explore, develop, and ultimately expand their individual potential. As a direct result of an authentic leader's service, commitment, and their consistent example, those served should be on the path to becoming better leaders *and* better human beings.

How will you know if you are leading well? There are many ways to measure this. Mission accomplishment and team performance metrics are important, since mission accomplishment is the "leadership top line." But you will also want to pay close attention to some other aspects of individual and team performance and health. Take measure of the individual performance of your teammates, and how they are progressing in the development of their individual skills, knowledge, and confidence. In addition, pay attention to their willingness to take on leadership responsibilities, and observe their ability to lead; these are among the strong indicators you are succeeding. Observe how well they work together, communicate, and collaborate. Take a measure of the team's morale and its level of energy. Finally, evaluate the culture to determine whether it supports the mission and properly reflects the values and ethics you seek. Develop some of your own indicators. Check them regularly. And don't shy away from seeking direct feedback on your leadership from your teammates.

The authentic leaders we served with over the course of our lives shared some important qualities. Chief among these was a deeply held passion to serve others. These leaders consistently sought opportunities to serve their teammates in a variety of ways and in every interaction. They placed a primary emphasis on how they could best serve their teammates, not on how they could be served. They clearly embraced a servant leader perspective, evident in their actions and decision-making, and considered their responsibility to lead to be a sacred privilege rather than an onerous burden. Every authentic leader we encountered was primarily moved to lead by a strong personal drive to serve others in accomplishing a shared mission.

At its heart, leadership is a responsibility of service, one that naturally results in profound acts of service. It is not something done *to* others but something done *for* and *with* others. To understand the nature of real leadership, you've got to appreciate that the influence you seek to have with the people around you arises from your *service* to them. This servant leadership approach is at the opposite end of the spectrum from the autocratic, command-and-control approach most of us see and experience.

Leadership is sometimes mistakenly viewed as an exercise of power *over* another person: a matter of control. The question people who hold such a belief ask of themselves when considering how to engage as a leader is also flawed: *What must I do to make this person do what I want them to do?* Servant leaders, on the other hand, seek to answer a different question: *How can I best serve my teammates so they are more capable, more committed, more responsible, and better able to lead others in accomplishing our mission?*

If leading as a servant is a new concept to you, you are not alone. You may not have heard of it before now, and it is likely you have rarely seen it in your personal or work world. Even though it may seem foreign right now, stay with us. Your path to becoming an authentic leader begins and ends with the desire to serve. Service is the essence of authentic leadership. Everything rests on that perspective.

PEER LEADERSHIP

The young adults I work with in leadership development programs often express hesitancy or anxiety in leading their peers and tend to feel inadequate, acknowledging they don't know more than those they are being asked to lead, or they feel they aren't "better" than the others. Some fear coming off as "bossy." I remind them these feelings result from a misunderstanding of the role leadership plays and the central principle of service required of leaders. Leadership is an essential and shared team function. Anyone who takes on the role of a leader is *serving* the team—not *imposing their will on* the team. Leadership is a service to others, not an imposition on others.

–John

THERE ARE NO BORN LEADERS

This is a perfect time to dispel a common notion that certain people are somehow born to lead. That idea is absolute nonsense. Reject it. Part of the problem with this idea is that it can become a self-limiting belief for those who may feel, for a variety of reasons, that they did not receive the leadership gene at birth.

Our experience has taught us something quite different: Leaders are made—and largely self-made. Becoming a leader is a continuous, creative learning process. It comes through a series of experiences (and your responses to those experiences), which shape you into a person who can build healthy relationships with others as you work to accomplish a shared mission. No one is born with that skill set. Those who become authentic leaders apply themselves in developing their inherent leadership capabilities through a lifelong, intentional process—through a learning journey.

THE LEADERSHIP GAP

The depth of your ability to lead matters a great deal, not just to you but to those around you. Let's put *you* in a broader perspective for a moment. Our society is suffering from a deep leadership effectiveness gap, one that runs across generations, disciplines, and organizations. We aren't going to dive into how this situation came about, because we are interested in finding a solution. We've had enough of the collective cursing of the darkness; it's high time to light a torch. We are all adversely impacted on every front by this lack of authentic leadership.

Unfortunately, much of the prevailing literature surrounding leadership development, along with most training programs, narrowly focus on the world of business. Leadership is not a responsibility limited to the business world, nor is it a responsibility restricted to a few members of an executive team or to those designated by the HR department as "high potentials." Leadership is a shared set of responsibilities; it rests with every team member, regardless of rank or title. Authentic leadership at every level within our teams, our organizations, and our communities and families should be fostered and developed as a priority. Navigating dynamic change and overcoming daunting challenges requires *leaderful* teams, teams filled with people capable of leading, rather than with only one or a few. A narrow focus on developing leaders at the very top of an organization is, quite simply, short-sighted and ultimately counterproductive.

Regardless of how we all got into this mess, it is now time to change the game. Leadership is a shared set of responsibilities carried by the many rather than the few. Those responsibilities arise across the spectrum of our lives and must be a core competency of people at every level on every team. We are beset by daunting challenges. It sometimes feels as though we are individually and collectively under attack and surrounded by seemingly insurmountable problems, with adversity weighing in from all sides. Shall we sit idly by and just try to ride out the storm? No!

Please don't get us wrong. Bad things, like a swiftly moving global pandemic, do occur. Such is the nature of life on Earth. Effective leadership is critical to a team's success, but it is not a panacea for all ills. Many outside forces which have nothing to do with the quality and depth of human leadership can adversely impact a team's performance, its ability to execute at high levels, and mission accomplishment. A rapid technological development can upend a once highly competitive business or render a product or service irrelevant overnight. Likewise, a lack of critical talent in a key position may stunt a team's ability to navigate through change or accomplish its mission.

When you peel back the layers, however, you will often find the absence of deeply imbedded, authentic leadership is a root cause of the failure to anticipate and overcome adversity. Regardless of the forces or conditions that oppose our progress, ongoing attempts to *manage* our way through a set of daunting challenges will fail without authentic leadership at every level. Our individual and collective ability to recognize opportunities, overcome obstacles, develop creative solutions to problems, and successfully navigate rapid change rests on the quality of leadership within us and around us.

Without authentic leadership, teams will not fully form in the first place, and those teams that do exist will be weak, incapable of operating at their highest levels. Without authentic leaders, they will not be able to cooperate and collaborate at the level required to adapt to rapid change and overcome daunting obstacles. Instead of advancing with purpose in the direction of its mission, such a team will be paralyzed or crushed by adversity. Positional leaders who have not developed the understanding of and capability to lead authentically will be frustrated by their inability to constructively influence the members of their teams. They will find it virtually impossible to create the environment and strengthen the culture necessary to make meaningful progress and take advantage of opportunities as they arise. While some individuals may find ways to improve their own performance, without a mission-focused servant leadership presence, the team will be unequal to the task.

REFLECTION

✓ Do you expect yourself and others to lead?

✓ Do you believe you have the potential to lead?

✓ Do your teammates have the potential to lead?

Your answers to these questions will reflect the value you assign to the importance of leadership in general and to your personal leadership development. If you regard leadership as important to team performance, you are much more likely to meaningfully work toward your leadership development.

YOUR LEADERSHIP COMPETENCE MATTERS

Leadership is key to the success of every highly functioning team. Authentic leaders, through who they are, what they know, and how they engage with their teammates, can strengthen their teammates' commitment to the team's mission. Authentic leaders help transform a mere group of individuals into a team, they inspire higher levels of mission-aligned individual and collaborative performance, they create and strengthen healthy cultures, and they develop people both personally and professionally.

Such teams have higher levels of resilience, are more capable of responding constructively to change, and are ultimately more successful by a significant order of magnitude. Teams filled with authentic leaders execute at levels that consistently surpass groups operating in a leadership vacuum. Leadership is *critical*. Virtually everything you accomplish in life is done by, with, and through other human beings, in pursuit of a common mission.

In essence, leaders *enlist* others to join them on a journey to accomplish a shared mission that is compelling, one that is beyond the capacity of any single individual or group of individuals. Those who agree to join the adventure choose to commit, to one degree or another, to that mission. Leaders then engage with their teammates in ways that deepen that level of individual commitment to the common enterprise. Members of the team then focus on finding ways to bring more of their skills, talents, hopes, aspirations, energy, and strengths to the effort. Leaders help create that environment by embracing their sacred responsibility to *serve*, which allows them to tap into the best of who their teammates are and what they can contribute to support mission accomplishment.

WHAT'S THE PAYOFF?

So, what's in this for *you*? That's a fair question! Although leading authentically requires you to move in the direction of selflessness, putting the interests of your teammates ahead of your own in the context of the team's mission, there are many reasons to become an authentic leader. The bottom line is this: You will develop the ability to have a greater impact on individual and team outcomes not only at work, but at home and in your community. Leading as a servant is both a perspective and a skill set that can enrich relationships across the entire spectrum of your life. Developing your leadership competence and confidence can be a game changer for you, both personally and professionally. When you become more comfortable carrying your leadership responsibilities, you will find ways to serve that have greater meaning to you. You will literally become more valuable to the people in your life and the teams on which you serve. You will find that your relationships will strengthen, and your experiences will deepen. Authentic leaders are rare in this world (a reality you will begin to understand as you lead as a servant), and embracing leadership as a deeply held personal responsibility can open doors to opportunities which would otherwise be closed.

We have seen many situations where extremely intelligent and highly experienced people hit a wall in their personal or career progression because they lacked real leadership competence. You can only go so far as an individual contributor, regardless of the level of your gifts and talent, before you hit that wall. Your ability to lead, to influence others in the pursuit of a shared mission, enables you to operate at a higher level and with a greater impact on a team's performance. The more competent and confident you become as a leader, the more valuable you are to any team, organization, community, or cause.

When you learn to lead authentically, you will find yourself living more deeply and engaging at higher levels with the people around you. Leadership is a relationship built on trust which comes with certain responsibilities. When you have earned your teammates' trust, they will more readily permit you to influence their behavior. As you move forward on your learning journey, you will find yourself seeking opportunities to stretch your capabilities, and you will take on roles of greater responsibility. This will present you with more opportunities to have a constructive impact on the people you serve and the team around you. You may very well find, as we have, that your ability to lead authentically will be one of the most significant factors in your professional growth and in the richness of your personal life. We've seen this play out time and again in many different situations, for ourselves and others.

CHAPTER 3

It May Not
Be Your Fault

While it may not be your *fault* that you were not properly prepared to lead, it is your *responsibility* to prepare yourself to
lead. Virtually every human being has the potential to lead
authentically, but many fail to commit to developing that potential, or once
developed, allow it to atrophy. It's highly unlikely that someone will come
floating into your life, take you under their wing, and walk you through a
structured set of experiences to help you build your leadership competence
and confidence. That's dreamworld thinking. You are going to have to take
the initiative and run with this. Your leadership development is up to you.

This is probably the point at which you want to shout out, "But you don't
understand! Not only have I not been properly prepared to lead, I don't think
I have what it takes to be a leader!" Sorry, but we're not letting you off the
hook. These unfounded perceptions about yourself are largely your own creation, and you must get them out of the way, now. Self-limiting beliefs only
serve to hold you back from achieving what you otherwise could.

When you equip yourself with a firm resolve, develop an empowering service perspective in your leadership, bolstered further with a clear mission-focus, you can overcome your own self-imposed limitations. Like all doubts that seek to hamper our growth and performance, if they are not put in their proper place, they will become well-entrenched excuses to justify inaction. We (you and us) are simply not going to allow that to happen.

Since your limiting beliefs are ultimately self-defeating and counterproductive, and since they don't hold up under scrutiny, we've taken the liberty of compiling a list of common self-limiting beliefs, along with some sample rebuttals. We encourage you to add your own:

I DON'T HAVE THE PERSONALITY TO LEAD

There is no right personality for leadership. Your unique personality is an important aspect of who you now are and how you engage with the world. Continue to refine and improve yourself, but be real. Be authentic. Leadership is less about your personality and much more about your perspective, your thought process, your level of resolve and commitment, and your behavior.

I'M AN INTROVERT

Whether you feel you fit in the introvert or extrovert category, you are in good company when it comes to authentic leaders. Some of the world's best leaders are introverts, and some are extroverts. The rest fall somewhere in between.

I LACK CHARISMA.

Authentic leadership does not spring from your innate charm or magnetism. Focus, instead, on being a fully formed, genuine human being, one who carries their responsibility to serve others with humility.

I'M THE WRONG GENDER, RACE, OR ETHNICITY; I'M TOO OLD

There are no right physical attributes for leadership; leaders come in all appearances, shapes, sizes, and ages. Physical characteristics do not, in any way, make or define a leader. You can be an effective, authentic leader regardless of your gender, your race, or your ethnicity. And you're never too young or too old to learn, grow, serve, and lead.

I LACK THE NATIVE ABILITY TO LEAD

If you are truly interested and willing to commit to your learning journey, you can learn to lead. There is no such thing as a leadership gene. Scientists have searched for it and have not been able to find it because it does not exist. Every leader is made and largely self-made through their own experiences and intentional effort.

I LACK SELF-CONFIDENCE

Good. That's the perfect place to start. Authentic leaders are humble, and confidence must be earned. Sacrifice who you are for who you wish to become. But you should also remember that the notion that a leader must be the smartest or most talented person in the room is a myth.

I'M A POOR PUBLIC SPEAKER

Leaders focus on real communication, the kind that builds authentic relationships with other human beings. Leadership effectiveness does not rest on your ability to give speeches before large crowds. Communicate clearly and keep it simple if you wish to connect.

I DON'T HAVE THE RIGHT PERSONAL BACKGROUND

There's no such thing. It doesn't matter where you came from. Leading has nothing to do with your heritage or social standing in life. We have all experienced unfortunate circumstance and adversity in our lives. Tough experiences can reward you with deep insights about yourself and compassion toward others. Actively mine those experiences and collect the invaluable wisdom that can often only be gained through adversity. Your family background also doesn't matter; leadership does not spring from a pedigree. Even your education doesn't matter; you don't need a certificate or degree to become an effective leader.

I'VE HAD POOR LEADERSHIP ROLE MODELS OR NONE AT ALL

Welcome to the experience shared by most leaders. You can learn valuable lessons about leadership from those who led poorly. You can also understand, in no uncertain terms, the impact poor leaders (or an absence of leadership) can have on a family, a team, or an organization. Mine those experiences. As you move forward on your leadership journey, keep your eyes open. Good role models are out there, and, if you seek them out, they can be readily found.

I'VE HAD NO FORMAL LEADERSHIP TRAINING

Good. You and over 7 billion other people on this planet are in the same boat. That is a great place to begin an intentional learning process.

MY ORGANIZATION DOESN'T SEEM TO VALUE LEADERSHIP

The truth of the matter is every organization places great value on leadership, although it may not express that value or invest in its development. If you will commit to your learning journey, the people around you will recognize your leadership impact and will come to appreciate it.

I'M NOT IN A LEADERSHIP POSITION

Perfect. Leadership does not spring from, or rest upon, a title or position. Leadership operates through your relationships in the way you think, serve, and engage with others. If you will lead authentically in the direction of a shared mission, you can and will influence others.

I'M NOT ON A TEAM, OR I DON'T THINK MY TEAM HAS A MISSION

Yes, you are, and yes, it does. So long as you are connected to other people with a shared purpose, like family, friends, colleagues, or community members, you are a part of a team. And every team has a mission, whether it has defined that mission or not. All you have to do is understand what that team is and what it exists to do, and find your leadership role.

I'M NOT IN BUSINESS OR IN THE MILITARY

The nature of your mission doesn't matter. Leadership is desperately needed everywhere.

REFLECTION

- ✓ Write down your own self-limiting beliefs. Be honest about naming what you think is holding you back.
- ✓ Take a few moments to challenge those beliefs and craft a rebuttal to each.

Do you see how this plays out? None of these potentially crippling beliefs stand up to close scrutiny when it comes to your ability to become an authentic leader. If you want to develop your capability to lead, and if you are willing to commit to your journey, you can make it happen. The life events that have happened to you, and the decisions you've made on your journey so far are valuable. They brought you to this point; they served to shape you and make you unique. They've given you a perspective and provided you a set of human experiences unlike anyone else's. So, bring those unique experiences, insights, knowledge, and your heart and hands to this learning process. During your leadership journey, you will come to understand deeply and without question the nature of leadership and why there may be many *reasons* but *no excuses* for not developing your leadership capabilities.

WHO YOU ARE IS WHAT YOU DO WITH WHAT YOU HAVE

You can learn something valuable from every person you encounter and from every experience you have. Once you understand the leadership essentials and commit to your development journey, you will realize that school is in session every single day and in virtually every situation. With a heightened sense of awareness and a greater understanding of what leaders do, daily interactions with others will yield valuable insights and provide critical instruction for you on your leadership journey.

To take full advantage of your learning process, keep the following in mind. Although these points may seem simple enough, they will require a sustained level of work and attention:

- Commit and open yourself up to being an active learner.

- Pay attention to those behaviors that inspire and strengthen individual and team performance and create an alignment with the shared mission.

- Take note of behaviors that impede individual and team performance and that serve to diminish morale and undermine mission accomplishment.

- Reflect regularly on your observations, and take mental and written notes on your leading and following experiences.

- Learn from everyone you encounter.

- Act on your learning.

To develop your leadership capabilities more fully, you must take an active role in your development. Trust us: Nothing less will suffice. Your life is your school, and school is always in session. The process of becoming a leader and developing your ability to serve your teammates as a leader requires a great deal of work and attention.

Authentic leaders seek out learning opportunities to obtain deeper professional and organizational knowledge. They find ways to practice and refine their leadership craft, regardless of their rank or title. But leadership is not the responsibility of a few; it is the shared responsibility of the many, of every member of the team. When leadership within a team becomes a core responsibility and competency of as many people as possible, remarkable outcomes are likely. Leadership can and must be democratized and spread everywhere. *Leaderful* teams can include our families, our communities, and our places of work. Such teams are stronger, healthier, more capable, and more resilient when authentic leaders recognize their responsibility and opportunity to lead, in real and powerful ways, at every level and in every place.

You have experienced what happens when leadership responsibilities in a family, a workplace, or a community go unrecognized or ignored entirely. You may have watched a talented, even brilliant individual contributor with an impressive title who failed to constructively impact the performance of individuals and teams. For a myriad of reasons, most of which are self-imposed, this person was unwilling to embrace their personal responsibility to lead or to commit to their own leadership development. The result was likely a series of personal and professional failures. Such people never made the critical leap from *individual contributor* to *leader*. This need not be your story. If you choose to embrace your leadership responsibilities, and if you intentionally commit to your leadership development journey, you can write a new chapter for a richer life.

NO EXCUSES

I had grasped the concept of taking complete responsibility for my own actions before I entered the Naval Academy. But taking full responsibility for results that were outside of my control without making excuses was a new concept. During my first year at Annapolis, we were limited to one of five basic responses in replying to upperclassmen: "Yes, sir (or ma'am)!"; "No, sir!"; "I'll find out, sir!"; "Aye, aye, sir!"; and "No excuse, sir!"

It was the last of these, "No excuse!" that sometimes struck me as unfair. What if the real reason I couldn't get something done wasn't my fault? What if I had personally done everything in my power to accomplish the required outcome, but it didn't happen due to forces (or persons) outside of my control? What if the task was poorly defined or impossible to accomplish with the time and resources available to me? What if the cause of the failure was another person's inaction or negligence? What if I had not been trained or prepared sufficiently? What if I actually had an excuse?

After some hard experiences and considerable reflection, I finally figured out what the upperclassmen were trying to teach us. They were trying to teach us a critical lesson about the often-unforgiving nature of a leader's responsibility. They were imprinting on our minds and placing in our hearts a fundamental truth about the nature of leadership: Leaders are accountable and responsible not only for their own individual performance but for the performance of their teammates and for the team as a whole.

There may be *reasons* why you have not developed your leadership abilities, but there is no *excuse*.

—Sean

Similarly, leaders can claim no excuses for failing to accomplish the mission. Leaders own their actions and the outcome. While there may be many *reasons* behind a particular failure, there is never an *excuse*. Failure must become an opportunity to learn, recommit, and grow.

CHOOSE TO LEAD

Many things in life don't unfold unless you first make a choice. Once made, that choice and your related commitments alter everything that follows. Leading is an important personal decision, but unless you consciously and intentionally decide to lead and take ownership for your leadership responsibilities, your positive impact on those around you will be significantly and unnecessarily limited. Opportunities, both personal and professional, will be lost as a result of your decision, and your relationships will shallow rather than deepen. Those around you will suffer as a result of your failure to show up in life as a leader, in ways both big and small.

In a very real sense, *you* define your life's roles and determine the nature and extent of your responsibility toward others. This is one of those often-overlooked realities in life. But as soon as you embrace your leadership responsibility, some fundamental choices appear. For example, if you envision yourself as a person who is independent of and untethered to those around you, with little or no accountability to anyone else, you will likely conduct yourself in alignment with that perspective. Your view of your place in the world directly shapes your engagement with the people around you. This is what we mean when we say that the roles you embrace and the corresponding responsibilities you attach to those roles materially shape how you engage with others. This applies in our family, in our community, and with our teammates in the workplace.

To help you more fully understand the roles you hold with your teammates, ask yourself two important questions:

- What is the nature of my relationship to this person or that person? To all of my teammates?

- How do I define my responsibilities to them, if any?

Don't skip past your answer to that first question. It is a key part of how you decide to engage with those around you. This is how you define, build, deconstruct, or strengthen your social network (which, dare we say, extends well beyond your social media presence). We all continuously define and redefine the extent and nature of our relationships with the people in our world.

REFLECTION

✓ What is the nature of my relationship to my teammates?

» Independent or interdependent?

» Subordinate, coequal, or superior?

» Close or distant?

» Trusting or guarded?

» In what other ways do I define my relationship with my teammates?

In light of the nature of your relationship with your teammates, consider your responsibilities. What responsibilities do you recognize, accept, and act upon? Once you have thoughtfully answered the relationship question, you will need to consider the responsibility question. Answering this one is far more than a mere conceptual exercise; you are then going to work to meet those responsibilities.

How you define your relationships with others and your responsibilities toward them will shape your behavior. For example, while you may admit that you have a neighbor or child or significant other or teammate, you may define your set of responsibilities toward that person in ways that may or may not include leadership. Your personal definition of the roles and responsibilities you embrace serves to clarify your focus, your attention, your energy, and your actions. Choose carefully. Be thoughtful in how you define yourself with respect to the people around you. Everything you are and everything you do hangs on that definition. We firmly believe we are all called to lead in our lives. How you answer that call will make all the difference in the depth of your relationships and the quality of your life.

When you humbly and sincerely add "a person with leadership responsibilities" to the definition of who you are, pay attention to how the world transforms. You may be asking whether it is presumptuous for you to declare yourself a leader or to include leader in how you define yourself. Presumptuous? No. It is, in fact, *courageous* to do so. It is actually irresponsible not to define yourself as a person with leadership responsibilities in your life. Embracing your personal responsibility to provide leadership for the people in your personal, community, and professional life is critical.

Leadership doesn't spring from title or rank. You don't have to have some puffed-up belief in the extent of your own excellence or intellectual abilities. Just the opposite: To lead in an authentic way you will need a deep humility that makes it possible to place others above your own self-interests. Embracing your leadership responsibilities doesn't mean you must be in charge of any particular team. Defining yourself as a person with leadership responsibilities simply means you accept and embrace what already exists.

Once you make the decision to embrace your leadership responsibility, you can then fully commit to the exciting developmental journey that lies ahead. Few people, even those with impressive titles or positions, truly embrace their personal responsibility to lead. Be rare. Be special. Step up and lead. The way you define who you are and your responsibilities in those roles will directly shape your conduct and your engagement with your world. Choose to *lead*.

CHAPTER 4

It Starts with Your Commitment

While this learning journey may have been triggered by the desire to become a more authentic leader, your journey's ultimate goal is something even more significant: to become a more authentic human being, capable of leading in an authentic way. No, we didn't just move the goalpost. It was always there. Your journey will lead you to a deep and personal internal transformation in how you view yourself and your relationship with the people around you, especially those you share a common purpose or mission with. Although it will certainly transform the way you lead in your life, it will also impact every relationship in your life. You will be different. The real point of your learning journey is to develop yourself as a human being, so that you can bring your best self to a deeper level of engagement with those around you as you serve them to accomplish your team's shared mission.

To learn to lead authentically, you will be asked to bring your whole self to the task: heart, head, and hands—all that you have and all that you are.

REEVALUATE YOUR LEADERSHIP OPERATING SYSTEM

During your journey of development and discovery, you will unpack and reevaluate some of the basic leadership beliefs you've allowed to take root in your mind. We all have a system of assumptions and beliefs that drive our interactions with the people around us. We are often not fully aware of them all, but they still shape how we think and act. Whether sound or not, productive or not, based on solid principles or faulty thinking, these working assumptions have effectively become a part of your personal leadership operating system.

Many of our beliefs about people, relationships, and responsibilities sit just below the surface in our mind. As a result, we tend not to reevaluate them. They solidify early in life to form our working foundation for what it means to be in relationship to others, to follow and to lead. They help shape and define the nature and scope of our relationships with the people around us, informing our thoughts about human nature and fueling our understanding about what moves people.

But your understanding doesn't have to end there; you are now on an intentional and deliberate learning journey. Rather than merely accepting an accumulated collection of assumptions and beliefs, we challenge you to exercise a more disciplined approach. Take a closer look at the mental constructs you've allowed to take root in your head. Get them out and set them on the table. Put them to the test in a variety of situations. Just because they appeared to be true in one situation doesn't mean they are applicable to most people and situations. Be willing to analyze and reprogram your leadership operating system if necessary. Since leadership centers on building authentic relationships with people in the context of a shared mission, a realistic understanding of human nature—yours and others'—is required. This is an ongoing part of your journey. Leading is not about you (in that you are at the center); it is about your teammates and about the mission.

Learning how to lead, however, is about you; you must take personal responsibility for your growth.

Your developmental journey will take dedication and intention, and it will not happen overnight. No single coach, certification or degree, promotion, book, blog, podcast, webcast, seminar, or leadership development program can magically transform you into a leader. To be clear, we encourage you to thoughtfully incorporate all of those things into your learning journey; they can accelerate and deepen your development and also refine your understanding of leadership and of who you are as a leader. However, there is no shortcut. If anyone attempts to sell a one-stop solution to you, we strongly recommend that you save your money, time, and attention and step quickly away.

Your real development as a leader can only come the old-fashioned way—through a combination of active study, challenging training, out-of-comfort-zone experience, and purposeful reflection. One of the toughest lessons we learned during the course of our own intentional learning journeys was this: You must *earn* the ability to lead, every single day, through focused effort, dedicated study, meaningful reflection, and a thoughtful consideration of feedback, with a high level of personal commitment.

UNDERSTANDING, THROUGH EXPERIENCE, LEADS TO WISDOM

The purpose of your learning journey is to understand who you are as a human being; that understanding then moves you closer to who you are as a leader, and from that place, you can lead with wisdom. Gaining that wisdom requires you to actively learn from your own experiences. Experience develops the muscle memory you will need as you serve others in your shared mission.

Like Lewis and Clark, you will often find yourself in unknown territory, *terra incognita*, navigating without the benefit of an accurate map. Courage will be required. Press on. Seek to gain meaningful experience, whether in actively following another's lead, serving as a teammate, or in a leadership role. Keep your eyes and your heart open to what is happening in you and in those around you. Certain portions of your journey will be tough. They will be difficult. They will test who you think you are and what you have long believed. Don't despair. This is as it should be. The lessons will become clear over time, and the wisdom will accrue as you reflect. That's how we learn. We are each more courageous than we often believe. You will find the courage you need to navigate the course of your journey.

On a true journey of discovery, your mind is alert, and your heart opens up. As you pay closer attention to every experience and situation you encounter, you will notice what seem to be new sights, sounds, and feelings, even if you remain in the same physical or relational space. As with any journey of discovery, your purpose is to do much more than merely progress from one point to the next. Your purpose is to learn as you go, to understand more about yourself and your environment, to come to grips with what you really value as you clarify your core principles, motivations, strengths, hopes, fears, weaknesses, and explore your real and perceived limitations. You will inevitably encounter obstacles and those who will question your motives or express doubt, but you will also find supportive circumstances and allies. Press on. We assure you that you will find ways to engage with them in practical and creative ways, gaining invaluable experience and knowledge along the way.

STEP BEYOND YOUR COMFORT ZONE

Like most people with leadership responsibilities, you are probably settling somewhere within your leadership comfort zone, safely within the bounds of your own self-imposed (or other-imposed) limitations. We understand. It's warm and relatively safe in that place; you won't have to test your thinking or reevaluate your behavior. In fact, you may have worked hard to get to that safe place, to get that promotion, to get a spot on that team, to enter that relationship. Why not rest there for a little while? The answer is simple: There is no growth in your comfort zone. You must move beyond it to begin your learning journey.

To grow as a leader, you must also move beyond your current leadership mindset. If you don't, you will effectively place a ceiling on your development as both a human being and as a leader. When you are tucked comfortably in your personal and professional comfort zone, there are few challenges and little adversity. There is virtually nothing more to learn about yourself, about those around you, or about the environment in which you operate. In that place, there is no way to expand your capabilities or deepen your understanding of leadership. Most of us spend a great deal of time and energy protecting and defending our comfort zone, leading and operating from what we perceive to be a place of certainty. We challenge you to move beyond. Get your gear together, pack your bags, and move out. This is an exhilarating opportunity.

To effectively navigate your learning journey, you will need to have a personal stake in its outcome. You've got to bring a high level of desire, self-motivation, and personal commitment to this learning process—as well as a fair amount of courage—to move from what has likely been an accidental and unintentional collection of experiences to an intentional leadership development journey. Take a close look at your current assumptions and understandings about leadership and the behavioral patterns you've developed (or allowed to develop) in how you interact with your teammates.

We understand that most people don't like looking in the mirror for any length of time. The person staring back at us is not always the person we'd hoped to see. Becoming *authentic* about who you are and how you will lead requires you to fundamentally understand what you truly value, what motivates and demotivates you, what scares and inspires you, and what makes up your strengths and weaknesses.

If you are among the few and the fortunate, you have been given access to some level of ongoing leadership development support at your place of work, in your community, or from a coach or mentor you respect. That's great! Good for you! Take full advantage of that support and work hard to be an active, highly engaged student. But even if this is your situation, don't kid yourself. Regardless of the level of external support available to you, the final responsibility for your growth as a leader still rests with you. You will be the one to apply lessons learned, to press on during the remainder of your learning journey, and to fail and succeed and learn and try again. And remember, the absence of others to help you to learn how to lead or to otherwise support your leadership development is merely a fact, not an excuse. When you take full responsibility for your own intentional journey, you will learn and grow in an intense and authentic way.

Your leadership journey will require three key things from you:

- **Ownership:** Own your responsibility to lead by recognizing, embracing, and stepping up to meet that leadership responsibility.

- **Commitment:** Commit to your intentional leadership development journey.

- **Application**: Apply yourself in an intentional way to progress toward the goal of becoming an authentic leader.

Learning *about* leadership is essential to your development, but it is only the beginning. Learning *how* to lead is even more important. Your overt behaviors—what you say and what you do—have the greatest impact on the people you seek to influence. Your behaviors drive your leadership effectiveness, which is the ultimate goal. Your consistent behaviors and actions are what influence the members of your team to commit and act in alignment with your team's mission, and that is what leadership entails.

So how do you shape your own consistent behavior and develop constructive leadership habits? This is something you already know, but you may not have put it in words before now. First, *intention*. Second, *commitment*. The first step in shaping your behavior is to set an intention to learn how to lead. You must then commit to carrying it out.

If you are serious about squeezing all you can from your journey, which is precisely what we are challenging you to do, you must recommit every day. In the beginning, it may feel like a grind. You should expect that feeling. But you can be assured of this: Your transformation will come from that daily commitment and follow-through.

We have good news. Once you commit—*really* commit—magical things will begin to happen. Allies you had never recognized before will come to your aid. Resources you were previously unaware of will appear in your life. Opportunities to further your leadership development will begin to come into full view.

One of the ways authentic leaders influence their teammates is through their own level of personal commitment to the team's mission. When others sense your deep commitment, they tend to align with you, moved to step forward and offer their support. We are not suggesting you should simply kick back in hopes the universe will magically align; you've got to kick in with your own serious effort. Our strong conviction, based on long experience, is that your commitment will create an environment in which opportunities begin to conspire to carry you forward.

We've experienced the power of real commitment ourselves. This book and the leadership development team we've put together began with an idea; that idea has come to life, resulting in our growing impact on leadership development on a much wider scale. Once we made a real commitment and engaged in the hard work required to create a vision and build a team, opportunities to share our learning appeared and compounded.

WHAT IF I FAIL?

Commitments are not contingent on *what if*. Full commitments look forward and require confidence; they are made without debilitating doubt or worry. You decide you will do the thing, and then you commit to do the work. When you truly commit to your deliberate learning journey, don't leave yourself the option to turn and run, and don't play the what if game.

REFLECTION

✓ What does commitment mean to you?

✓ Where are you on a scale of 1 to 10 on your commitment to becoming a better leader?

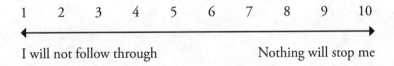

| 1 | 2 | 3 | 4 | 5 | 6 | 7 | 8 | 9 | 10 |

I will not follow through   Nothing will stop me

✓ Why did you pick the number you did, and what does that number say about your level of commitment to your journey?

✓ If you're not yet fully committed, what is holding you back from selecting a 10?

✓ What steps can you take right now to move yourself to a higher level of commitment?

FIND SOMEONE TO HOLD YOU ACCOUNTABLE

Accountability is a key element in strengthening your commitment. It requires you to answer to another human being (or team) for what you do and for your follow-through on what you say you will do. Leaders hold themselves accountable to their teammates for their example, behavior, and performance.

As you progress along your learning journey, we strongly recommend you find a supportive ally to hold you accountable as you implement the action steps necessary to achieve your goals. Choose someone who cares for you, someone you respect and trust. This person could be a family member or a close friend. Explain the commitment you've made to lead more authentically and share the intentional leadership journey you are now on. Enlist them to be a part of that journey as someone who will hold you to account for your progress.

REFLECTION

✓ Are you willing to ask a trusted colleague, close friend, family member, or coach to hold you accountable for implementing the commitments you've made?

✓ Who will you ask?

✓ How and when will you ask them, and what will you ask them to do?

ONE HARD THING

It all began with a simple comment. While playing catch with my stepson, who was nine years old at the time, I casually mentioned that I was going on a long bike ride that afternoon so I could complete my one hard thing for the day. He stopped mid-throw and asked me what I meant by "one hard thing." I explained that I'd made a commitment to myself to do something personally challenging every day, something I knew I needed or wanted to do, but that might be difficult or uncomfortable for me to complete.

"Like what?" he asked.

"Well," I said, "it could be something simple, like working out when I feel tired or tackling an issue at work that might be uncomfortable, like having a tough conversation with one of my teammates."

He nodded, and we continued to throw the ball back and forth.

The following day, when I got home from work, the first thing my stepson did was ask me, "What was the one hard thing you did today?"

Not only was I surprised he had actually paid attention to our discussion (you can't always tell with a nine-year-old), he seemed genuinely interested in my answer. I thanked him for asking me and told him I had put the finishing touches on a project at work that had been sitting on my desk longer than it should have.

He asked me the same question the next day, and the day after that, and the day after that. It became a wonderful part of our daily ritual. He was holding me accountable. Every day, he would ask me about my one hard thing for that day.

Since I knew he was going to ask, I made certain I had accomplished something that was above and beyond each day, something I likely wouldn't have done otherwise. Whether he asked or not, I was going to have something to report back to him. Accountability is a powerful and necessary aspect of your successful leadership development journey.

—Sean

To this day, your authors continue to navigate our own leadership journeys, deliberately and with intention. We can affirm your journey will be a deeply satisfying growth process and unique to you. While we have had many common experiences, our own leadership journeys have taken very different paths. Along the way, we have observed some common features and milestones that we will share so you can more effectively navigate your own journey. Like us, you will quickly grasp some leadership concepts and grapple longer with others; you will practice leading and following, learn and practice more; you will succeed and fail. You will try, observe, and question, and all the while you will grow and build real competence. This process will continue until you are up and walking on your own. In the end, you will find yourself properly equipped to lead, aimed in the right direction, and moving forward with a profound sense of mission. Welcome to your journey! Now let's get oriented.

Part 2

Orientation

CHAPTER 5

Laying a Solid Foundation

I f you've made it this far, you're making serious progress. Beginnings are often the most difficult and important part of any journey. Keep it up; you're well on your way to leading in a more authentic way! Let's take a quick look at where you now stand and what you have already accomplished. First, you've chosen to take ownership of your leadership responsibility. That important choice was the result of another critical decision: to humbly define yourself as a leader in your life. You've also taken a critical step forward by committing to your leadership development journey. That intentional journey is now officially underway. Congratulations! Your internal motivation to keep learning and your commitment to the journey will drive you forward.

We now want to help you gain clarity on what it really means to lead, the proper leadership perspective you must adopt to lead authentically, the essential leadership concepts you will be applying in your life, a leader's role and what a leader does, and the nature of the leader–follower relationship. To help you approach leadership with a fresh perspective, we will also address what leadership is *not*.

To lead authentically, you must have a central, unifying perspective from which to engage with those you seek to lead. Along with this perspective, you will need a solid understanding of the core leadership principles—the fundamentals—to put into effect as you carry your leadership responsibility. As the saying goes, you can't build a solid house on a defective foundation, so it would be pure folly to embark on your leadership development journey if your underlying beliefs and attitudes about leadership are uncertain or flawed.

WHAT IS LEADERSHIP, AND WHAT IS A LEADER?

Let's restate our definitions of *leadership* and *leader*:

> *Leadership is who you are and what you do to influence others to commit and act in alignment with the mission.*

> *A leader is one who carries a personal responsibility to serve others in support of a shared mission.*

If you look closely at these definitions, some key words stand out: *do, influence, commit, act, responsibility, serve*, and *mission*. These words highlight the true nature of what it means to lead.

How, then, do I lead? Great question! You lead through your relationships, in service to others, in support of your shared mission. What is it that a leader does to influence another person to follow their lead? In short, leaders act and behave in ways that *serve* their teammates. Through the impact of your consistent, service-oriented behavior and your personal example, you will build relationships and model behavior that influences the behavior and commitment of others in support of the shared mission.

Authentic relationships are built on mutual trust; there is no real relationship without it. A leader's influence develops largely through the impact of their exhibited behavior, the consistent example they live, and their level of engagement with those they serve, along with their commitment to the team's mission. Your leadership influence is directly related to the depth of your relationships with those you lead.

Look more closely at the dynamic between a leader and a follower. In a very important sense, the relationship is permissive in nature. Someone must choose to follow your lead; they must permit you to influence their thinking, behavior, or their commitment. Influence cannot be demanded, although many would-be leaders attempt to do just that. For a variety of reasons, I may choose to follow you or emulate your behavior. At the same time, if our relationship is nonexistent, weak, or trust or respect has not been earned, I may choose to dismiss you, ignore you, confront you, or challenge you rather than to follow you. Leaders are equipped with no magical power to force another human being to follow their lead. In the end, those you seek to influence must permit you to enter their head and heart.

The degree to which another person permits you to influence their behavior or commitment is based in no small part on the nature and quality of your relationship with them. The reality is that you do not ultimately decide whether you are a leader in any situation. That's not how a leader–follower relationship works. The person you seek to influence is the one with the power to decide whether and to what degree you will influence them. You've got to *earn* it.

Your values, beliefs, and intentions are important; they are the engine powering your observable actions. Your words and deeds reflect your intentions. Your teammates, those you seek to influence, are always evaluating you, weighing whether you are real and authentic, discerning whether your actions are congruent with your stated values. Your intentions literally come to life in your actions and behavior, and your actions and behavior are what most impact those you seek to influence. Clarify your values, beliefs, and intentions, because they come to life in your words, your actions, and your behavior. Be clear. Integrate them deeply in who you are as you find ways to serve and influence your teammates.

STRIVE TO BE *A* LEADER, NOT *THE* LEADER

Over the course of our lives, we've consistently observed that highly functioning teams are made up of multiple leaders, people who are capable and competent to lead. These teams have a rich reservoir of leadership, with people willing and capable of stepping into a leadership gap as quickly as it appears. This is strikingly different from the top-down, authoritarian model in which a positional leader hoards leadership, issuing orders and assignments to subordinates from on high. The world we live in is complex and rapidly changing. Meeting the daunting challenges facing any team in such a dynamic environment requires a dance of leadership: a fluid interplay between leader and follower where roles shift and evolve as needed depending on the present circumstances. Leadership responsibilities, then, are shared among the interdependent members of the team. In this dance, sometimes you will lead and I will follow, and in other circumstances, our roles might reverse. But to make this work, both you and I must be prepared to both lead and follow.

These moments can take place at virtually the same time and without clear demarcation. Team execution at the highest level cannot rest on a single leader regardless of how talented they may be; it rests on the capabilities of leaders throughout the team. The likelihood of a mission's success increases dramatically when there are more people capable of leading and confident in doing so rather than when a single positional leader is surrounded by a group of followers with limited, narrowly defined roles. When leadership responsibilities are shared, a team can be agile and resilient and will more effectively adapt, respond, and act in powerful and timely ways, unconstrained by the limitations of any single person.

Do you see how leadership is a shared set of responsibilities that must be distributed widely within a team? While a single person may have primary or ultimate authority over others, with the corresponding responsibility and accountability for the entire team's performance, true leadership acts at a much deeper level. Even absent a formal designation or leadership title, any member of the team can effectively influence those around them to move the team forward in accomplishing its shared mission. The team leader (position) should not be the only leader (shared responsibility) on a team.

Love is a pertinent analogy. Two people can love each other. It is possible to love another person without diminishing their ability to love you. Love is infinite; there is no cap on the amount of love shared in a relationship. And when love is mutual, the relationship is strengthened. So, too, with leadership. You can lead another without diminishing their ability to lead you. Leadership is unbounded; there is no cap on the amount of leadership which may be shared among teammates. Leadership is a powerful combined and shared resource that is strengthened, not diminished, when there is more than one leader on a team.

SHARING POWER

Leadership is often discussed and considered in terms of the exercise of power over another person. We disagree with that perspective. Power, as it relates to human interactions, is simply what fuels one person's influence on another.

Broadly, there are two types of power—personal power and positional power. Personal power comes from a person's being (their character, qualities, competencies, and behaviors). Followers are inspired by a leader with personal power and voluntarily choose to follow them. Positional power, on the other hand, comes from an organization, reflected in a leader's formal rank and authority. People are influenced not by the leader themselves but by the leader's status or ability to grant reward or impose penalty or punishment. Those in a position of authority can wield that power with those who have less authority. Positional power can be hoarded or shared.

Power properly distributed and shared within a team, among teammates, when further supported by meaningful preparation, a level of accountability, and role clarity, will dramatically increase the team's overall effectiveness. You can see this in most highly functioning teams. Limiting organizational power to a single person or a small leadership team unnecessarily diminishes and constricts overall team effectiveness.

We have all observed instances where people in positions of power hoard that power in the form of information, rewards, recognition, incentives, authority, and the like. They may do so out of ignorance or a lack of self-confidence or in an unhealthy attempt to drive behavior or exercise control. The unfounded belief among such would-be leaders is that "giving power away" by sharing it with a teammate will diminish their own power. They believe it's a zero-sum game, which is a serious misunderstanding of team dynamics.

Authentic leaders, on the other hand, do not withhold or hoard; they share. Rather than diminishing your leadership influence, sharing power strengthens both your relationship with your teammates and the team's ability to respond and execute.

PERSONAL RESPONSIBILITY, ACCOUNTABILITY, AND AUTHORITY

The concept of *personal responsibility* is at the heart of what it means to lead; it is a concept found no fewer than three times among the eleven battle-tested leadership principles of the Marine Corps: "Take responsibility for your actions," "Develop a sense of responsibility among your team," and "Seek responsibility." Authentic leaders take personal responsibility not only for their own behavior but also for the team's overall performance. When leading, you will share the responsibility for everything that happens within your team.

Accountability is another key element in how leadership operates in real life. Authentic leaders have a strong sense of personal accountability to those they serve. Leaders don't shrink from that accountability; they embrace it. When leading, you must always remember that those you serve have the right to—and certainly will—hold you accountable.

THEY ARE ALWAYS EVALUATING YOU

As the senior ranking Midshipman on duty that weekend, it was my responsibility to conduct a uniform and readiness inspection to ensure my colleagues were prepared to stand watch for the next twenty-four hours. As I made my way through the formation, from person to person, I tried to move quickly while being thorough. No one likes to stand at attention in a formation, especially on a weekend.

Our uniform included a white cap with a gold band around the front and above the bill. The band was secured by two posts that screwed into the cap on either side. Stamped on each post was an eagle with wings spread wide. If the post was correctly seated, the eagle's wings would be parallel to the ground. If misaligned, which happened easily, the eagle's wings would tilt, a condition known as a "drunken eagle."

After a brief greeting, I would scan each person's uniform from their cap to their shoes. After coming to attention in front of a particular Midshipman, I leaned my head to the side, and noticed the eagle on the right side of his cap was tilted. It wasn't a huge deal, but attention to detail is important in the military, and it was a uniform issue I felt I needed to address. I moved my head back in front of the young man and calmly informed him he had a drunken eagle on the side of his cap. In response, he smiled and said, "So do you, sir." I thanked him for the feedback and said, "Good attention to detail. Let's correct this right now." I took off my cap and corrected it while he adjusted his.

Humbling? Yes. But here's the thing: Although I was the senior inspector, I was also being inspected by every member of the team. I had fallen short of the very standard I was demanding of my teammates. It was appropriate for them to hold me to account for measuring up to the same standards.

—Sean

As a leader, you are responsible both for your own performance and for the performance of the team. You will hold your teammates accountable, in respectful ways, but remember that you are accountable to them. And don't fool yourself; they are always inspecting you, your behavior, and your performance.

Authority is an important concept to consider when thinking about leadership. We've all heard the following phrase from a parent or coach: "Do it because I told you to do it!" That approach usually comes from someone who has a formal or informal grant of authority. It is important for leaders to understand both the extent and limits of their own authority, so they can best deploy any positional power they may have in service to their teammates while leading.

However, your ability to lead is not dependent on your level of authority. Leadership does not spring from a title or a rank. Authentic leaders learn how to effectively use their formal authority, if they have such authority, in service to their teammates and in accomplishing a shared mission. Authentic leaders never abuse their authority; they use it in service to their team.

CHAPTER 6

Leading as a Servant

Patrick Lencioni, author of several bestselling books on leadership, captured a key point when he observed that servant leadership is the only type of leadership. Servant leadership is not a style of leadership; leading as a servant is the very essence of what it means to lead in an authentic way. Serving your teammates, individually and collectively, in alignment with the team's mission in each and every interaction, large and small, is what it means to lead authentically. Your attitude, your perspective, and your philosophy are anchored to leading as a servant. There is no other kind of leadership, and leading authentically requires you to embrace this approach.

Authentic leaders view their responsibilities from the perspective of a servant as they interact with their teammates in support of the team's mission. Real leaders don't lead to serve their own interests. Servant leaders seek to accomplish the team's mission by building and maintaining supportive relationships with their teammates. As a servant leader, embrace your personal and professional responsibility to serve your teammates; they do not exist to serve you.

Your ability to lead others—to deeply influence their commitment and behavior in support of the team's mission—rests on this understanding. In all you do as a leader, you must remember that your core responsibility is first and foremost to serve your teammates. Notice we said "serve," not "coddle." More on that later. Servant leadership is a core perspective so important that it is the foundation on which your leadership rests. Do what you must to fully wrap your mind and your heart around this concept. We assure you that embracing this orientation will be well worth the effort.

A servant leader perspective is a characteristic of every authentic leader we have ever observed. To understand how to lead, you must put this mindset into practice. Here's a bit about how we began to understand it during our own leadership journey.

The first and most important leadership insight we gained in the Marine Corps is captured in the phrase "Leaders eat last." This was much more than a catchphrase in the Marines; it became the very hallmark of how we would lead. By embracing the sacred responsibility to serve our Marines in carrying out the team's mission, our own self-interest was subordinate and came into consideration only after we had done all we could to support the team's mission and attend to our Marines' needs. We were learning that leading was not about the leader; leading was about those served.

In a literal sense, "Leaders eat last" means exactly what it says: A leader follows their team through the chow line, and by so doing, ensures their teammates partake of the best of what is offered. Without exception, leaders see to the needs of their teammates before they think about their own. If there are no pancakes left by the time a leader presents their plate, then so be it; leaders take it in stride. Without complaint, a leader will open a can of peaches if that's what is left.

Of course, there is much more at work with this concept. "Leaders eat last" evokes a philosophy of service that impacts everything a leader does and says. With this philosophy, a leader's primary focus is to see to the needs of those served. As a leader, you will naturally shoulder the burdens required to fully serve your teammates in accomplishing the team's mission. It represents a philosophy that requires you not only to subordinate your personal interests but to exercise real humility in doing so, sacrificing when necessary, sharing the team's burdens, and working longer and harder than the people you serve. It requires you never to ask more of your teammates than you are already giving. When you embrace this perspective on leadership, you will do what it takes to consistently set the example for your people and to look out for their best interests as you serve them in accomplishing the team's mission.

When the people you serve experience a consistent "Leaders eat last" approach on your part, their respect for you will strengthen. You will find them responding in remarkable ways, working harder, sacrificing more, and looking out for you in quiet ways to ensure your basic needs are met. When those who follow your lead see you looking out for their interests first, they will reciprocate. It's one of those magical human things. The greatest praise a leader of Marines can receive is perhaps this: "They took good care of their Marines."

The servant leadership perspective is actually quite simple to understand. Your commitment and dedication to your teammates in the context of your team's mission must be unquestioned. Authentic leaders are the first to show up in the morning and the last to leave at the end of the day (or upon completion of the mission). No task is beneath them. The team's work is not to improve the leader's lot. Authentic leaders serve in many ways, ensuring their teammates are properly selected, trained, prepared, and supported for what lies ahead. Authentic leaders neither seek nor accept perks for themselves; instead, they seek such advantages for their teammates, when appropriate. Authentic leaders never take the credit as if it belonged to them individually; they shine the light on their teammates, deflecting the credit to its rightful owners. Authentic leaders don't think or talk in terms of *I*; they think and talk in terms of *we*. Without exception, authentic leaders think and plan and work in their teammates' best interests rather than their own. Authentic leaders sacrifice and subordinate their own needs and desires in service to their teammates in support of the team's mission.

Several theories have been proposed to describe distinct leadership styles for various situations. While they are interesting, these situation-based theories are not only confusing and difficult to apply in a dynamic environment (the real world), but they miss the most important point: authentic leaders serve their teammates in alignment with the team's mission. Don't focus on a style of leading. Instead, focus squarely on becoming a human being capable of leading others authentically. Authentic leadership never goes out of style.

THE SERVANT LEADER'S PERSPECTIVE

To help illustrate your core leadership perspective and fully embed it in your mind, we've created a simple visual model. You can literally draw this on the back of a napkin, and we recommend you draw it in your journal. This model has served us well in virtually every leadership situation we have encountered, both in the military and civilian contexts. The visual below will help you keep a proper leadership perspective clear in your mind and will serve as a powerful aid as you engage as a leader in your life.

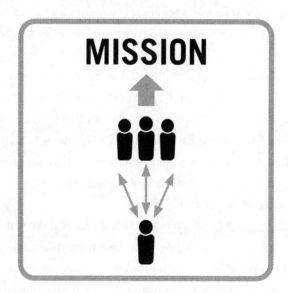

Let's look more closely at the three essential components of this leadership model.

MISSION

At the top is your team's shared mission. A clear, compelling mission is the very reason we create and work as a team. Its mission is the purpose for which the team exists. Your team's mission provides an aligning context for everything you do as a leader. It unifies the focus for all that your teammates do as you work together to accomplish that shared mission. When you are leading, you will keep the team's mission in your line of sight as you consider and carry out your best and highest role in serving your teammates. This mission context is critical. When you are leading, incorporate the team's mission into everything you do; put the consequences of your actions and those of your teammates squarely in that context.

TEAM

The next element, at the center of the model, are your teammates and the team. Leading is about people; they are at the center of your leadership model for all the correct reasons. As individuals, your teammates are *interdependent* contributors, not independent contributors. They are responsible for their own performance, but they also have responsibilities to their teammates. They are not only bound together by the team's mission; they are literally dependent on one another to carry out their primary responsibilities on behalf of the team. Each member of the team is accountable not only for their own behavior and performance; they are also accountable to one another. This interdependence and shared accountability strengthens the connection between members of the team.

People join together in a team to do the individual and collaborative work necessary to realize the team's mission. They bring their collective experiences, strengths, passions, aspirations, skills, energy, intellect, efforts, and commitment to the shared enterprise. They form and move as a team to accomplish what is beyond their individual reach.

YOU

The third and final element, at the very bottom of the model and subordinate to both mission and team, is you, a leader. This captures the correct orientation you must embrace as a servant leader: Your operating perspective on everything you do in leading is bottom-up and not top-down. This leadership perspective holds true regardless of whether you hold a senior title or position or none at all. From this humble position at the bottom, with your feet firmly planted on the ground, you are looking up with your focus on serving your teammates, in the direction of the team's mission.

When leading, you serve from who you are, through what you say and do. The two-way arrows connecting you to each of your teammates symbolize your authentic relationship with each of them, with responsibility, accountability, and genuine trust flowing in both directions. When you approach leading in this way, you will begin to understand that the responsibility to lead is a real privilege rather than a burden. Your awareness of the importance of this relationship is essential to your ability to lead authentically.

There you have it. You are now properly oriented with a simple but powerful conceptual model you can apply regardless of the nature of the team or its mission. Yes, it can be that simple. Your challenge, during the course of your leadership journey, is to keep this perspective in your mind's eye as you interact and engage with your teammates. This is the orientation of an authentic leader, an essential perspective you must embrace as you lead in the direction of your team's mission. Only when you lead as a servant can you begin to tap into and develop the real potential that often lies dormant in individuals and largely goes undeveloped in a team. Your impact does not come from an autocratic, top-down, "follow my orders" approach. With a true servant leader perspective, you can begin to move yourself and your teammates into extraordinary individual and collective team performance.

REFLECTION

✓ If you truly adopted a servant leader approach in your current environment, what would that require of you?

✓ How would you conduct yourself differently? What would you no longer do? What would you start doing?

✓ How would behaviors consistent with this model impact the people around you?

THE SERVE-ME LEADER

Now that you have a clear picture of the servant leader model, let's consider the opposite approach, the "leader-first" model. What's the problem with the "leader-first" model? In short, this approach limits what the team can accomplish due to the positional leader's limitations. When a "positional leader" (a person who holds a title, rank, or place of authority—an entirely separate matter from whether they are leading) operates as the sole source of leadership within a team, many problems arise, all of which can adversely impact the performance of individuals and the team.

Rather than bringing the team's combined and shared capabilities to bear on the challenges and opportunities they face, a top-down "leader" restricts the team's individual and collective performance. Creativity, initiative, and energy is stifled, as the members of the team respond and react only to the wishes of the leader. Leadership development and learning opportunities within the team become an afterthought, power is hoarded at the top, and individual and team capabilities typically plateau or decline. This top-down approach places an artificial and unproductive ceiling on what the team can accomplish, since it now must operate in a debilitating culture literally capped by the ability, vision, talent, energy, commitment, initiative, and intellect of "the leader." A top-down leadership model creates numerous obstacles to high performance, serving as a sort of "governor" on how effectively the team can operate. In effect, the team is held hostage and *limited to the capabilities of the positional leader*. This limitation can be a death knell for any team, especially those that operate in a competitive, dynamic environment.

When leadership flows solely from the top, from a single person or management group, the people below are reduced to acting in ways that are best characterized as compliant or reactive rather than empowered and fully engaged. There is little reason for a sense of urgency, creativity, initiative, or shared ownership. The positional leaders' "subordinates" are now restricted and limited by their "superiors."

By the way, we urge you to avoid using the words *subordinate* or *superior* to describe leadership relationships in your life. Strike these common terms from your vocabulary. Discourage others from using them as well. In that construct, the interests of the positional leader (or management group) often supersede the interests of the very teammates these leaders should be serving.

Autocratic leaders who may or may not have the level of intelligence, experience, vision, commitment, or heart to lead the team authentically often fall into a downward spiral, using performance-stifling management methods to control their team members' behavior. Controlling is not the same thing as leading. As a direct result, the team's morale, its level of energy and engagement, will naturally take a nosedive—as will the quality of its work. The culture created in such an environment places a premium on carrying out orders and restricting effort and attention to what is set forth in narrowly crafted job descriptions. This type of a culture is, quite frankly, doomed to fail. Autocratic leaders often revert to demanding a specific level of performance rather than inspiring, supporting, and elevating a higher level of performance. There is a world of difference in the impact created between these two.

Rather than the empowering servant leader perspective in which a leader carries a deeply held, sacred responsibility to serve their teammates in the direction of the team's mission, an autocratic leader often operates with a belief that "their people" exist merely to serve the leader so that the leader can accomplish the team's mission. In addition, information generally flows downhill when it flows at all. Any information transferred uphill is often heavily filtered and fragmented. "Subordinates," who generally are the people in direct contact with processes, customers, and clients, live in that critical gap where the product or service meets the customer or client. They feel distanced from more senior management because they have little contact or engagement with the mysterious figures "in charge" of the organization. Direct interactions between senior management and their teammates on the front lines become episodic and even rare. The positional leader whose responsibility includes determining what performance should be credited, recognized, and rewarded often has a difficult time getting the real picture. That is just one of the problems—and one which requires authentic leadership to overcome it.

In the servant leader model, where a leader is conceptually at the bottom, serving their teammates in the direction of the mission, the world is quite different. The servant leader's focus (and that of the entire leadership group) is upward, on their teammates, in line with the mission. The servant leader acts with a strong sense of humility, putting the concerns and interests of teammates above their own concerns and interests. The servant leader works hard to build and maintain authentic relationships with the people they serve

and continuously evaluates and chooses their best and highest role in support of their teammates' efforts and the work of the team. This authentic
leader is moved to ensure their teammates have the information, resources,
culture, and support they need to do the work required to advance in the
direction of the team's mission. The servant leader is always seeking ways to
serve and support their teammates as they work together, share information
and resources, and accomplish what needs to be done.

EMBODYING SERVANT LEADERSHIP

Now that you have clarity on what it means to lead as a servant, it's time to
embed the servant leader model in your being. To move through this brief
exercise, take a deep breath and relax. In your mind's eye, envision yourself
standing with your head back and looking up, your attention and intention
focused upward on the teammates you serve. Your feet are solidly on the
ground, your head is high, and your focus is upward, on your teammates, in
alignment with your team's mission. Envision each member of your team (or
your family, community organization, etc.). Your responsibility, your duty, is
to begin to envision all you can do to serve your teammates in ways that align
with your team's shared mission.

Keep it simple; the world is complex enough. Leadership will not always
be easy, and you will have to work at it, but the concept is simple. Your chief
responsibility as a leader is to ensure your team has the resources, authority, clarity of responsibility, training and education, support, feedback, and
opportunities required to accomplish the mission.

REFLECTION

✓ Sketch the organizational chart of your team, business, board, committee, classroom, or family—any relationship or team in which
you regularly participate.

✓ Instead of writing job titles in the boxes, use people's names—the
individuals or team leaders you deal with directly.

✓ Now, literally flip the org chart upside down. (You may need to
    rewrite the names to avoid straining your neck.)

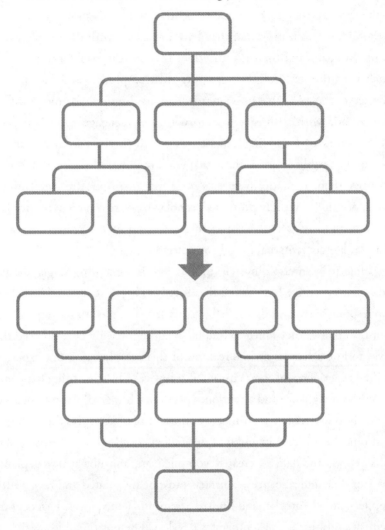

✓ Spend some time analyzing the new diagram and consider the fol-
    lowing questions:

  » What was inferred in the first diagram that is absent in the second?

  » What is apparent in the second diagram that was unclear in
    the first?

  » In what ways does this new paradigm change your thinking?

STAY ENGAGED WITH YOUR TEAM

You may be familiar with the television show *Undercover Boss*. The basic premise involves a CEO or senior executive of a large company who comes to the sudden realization that they have lost touch with the people who are on the front lines of their organization. In a last-ditch effort to get back in touch with the key realities impacting their employees and the customers they serve, the executive puts on a ridiculous disguise, assumes a different identity, and with a flimsy cover story, tries to reengage with their people. After a series of humbling experiences in which the executive concludes they are incapable of doing the actual work required of their employees, the executive then dramatically reveals their true identity. After the emotional reveal, people are rapidly promoted, scholarships are awarded, money is distributed, and the executive comes to understand that they need to lead this group of largely remarkable and committed human beings.

While it is entertaining television, there is something tragic about the show. The executive has created the tragedy. They lost sight of their leadership responsibility, and they failed to carry it; they failed to stay engaged with their teammates; they failed to lead in an authentic way. They allowed themselves to lose a handle on the realities of their employees' work experiences and the experiences of their customers. How could such a thing happen?

Without vigilance and attention, a positional leader's isolation can develop gradually, one decision at a time, over the course of years. It's the boiling frog syndrome. Priorities shift and morph, strategy meetings take the place of field visits, reports and data are created, compiled, and must be analyzed, planning takes up time and resources, contracts must be negotiated and reviewed, and suppliers and clients demand limited attention. Time passes. Layers of management and bureaucratic processes develop. The positional leader relies on subordinate managers to maintain the culture and manage the people closest to the work that really matters.

It does not have to be that way. There is another approach, and it's relatively simple, but you will have to fight for it, and the world will often seem to conspire against you. It requires authentic leadership.

Exercise an ongoing discipline. Don't allow yourself to become estranged from your teammates. Spend time with and among them, in their environment, on their ground. Do it frequently. Make the effort to build and maintain your relationship with your teammates, regardless of the size or complexity of your organization. Understand the reality in which they operate by engaging with and spending precious time in that reality. Get out from behind your desk. Lead by example and ask for the same discipline of the other leaders on your team.

A MISGUIDED APPROACH TO LEADING

Marines take leadership seriously and talk about it frequently, even when off duty. I was with a group of junior officers one night. We had only recently been commissioned and, after years of education and training, were finally leading real Marines on real missions. While sharing some of our limited leadership experiences with one another, one of my colleagues clarified his philosophy on leading his Marines. He said, "I want to remain an enigma to my Marines. I want to be a mystery. I don't want them to know me. I want them to *fear* me. That's how you get people to do what you want them to do."

I nearly choked on my beer. I thought his approach was completely off the mark, going against all we had learned about leading Marines. But he seemed so sure of himself. I didn't know him well, but I respectfully told him I didn't agree. I explained that my experience taught me that fear creates a toxic environment, and a fear-based approach to leading will create a situation where his team and his Marines will be limited to merely following the letter of his orders. He would never get more than mere compliance. I explained that, in my experience, fear doesn't inspire the best in a person, but a sense of respect does tend to bring out one's best. Fear doesn't encourage acts of initiative; it only leads to compliance with orders given. I also added that I thought his approach would set a poor example for his Marines as they developed their leadership skills. I told him I certainly wouldn't be inspired by that kind of approach. I recall him looking at me with some disdain, and I think it was the last time we ever got together for a beer.

—Sean

Whether you attempt to lead with the hope of seeking popularity, love, or the admiration of your teammates, or you try to shape your teammates' performance through fear or intimidation, you are leading from the wrong place. Those approaches are centered on you. To serve in your leading, you must center your attention and energy on those you serve. You can't lead in an authentic way if you engage with your teammates out of a need to fuel your own ego, beef up your resume, obtain admiration or love, or simply get people to merely follow your orders, however brilliant they may be. Seeking popularity or looking to impress or even overwhelm another with your brilliance or your strength is really all about you.

There will certainly be situations when your best and highest role is to lead from the front and ask your teammates to follow. But when you step beyond the need to be the sole source of leadership and the dominant force on the team, you will quickly find your teammates taking on more responsibility for the team's performance and its success. That is the environment real leaders seek to create. Authentic leaders understand they cannot accomplish the team's mission through their own brilliance, using the services and efforts of their teammates as merely a supporting cast. Authentic leaders engage with their teammates in ways that foster team ownership and enable leadership at every level. Mission accomplishment becomes the team's accomplishment, not solely that of the leader.

Authentic leadership works through action and behavior, not through the mystical power of one's perceived charisma. Leaders work to create a supportive environment, a culture that elevates the passion, performance, and capabilities of every member of the team. Authentic leaders don't seek to elevate themselves, nor do they seek credit for the team's accomplishments; authentic leaders seek the highest level of service to their teammates in support of the mission.

As your teammates continue to develop both individually and collectively, and the team strengthens and performs, your prominence in their eyes will diminish for all the right reasons. That is as it should be. The team's performance and success never really was about you in the first place; mission accomplishment becomes less about you as leader and more about the team. Successful leadership is measured by the growth of the team and the team's execution, not by how brilliant or charismatic an individual in a leadership position may be. If you lead well, the team's culture strengthens, and your teammates develop a well-deserved sense of pride earned from their individual and team's work, progress, and success. While you are contributing to it all in important ways, you are placing yourself in roles where you can serve at your best and highest, moving in and around the team, serving their growth and performance, often in the background. At the end of the day, leadership is not solely about you; it is about how you have impacted the team.

IT'S NOT ABOUT YOU, SKIPPER

As a young officer, I was given the opportunity to command a company of Marines. For several years, I had been working toward and anticipating my shot at being promoted to a position of company commander. When it finally happened, I was very pleased with myself. On my first day, I drove to my new headquarters and parked in a space with a sign clearly labeled *Company Commander*. I walked into the building and entered the office labeled *Company Commander* and sat down in the leather chair behind the desk adorned with a *Company Commander* placard. I was quite proud of my newfound status.

My self-satisfaction evidently showed. The company first sergeant, an experienced veteran, came into my office and quietly said, "Sir, that isn't your parking space, this isn't your office, that's not your desk, and these Marines aren't yours. They belong to the Marine Corps. Never forget that."

I never did forget his advice. The first sergeant, who was to become one of my most important mentors, was teaching me (thankfully I was a quick learner) that the perks were merely entitlements of the position. What was much more important were the responsibilities of the position. The company commander position wasn't about what I had earned but, rather, the leadership I was expected to provide.

—John

In the modern leadership classic *Leadership Is an Art*, former CEO Max DePree offers a powerful, succinct summary of the scope of a leader's responsibilities: "The first responsibility of a leader is to define reality. The last is to say thank you. In between the two, the leader must become a servant and a debtor." This quote is quite nearly a drop-the-mic moment. We recommend you write it down in your journal. In three brief sentences, it captures the essence of what it means to lead.

DEFINE REALITY

First, a leader is responsible for defining reality. Defining a team's "reality" may sound simple, but it requires some real work. A leader must clarify and communicate to their teammates the relevant realities that are at play as the team moves to accomplish its mission. Leaders must clarify the scope of the team's mission, and what is outside of its mission. Since a broader understanding of the wider operational context is always helpful, leaders should work to make those realities clear. Expectations relating to team culture, performance standards, ethics, values, and behavior must be clarified and understood. Each member of the team must understand their primary role and responsibilities and how those align with the team's mission. They must know what to expect of their teammates and of those leading. Resources and assets, threats and opportunities need to be identified. Failure and success must be explained and made clear. Don't make your teammates guess about what matters.

EXPRESS GRATITUDE

A leader is responsible for bringing their gratitude to light. Sometimes, it is as simple as saying the magic words at the right time and place, when appropriate: "thank you." Leaders don't simply feel a sense of appreciation for their teammates; they find ways to express that sincere gratitude. Don't simply think to yourself, *I'm grateful for their effort, their commitment, and their contributions.* Say it. Express it in a variety of ways. Make it clear. Don't make them wonder whether you are grateful.

SERVE

Serving is where the hard work comes in. As an authentic leader, your effort and attention are fueled and shaped by your deeply held orientation as a servant and debtor to your teammates. Once you've embraced that perspective, you will act in alignment with those intentions; everything you do and think as a leader will be shaped by that powerful perspective. This perspective is heightened further by the acceptance that you are literally indebted to your teammates. Consider how little you could accomplish on your own. Keep in the forefront of your mind the debt you owe to your teammates for all that they are and all that they do. Let this perspective shape your thoughts, guide your decisions, and accelerate your actions.

SHIFTING YOUR FOCUS

In adopting this philosophy in how you lead, your focus will naturally shift from a narrow and limiting "What's in it for me?" to a broader and more empowering "What's possible for us?" Your efforts will start to align with your team's mission, and you will find your best and highest role in service to your teammates. When you wholeheartedly embrace the understanding that mission accomplishment does not rest solely on your own limited capabilities but on the combined and collaborative capabilities of those around you, you will begin to see the practical wisdom behind leading as a servant. You will then be able to tap into that deep reserve of self-motivation we all have inside when we serve something beyond ourselves.

You can now engage intentionally with your team, using all that you have in all the ways possible. Do the hard work required to know your teammates, and let them come to know you. Find ways to help them build their individual capabilities and support them in connecting with and serving one another as members of a highly functioning team. Understand that you are not always leading; you also have a continuing responsibility to be a good teammate. Work on your own performance, and continuously find ways to contribute to the team. Take full responsibility for the health of each relationship you have at every level to include your peers and those you serve.

To lead in an authentic way, you do not have to be the source of all wisdom, and you don't need to have all the answers. In fact, as you embrace servant leadership, you will begin to shed the need to be (or to *appear* to be) the wisest, most talented, most valuable person in the room. Even if you are any or all of those things, that's not where your leadership power comes from. Mission accomplishment requires a focused team *effort*. Your team's progress rests on your actions and behaviors as they support the actions and behaviors of your teammates as you move together as a highly engaged and mission-focused team.

So, relax. Get over yourself. You are important, but your teammates are just as important. Shift your focus onto them. Roll up your sleeves and get down to the real work of leadership: serve.

CHAPTER 7

How Leadership Really Works

L eadership is relational, not transactional. Authentic leadership is only possible when you engage in real relationships with the people you share a mission with. When you lead, you move beyond a merely transactional arrangement: the giving of this in return for that. In leading, the arrangement takes on its true character and becomes a human relationship—one not centered on me but on what we can do, together, to accomplish our mission.

Your ability to lead is founded on the strength of your relationship with others. This relationship allows you to truly influence the actions and commitment of your teammates.

For far too long, leadership has been practiced and discussed as if it were merely transactional in nature, an exercise of power over those with less power in return for a certain level of effort or work. Positional leaders wielded their power or authority like a weapon, as if leadership were something done to "subordinates" by persons who "know better" or simply considered themselves "superior" because of a job title. That is no longer the norm.

Unfortunately, many people are placed in positions requiring the ability to lead predicated on little more than "seniority" (the mere fact that they have been around longer) or a certain level of experience (regardless of the *value* of that experience). Real leadership isn't limited to a senior–subordinate construct. That's a management approach, built on a belief that "subordinates" must be closely managed to reach their maximum work output. With little leadership preparation and no clear expectation to lead, many managers fall into a transactional arrangement trap. Rather than leading with humility through relationships built on service, they try to drive performance using a system of reports, analytics, key performance indicators, and systematic incentives and disincentives. That is not leadership, and it cannot serve as a substitute for the real thing. It is merely an attempt to shoehorn management principles into a leadership vacuum.

Leading a team to a high level of execution requires the application of both management skills (managing work processes and resources) and leadership skills (influencing human performance and development). Ignoring or misapplying one or the other is a certain recipe for failure.

Transactional arrangements are not necessarily bad. Incentives and disincentives can have a real effect on human motivation and do have a place in managing a collective effort. But if you do not lead, and an incentive plan and a disciplinary policy is all you've got, you cannot maximize human effort, you will never build real commitment, and you will fail to tap into the deep potential of your team. Doling out financial or psychological happiness and pain is not leadership and is no substitute. Transactional arrangements do not create teams with the resilience to endure the stress test of adversity, nor do they engender deep commitment among human beings. We've all seen examples of employees who work for a paycheck, despise their boss, and do exactly as they are told—but certainly no more than that. This is mere compliance, and it does not make for a pretty picture. There is a world of difference between: "I am only responsible for X and Y," and "My *primary* responsibility is X and Y, but I am also responsible for my teammates and our team's mission." Leaders are responsible for creating the environment that results in that difference.

From the "leader's" perspective, the transactional arrangement goes something like this: "I am your boss. As you know (although I'd be happy to remind you), I have a superior title, more worthwhile experience, greater talent, deeper knowledge, heightened creativity and insight, and more organizational authority than you do. I have the power, along with an impressive title, which you do not possess. Therefore, I will be the one to manage you and your work. So here's the deal, and it's pretty simple: You will produce X effort and complete Y tasks, in ways and by means which will be made clear to you or otherwise dictated by me. In return, I will compensate you with $Z and certain specific benefits. One day, if you impress me enough, meet established goals, and work in accordance with our standards, you may get to keep your job, you might be considered for an incentive bonus, and you could possibly even obtain a promotion to middle management." No wonder our teams are in trouble.

Learning how to lead is much more than an intellectual process. This is because leadership is not an exercise of power over another human being. Leadership is a relationship with responsibilities, not merely a transaction. Authentic leaders are responsible for creating an environment in which people want to apply their talents and energy in pursuit of a mission. Authentic leadership encompasses the heart, the mind, and the hands. It enables people to pursue the completion of complex tasks in dynamic environments in ways that tap into their deep potential. Authentic leadership is powerful. Leadership is a sacred, shared responsibility in highly functioning teams. It is the difference maker in those teams that succeed.

Leadership is a uniquely human emotional and intellectual process with a foundation of practical human interaction, which is why it cannot be fully understood in a purely intellectual way. You will not become a leader by merely trying to adopt certain generally accepted "leadership attributes" or by mechanically applying leadership techniques. If it were that easy, every family, community, and organization could simply stamp out more leaders like an assembly line.

"WELCOME TO THE COURTROOM."

As I entered the courtroom for my first contested court-martial as a newly minted Marine Corps trial counsel (prosecutor), I felt a level of excitement and

continued

nervousness—that feeling you get whenever you do something for the first time. Over the next two agonizing days, I would learn I had failed to effectively prepare for trial.

As the trial wore on, I knew things were not going well, and I was certain everyone in the courtroom knew I was falling short. After I had presented our case, and after enduring the defense counsel's efforts to tear my case apart, we presented our closing arguments. As expected, the judge announced a verdict for the defense.

As the courtroom cleared, the judge asked me to approach the bench. He shared some candid feedback: He thought I had tried to finesse my way through some technical aspects of my case. He recommended I spend more time working through basic case preparation. I thanked him for the feedback and quickly gathered my files, trying to get out of the courtroom as quickly as possible.

Unknown to me, a senior officer on my trial team had attended the entire trial. Fortunately, he was more than just an experienced lawyer; he was also a leader. In my very public failure, he saw an opportunity to serve my professional development. As I began to leave the courtroom, he walked up and asked how I thought the trial had gone. I told him I was deeply embarrassed and disappointed with my performance.

"Good. That's a great place to start." He then said, "I want you to go back and carefully review what went well, what didn't go well, and how you would do it differently. Feel the sting for a while. Then let's get you back on the horse. I want you to come by my office on Friday. Let's go through your performance in this case and learn what we can from it. You are good on your feet, and you've got a good skill set, but you've got some work to do. I will help you. I'll see you on Friday."

After thanking him, he turned to me and said something I will never forget: "Welcome to the courtroom."

This leader's willingness to take the time to observe my performance, to hold me accountable in a constructive way, and to actively engage with me to help me learn through a trying experience set me on a solid path to becoming a capable trial lawyer. It also gave me a powerful leadership example to emulate and helped me to become a better leader in my own right.

–Sean

You can only lead authentically by being a fully authentic human being. Leading does not require you to be perfect, flawless, unblemished, all knowing, or untouchable. No person is any of those things, so how can we expect to influence others from such a pedestal? You will lead most effectively when you lead as a genuine human being, without pretense or posturing, in service to others.

When we say, "be authentic," we are not advocating that you rest where you are. You may have some things to work on that are impediments to your leading at the highest level, such as a lack of patience or an inability to manage your emotions. Work on those. Stay on a path of continuous improvement as a human being. The best of us are on a never-ending road to greater wisdom, increased maturity, and deeper levels of patience and grace. Learn from your experiences, continue to refine your skill set, smooth out the rough edges, and grow. The best leaders continue to develop their character and improve their own performance. So, lead from where you are, and focus on how you can best serve your teammates.

Remember to take your focus off yourself when leading. Focus on the person or the team you are serving, along with the team's mission. Mission first, people always. When you focus on how you look or how a situation might serve your own interests, you've lost sight of the very purpose of your leadership—to serve your team in accomplishing its mission. You cannot lead while serving yourself or your ego. When you expend energy and effort in posturing and pretending and trying not to look like a fool, you will be ineffective. Lead from a place of humility, instead. If you maintain an unsustainable, inauthentic stance in your effort to lead, you will not be able to build genuine connections with your teammates, and you won't be able to serve effectively.

Get real. Own your talents, capabilities, experiences, and strengths. Work hard to build on those and challenge yourself to fully realize your own potential. At the same time, be aware of your lack of experience, your opportunities, and your limitations. Since you are always learning and growing, you won't stay in that place. Trust us. You can lead authentically from a place of brokenness and incompleteness, so long as you serve with humility. You can still serve your teammates in your leading even though you have not yet developed a complete understanding of all the forces at play in a particular situation. With humility comes openness, a firm grasp on reality, greater capacity for learning, curiosity, and compassion.

A grounded sense of humility will also enable you to more easily put your ego in check so you can reach out and seek support from those around you, others who may be able to bring greater clarity or understanding or who may bring relevant expertise and experience to the table. Learn from them all. Engage with them. Involve them.

Even while leading, you will find you are sometimes a student and other times a teacher. You will be a resource to your teammates just as your teammates will be a resource to you. They can help you to increase your own understanding and competence in a particular area, serving you in ways that contribute to the team's ability to move toward the mission. Effective leaders create an environment; one that enables the team to move past a leader's individual limitations. If you are inexperienced or uncertain, own it. Understand your limits and engage with those around you in ways that support the team, despite your present lack of experience or understanding. Be humble. Be authentic. Persevere through these learning experiences. Your teammates will respect you more for your humility than they will if you pretend to be something you are not or claim to know more than you do.

WHAT IS MY BEST AND HIGHEST ROLE?

Once you've embraced the servant leader perspective, there are decisions to be made and actions to be taken. As we've emphasized, your leadership is manifested in behavior and action. There is a powerful yet simple question you must ask yourself to help you determine your next step:

> *"What is my best and highest role in service to this person and this team in alignment with our mission?"*

(To make it easier to remember and use, shorten it to "What is my best and highest role?") Exercise the discipline of asking yourself this question in every situation where you have an opportunity to lead. We call it a mirror check question, because you must answer it with honesty and candor, as if you were standing alone in front of a mirror. Trust us; this practice will soon become a powerful leadership habit, and then it will become second nature.

Write the question on a notecard or a yellow sticky note and put it in a place you'll easily see it every day. Practice using it. When searching for an answer, don't just take the first thought that comes to mind; if time allows (and it usually does) thoughtfully reflect, decide, and then act. Run through a range of potential answers and evaluate those possibilities. Remember that you don't have to be perfect, so don't strive for it.

Leadership opportunities will present themselves frequently, virtually every day. These moments will often come unannounced, and unless you maintain a high state of awareness, you will miss them. Most leadership failures come from leadership opportunities that go unrecognized and unaddressed. People in leadership positions either don't see these leadership moments as they unfold or they decide to ignore them. Leadership failures are often the result of misfeasance (a failure to recognize a responsibility or to take responsible action) rather than malfeasance (with an evil or malevolent intent). Keep your head up. Pay attention to what is unfolding with the people around you. Get creative in your response to the question. If circumstance allows, seek input, advice, or guidance from your peers, mentors, or coaches.

Leaders think beyond what is easy. Instead, leaders think in terms of long-term impact, deep influence, relationship-building, and capability development; they don't shy away from a longer timeline or a greater investment in time and energy if that is what it will take to impact their teammates in a particular situation. Leadership is not efficient, and it is not easy. Authentic leaders focus, instead, on thinking and acting in ways that bring the most value to the people and the mission they serve.

Here's a novel idea (sarcasm intended) to help you determine your best and highest leadership role: Ask your teammates how you can best serve them! Then listen. Really listen. They probably have some important insight on what they need from you. Once you've heard them out, you may decide you need more time to reflect or more information to understand the situation fully. You may ultimately decide to do something other than what your teammates suggest, but their answers will reveal what they think they need. That's valuable information. Prepare yourself; their answers may surprise you.

"SIX MILES. GRANNY GEAR. FOLLOW ME."

I brought my road bike on a recent trip to visit with my friend and coauthor, John. His family lives in the mountains of western North Carolina. I love to cycle, but I live in southern Indiana, where the land is flat as a table. Riding past cornfields is a Zen-like experience for me, but it isn't the best training to prepare you for the mountains.

As we got ready to ride one morning, I reminded John how little climbing I'd been able to do. He shrugged off my excuses and told me we were going to take a 100-kilometer ride through some scenic country. He explained we would be climbing up to the summit of Caesars Head Mountain. Because he was calm (he's always calm), I stayed calm. I've known him long enough to trust he wouldn't leave me on the side of the road, and I also knew he had completed that ride many times before.

The scenery was gorgeous, and my confidence foolishly grew as we rode. About halfway through the ride, we began a gradual ascent up the mountain. We then came to an intersection where an ominous sign warned us we were about to begin a six-mile ascent to the top of Caesars Head, one of the highest points on the Eastern Continental Divide, a climb of over 2,000 feet. I'm sure my face reflected a mixture of fear and self-doubt.

John looked at me and recognized my concern. In a firm, calm voice, he uttered six simple words: "Six miles. Granny gear. Follow me." It was exactly what I needed to hear. He was ready and willing to lead me up the mountain. He had conquered this ride many times before. Although I had serious doubts about my own capabilities, he appeared fully confident I could complete the ride. His confidence in me fueled my own self-confidence.

To be candid, had he not been there I would have quietly headed back down the mountain the way we came. There was no question he would take the lead and I would follow his lead. With him in front and me following, we, as a team, successfully completed the arduous climb to the summit, grinding in granny gear—the easiest gear to pedal in—all the way up. I simply couldn't have done it without his leading from the front.

—Sean

Sometimes, leading from the front and asking your teammates to follow will be your best and highest role. Exhibiting a sense of calm and quietly expressing your confidence in the untested capabilities of a teammate can lift that person well above their own self-imposed limitations. This is just one example of the impact you can have on your teammates through your leadership, by thoughtfully selecting your "best and highest role."

THE "CORRECT" DECISION

You will often question whether you've made the "correct" leadership decision about your best and highest role in a particular situation. Here are some practical suggestions to help you evaluate the quality of your leadership decision:

- Pay attention to whether and how your decision affected individual and team performance.
- Observe the short- and long-term impacts on attitude, behavior, and performance.
- Seek targeted feedback from your teammates.
- Determine whether your decision added to or detracted from the capabilities of the people you lead.
- Determine whether your decision served the team in advancing toward its mission.

As you consider your best and highest role in a particular situation, keep these clarifying considerations in mind. If you could have done something different to accomplish more, then learn from your experiences. Pay attention to what follows from your leadership decisions, including the impacts on performance. The answers will appear, your judgments will improve, and progress will result.

I JUST NEED YOU TO LISTEN

One of my key team leaders asked me if I had a moment to talk. I always kept an open-door policy, and I welcomed the opportunity to stay engaged with my teammates. We had a good working relationship, but she had kept me at arm's length

continued

since I'd started. She asked me, very directly, if I really wanted to know what was on her mind.

"Yes," I replied. "I think I could serve you better if I understood you more."

"Okay, then," she responded. "Here's what I need from you: I need you to listen." She continued, "I don't want you to say anything, and I don't want you to fix anything. I don't want you to make any suggestions or do anything in response to what I'm going to tell you. I just need you to listen."

For the next forty-five minutes, she shared, and I listened. I listened carefully as she talked about the pressures she and her team were under. Her team was lean, and their workload was substantial. She told me how proud she was of her people and their accomplishments, but she felt the company's senior leadership didn't fully recognize or appreciate the difficulty of their work. I listened intently, actively, and silently. She became emotional, and then apologized for her show of emotion. I was deeply impressed with the courage she showed in being so candid with me. I knew this was difficult for her. I felt fortunate to work with someone who cared so much—about her people, the quality of their work, and our team's mission. I knew this could be an important moment in our relationship, if I handled it correctly. I wasn't going to blow it by saying a single word. I was going to follow her instructions and *listen*.

She ended by saying, "Well, there it is. You asked for it. Thank you for listening. That is all I wanted."

I asked for permission to speak. When she nodded, I simply said, "Thank you."

After she left, I thought long and hard about what just took place. It was a wakeup call for me as a leader. I realized I had more work to do—to better appreciate and represent the work this team did to senior leadership. I also needed to more thoughtfully address some of the issues she raised, without immediately reacting to "fix" what might be broken. Some of her concerns had no quick fix and would need to be addressed over the long haul. I also had work to do in strengthening our team's culture, to ensure it was safe for my teammates to walk through the open door and share their concerns and disappointments with me. I learned many things about me and our team from that meeting. I also learned that the act of listening with the intent to understand may be one of the most important leadership responsibilities we have.

—Sean

CHAPTER 8

What Leadership Is *Not*

D uring your learning journey, you will continue to discover and clarify what it means to lead in your life. To help you with that, it is important to understand what leadership is not. This may help you purge some misguided assumptions about what leading entails. Recall our core definition: *Leadership is who you are and what you do to influence others to commit and act in alignment with the mission.* You will begin to distinguish behavior that does not fit this definition from that that fits squarely within it. You will refine your assumptions and understanding about human nature and find more authentic ways to influence those you share a common mission with. Again, keep in mind that you lead from the perspective of a human being serving your teammates toward their mission. Any behavior falling outside of that perspective will require your adjustment. Check your intent at every turn. Be humble and be authentic. Ask yourself whether your primary intent is to serve yourself or to serve your teammates and whether there is an alignment in that service in support of your shared mission.

LEADERSHIP IS NOT ABOUT TITLE, RANK, OR POSITION

A common misconception that must be dismissed if you seek to lead authentically is that the ability to lead depends on a title, rank, or position. The reality is this: Holding a title or obtaining a promotion will not magically transform you into a person capable of leading others. If it were that simple, the leadership gap in our families, our communities, and our work teams could easily be filled by simply issuing impressive-sounding titles! The Wizard of Oz (or some other high-level authority, governmental agency, or nonprofit organization) could simply dole out a range of fancy titles and ranks and distribute them far and wide, and all would be well. If this were true, we could then be on our way to resolving all manner of human and societal issues on every front. If only it were so! Of course, this is not reality.

Notice that title or rank is not referenced in our definition of leadership. If you do happen to hold a position or title in an organization that provides you with some degree of organizational authority, then lead with it! Use it to further the impact of your influence and its reach. But be clear as you walk your journey: Leadership does not arise from formal authority, nor is it dependent on it. We have all observed people who hold leadership titles or positions yet do not actually lead. Holding a title or position is entirely different from leading.

Opportunities to lead are all around you. Keep your head up and stay aware. You don't need anyone to grant you an opportunity to lead; you own that opportunity by virtue of your humanity. No leadership title or certificate is required, nor do you do you need a permissive nod from anyone above you in your chain of command. Prepare yourself for the opportunity, and when a leadership gap appears—and it will—step into the gap!

LEADERSHIP IS NOT ABOUT BEING THE BOSS

One word that needs to be removed from common usage is *boss*. Authentic leaders don't aspire to be a boss, nor do they boss their teammates. While being decisive and communicating clearly are indeed leadership virtues, barking out orders to "subordinates" is not leadership. Leaders work hard to build relationships with their teammates and strive to develop a high level of commitment to the team's mission among the people they serve. Involvement leads to commitment. Commitment fuels creativity, courage, and initiative, all of which are critical to mission accomplishment. That is precisely what authentic leaders seek to create. We implore you not to use the word "boss" and to ensure it isn't used by your teammates. Strike it from your vocabulary and throw a red flag in the air whenever it is used in any context. That's how we handle it.

Rather than merely issuing orders or instructions to be followed, the authentic leaders we've worked alongside engaged actively with us as important members of their team. They led by clarifying the team's guiding vision, making sure we were aligned with the team's mission, and they worked to ensure performance expectations were clear and understood. They involved us in developing solutions consistent with the team's culture, and they kept us on mission through the power of their consistent example, through coaching, and by providing us with timely, constructive feedback. These leaders made themselves available to us to help us carry out our responsibilities, work through issues, and define problems. When necessary, they would help us clarify priorities as circumstances shifted. They made sure responsibility and leadership was shared and distributed widely and deeply. They worked to ensure our team's culture—its social DNA—was clear and strong, so that we could align our own decisions and actions with our team values as we worked to accomplish our team's mission. Finally, they supervised appropriately, and held us accountable for the results we achieved, both good and bad. They always led with love, with genuine care and concern for our well-being and development. Finally, they worked to ensure we learned from and evolved as a result of our experiences.

Authentic leaders become a resource for the people around them, engaging in ways that result in best efforts and high levels of commitment. Leaders make this possible by providing encouragement and communicating convictions, and they never stop teaching and coaching. Feedback is always offered as a gift, in a timely and respectful way. While leaders generally have a strong sense of what needs to be accomplished, they are careful about how they shape the purpose, leaving the details up to their teammates who are directly responsible to carry out the responsibility.

When leading authentically, there is very little bossing going on. While clear communication is important, direct orders are generally unnecessary when trust among teammates is high, people are respected, the team's culture is supportive, and the mission is clear and in the line of sight. As we've stressed, the responsibility to lead within a team is a shared responsibility for the team. Ensure your teammates share in the responsibility to provide leadership within the team and support those expectations through both word and deed.

LEAD PEOPLE; MANAGE THINGS

There is an important point to make early in your intentional journey, one you must understand: Leadership responsibilities are distinct from management responsibilities. The roles, skills, tools, and mindsets associated with each are different. Leadership is about people, about influencing other human beings through relationship and human engagement in support of a shared mission. Management, on the other hand, relates to transactional functions, processes, and the use of assets and other resources. Unfortunately, many organizations use terms and titles that only serve to muddy the waters. Leaders are referred to as "managers," and managers (of processes or functions) are often called "leaders." Join us in keeping this important distinction in mind. You may be a manager of a function or a process that requires you to work with or through other human beings, but that simply means you also have an opportunity and a responsibility to lead. We raise this point to ensure you keep the distinction in mind, understand why both are important, and recognize when one or the other (or both) is required.

You cannot lead a budget, a performance metric, a supply chain, or any other inanimate object, process, or concept. Try to inspire a paper clip or a budget with the power of your personal example or the level of your commitment. It doesn't work. You can, however, lead people, who then move to maximize such things as a budget or a supply chain. Do not attempt to manage people.

We've heard executives admit that during their careers they've viewed people in their workplace as "cost centers" rather than human beings. To state what should be obvious, people are neither inanimate objects nor merely cost centers; human beings are not boxes on an organizational chart. Similarly, any attempt to *manage* the effort or commitment of another human being will have limited impact. You cannot lead through performance metrics, regardless of how brilliantly they are crafted.

Of course, most people who have the responsibility to lead people also have management responsibilities. Good leaders often have excellent management skills, and effective managers often have a level of competence in leading people. You likely have responsibilities in both areas: responsibilities to lead people and manage things. Management disciplines and their related skill sets are important, but they are different from leadership and cannot serve as a substitute for leadership. Our focus is specifically directed at your leadership skills. When people are involved, there is always an opportunity and a responsibility to lead.

THE THREE E-MAILS

Sometime after leaving the Marines, I practiced law with a civil litigation law firm. I had much to learn about what it took to succeed as a civilian lawyer. As I looked around the firm, I thought I could gather a great deal of that wisdom from the law firm's managing partner. It quickly became clear to me that he didn't fully embrace his leadership responsibility to build relationships and contribute to the growth of the newly joined lawyers. Perhaps he felt his primary responsibility was to manage the firm's business and to bring in the clients.

During my two years with the firm, this man never visited my office to engage in direct conversation with me, not that I required much one-on-one attention. This failure to engage stood in stark contrast to my experience in the Marine Corps, where more senior officers went out of their way to engage with junior officers on a frequent basis. In the Marines, senior officers embraced their responsibility to lead, which included building relationships with the members of their team and developing the junior officers at every turn.

I do, however, recall three "urgent" e-mails this partner sent to all the firm's lawyers over the course of those two years. They were the only general communications from him that stand out. In one, he set forth his clear expectation that any magazine taken into the restroom must be brought back out. In the second e-mail,

continued

he instructed all personnel in the law firm that the scoop for the ice machine must be placed in the holder *outside* the machine and not be left *inside*. Finally, in the third urgent e-mail, he warned us, his fellow attorneys, that client billing sheets must be submitted by a certain deadline or we "would be damned surprised by the results." That was it. Three e-mails over two years.

It seemed to me he had missed a significant leadership opportunity (I would characterize it as a responsibility) to lead. From where I sat, he had failed to communicate as a leader, to build and strengthen the team's culture, to teach and mentor the younger professionals in his firm, and to build a real team. His apparent focus on other aspects of the business sent a clear message to me that he might not even recognize his leadership responsibility. Of course, if he didn't even recognize he had such responsibilities, his failure to meet them is not surprising.

—Sean

We urge you to get clear on the difference between leadership and management. Remember the simple phrase *Lead people; manage things*. You will often have to do both, but you must remember that they are distinct responsibilities.

MANAGEMENT IS NOT LEADERSHIP

Consider your current situation. Are you being managed, or are you being led? Are you *leading*, or are you trying to *manage* your teammates' behavior or performance? For far too many, the attempt to manage people has become a default approach based on ignorance or a serious misunderstanding of human nature. Now is the time to prepare yourself to learn how to serve the people around you through authentic leadership. Start *leading* people. Stop *managing* people.

In this book, we are trying to prepare you for a deeper level of engagement with those with whom you share a common mission. You have a responsibility to influence those around you from a solid foundation, one based on a relationship built on trust and respect, rather than a merely transactional relationship built on the exchange of effort for something of value. Your leadership impact will arise from the strength of your relationships with your teammates. Think about how you engage and interact with the people around you, including your family members, your peers, your teammates, and the people you report to.

MANAGEMENT IS NOT LEADERSHIP

I once worked with a client who had a culture built on a highly evolved *management* model. As I came to understand how it really functioned, a clear pattern emerged: Its senior managers engaged with "subordinate" managers through a process they called "MBE," or management by exception. The senior managers sought to obtain defined performance results by focusing energy and effort in measuring and analyzing what was *wrong* with performance. While some attention was placed on what was going well, greater emphasis was placed on those who were not measuring up.

As it was explained to me, financial numbers and related data points were what really mattered to management. Since time was limited and management's energy and attention were at a premium, they had created a detailed set of performance metrics to drive performance throughout the organization. If something could be measured, it was measured. That data then became important because it would end up on a report for everyone to see. If an aspect of human performance was thought to be too subjective, or if it could not be measured or analyzed in some objective way, there was no reason to try to capture it. Why fix it if it ain't broke? Senior management had near real-time visibility into these metrics, and they took comfort in that. In one sense, it was a remarkable system, impressive in its depth and breadth. In another sense, it left many aspects of the human side of organizational reality in the dark.

As you might expect, managers down the line expended considerable energy on staying off the dreaded exception reports. If a subordinate manager fell outside of the expected results, a senior manager would call them out, often during group phone calls or open meetings, and the subordinate would be required to address the perceived shortcomings. These meetings were dominated by the presentation of endless slide decks comparing and ranking various teams against one another across a broad range of metrics. While accountability is necessary in

continued

every organization, and effective management of assets and processes is critical to success, the people side of the equation was being overlooked.

What about the people? What about their morale? Were they developing and becoming more capable? What was the quality of their daily experiences? Were they learning from one another and sharing best practices? Was there any real collaboration? Was energy being put toward creativity and innovation? Was there any attempt to try something new and learn from those experiences? What culture was being supported and strengthened?

The negative energy and sometimes harsh attention created in that MBE-based culture needed to be addressed, and I am pleased to report that this organization would evolve to balance the responsibility to effectively manage the business with the responsibility to serve and lead the human beings carrying out the business. You've simply got to do both: manage things and lead people.

—Sean

Your current responsibilities at home, at work, and in your community undoubtedly include both leading people and managing things, often simultaneously. Please don't misunderstand us. We are not suggesting that leadership is somehow better than management. We are emphasizing that leadership and management involve a distinct set of responsibilities and capabilities. Applying management principles to meet your leadership responsibilities will result in failure. If you wish to succeed, attend to both sets of responsibilities.

LEADERSHIP IS NOT ABOUT CONTROL

Authentic leaders don't try to control the behavior or performance of their teammates. People are sentient beings, capable of independent thought, judgment, and initiative. Instead, authentic leaders seek to influence and shape behavior through inspiration, example, encouragement, and by creating a team culture that elevates performance. Leaders don't think in terms of control. Control is a management consideration.

Authentic leaders never resort to manipulation, emotional or otherwise, to drive commitment and behavior. Efforts to manipulate will result in, at best, short-term responses with little constructive long-term effects. Authentic leaders consistently treat people with respect and dignity and recognize their innate potential and inherent value. Control, popularity, and manipulation have no connection to authentic leadership; pursuing them will only undermine your effort to develop real relationships with your teammates, a foundation on which your ability to influence must rest.

Managers, on the other hand, think in terms of control for good reason: Objects and processes can be precisely measured and meticulously managed. Human commitment and behavior, however, cannot. Leaders understand the only way to effectively and sustainably inspire commitment and influence behavior is through genuine relationships built on mutual trust and respect. Leaders seek to influence others in ways that move them to reach deeply into their own capabilities, ambitions, and sense of commitment. Since authentic leaders serve their team through relationships built on trust, their ability to influence others cannot be based on control.

LEADERSHIP IS NOT ABOUT POPULARITY

Leaders don't pursue popularity as an end in itself. Leaders who have gained a degree of popularity with the people they serve understand it is not a meaningful measure of their leadership effectiveness. Popularity is based on a shallow perception others may have of you. Popularity is impermanent, flimsy, and paper thin; it works in a very limited way until that moment when, well, you become unpopular. Seeking to lead with the purpose of gaining the love and admiration of others is an ego-driven approach that is very much about you rather than us. Authentic leaders engage with their teammates from an others-first perspective. A leader's primary motive is to serve others in building a relationship based on earned trust and respect. Relationships based on earned trust and respect provide the foundation for real influence, which enables you to lead toward your shared mission in an authentic way. That relationship then creates the potential for a lasting, constructive impact, through leadership, on another. Leaders don't seek popularity. Leaders strive to earn something higher. Leaders, through their service, humbly seek to build authentic relationships to influence others in a deeper way. Authentic relationships—not popularity—are what move people in the direction of positive action toward mission accomplishment.

LEADERSHIP IS NOT ABOUT MANIPULATION

Manipulative behavior is not the work of an authentic leader. Any effort to influence others using pain, fear, threat, punishment, humiliation, unsupported hope, or by playing on personal weakness or uncertainty is the work of an autocrat and not of an authentic leader. A stimulus generally produces a response. However, a mere response is not what leaders seek and does not serve as a foundation for healthy relationships. Leaders don't try to manipulate their teammates to accomplish a desired result. Authentic leaders work to inspire and move others through service, compassion, and authentic relationships. Authentic leaders work to voluntarily enlist the heart, mind, and effort of their teammates to merit a level of commitment and collaborative performance that would otherwise be impossible.

MANIPULATION IS NOT LEADERSHIP

I recently played a round of golf with a person I'd just met. As we began the round, I learned that he held a senior executive position with a local manufacturer. He told me they employed many "blue collar" employees, as he referred to them. I told him a bit about myself and shared a comment about my ongoing passion around leadership.

In response, he said, "Oh, I've figured out the easiest way to lead people."

I was struck by his use of the word *easiest* in relation to leadership. I'd been leading for decades in the military and the civilian world and had never thought leadership was easy; I'd always considered leadership to be a privilege and a sacred responsibility, but I'd never thought of it as easy. I asked him what the "secret" was, and he responded.

"It's actually pretty simple. You just have to use child psychology. You have to treat your employees like children." He went on to explain, "My people respond best to simple manipulation. You have to offer them a reward for good behavior or performance, and you have to ensure that they understand punishment will follow for poor behavior or performance."

I was so taken aback by his response that I looked more closely to see if he was being serious. Unfortunately, he was. As I selected my club for the next shot, I told him I respectfully disagreed with his premise, explaining that it didn't square with either my military or business leadership experience. I told him that what I had learned about leadership was completely different. My education and experience had taught me that leadership is about influence, and the ability to influence comes from serving your teammates in the direction of the team's mission.

I then addressed the ball for my next shot and ended the leadership discussion. It was clear to me that this was going to be a very long round of golf if we kept the leadership discussion going. Quite frankly, I wasn't interested in pouring energy into persuading this executive how his approach to leadership amounted to nothing more than a strategy of manipulation, so I decided to focus on golf. He clearly had no idea about what leadership required, and he certainly hadn't discovered the "secret" to leading adults. Reward or punishment, standing alone, is simply manipulation, not leadership.

—Sean

YOU CAN DO THIS!

We want to give you some encouragement as you navigate your intentional learning journey. Leadership has been described as one of mankind's most advanced social interactions. Humans are large-brained, complex creatures with the capacity for deep thinking, creativity, sometimes fickle emotions, and advanced communication skills—all contained within an intricate and often unpredictable social system. Leading people can admittedly be intimidating. Having said this, the core leadership principles are not complicated. You need not be a psychologist or social scientist to understand and apply those principles and lead effectively. All you need is benevolent intent, a deep personal commitment to serving others, and a basic grasp of human nature.

Leading authentically is within your capability. The essential leadership concepts are simple, knowable, teachable, and well within your reach. There are no leadership "secrets"; there are only time-tested and universally recognized principles. We are all (and this includes you) fortunate to be able to draw upon the powerful and foundational lessons of recorded human history along with our own experiences.

This is your journey, and—make no mistake—it will be a learning journey. No one can take this developmental journey of discovery for you. It's up to you and you alone to become an authentic leader. Now on to your journey to become a more effective leader.

Part 3

Becoming an Authentic Leader

CHAPTER 9

Write Your Story

W hat if you could start your leadership development journey over? It may surprise you to learn that you can do just that. In fact, you *must* start anew, newly armed with intention, a high level of awareness, and with a servant leader's perspective. During our life's journey, we amass a great deal of knowledge and wisdom. We also accumulate some excess intellectual and emotional baggage: unfounded rules, wrongheaded assumptions, poor habits, disappointments over bad decisions, and bouts of crippling self-doubt. We become accustomed to our journey's pace and direction as we adjust to the weight on our backs. We can easily forget we have the power to choose an entirely new route at virtually any point. Sometimes, wholesale change is needed: a complete resetting of our compass. For others, slight modifications will do—simply repacking our luggage with a fresh perspective and a good dose of resilience. Either way, we each possess the power to change the arc of our journey. We urge you to exercise that power.

As a testament to the power of starting anew regardless of where you are on your current life's journey, we decided to include a very personal account of how a letter to one of your authors some forty years ago profoundly impacted his lifelong journey.

THE LETTER

At eighteen years old, I was in the middle of an ordeal commonly known as *Plebe Summer* at the Naval Academy. Despite my best efforts to exhibit a stoic perspective in the face of what was the most trying time of my life up to that point, I let something slip in a call home about the intense pressure I was feeling, and my own self-doubt. My mother, who seemed to know me better than I knew myself, must have picked up on that anxiety, so she sat down and typed a letter.

In it, she gave me perspective on what I was going through by offering historical examples of how ancient societies developed leadership and instilled character in their young people through trial, hardship, and stress. She reassured me that what I was going through was a necessary part of becoming an adult and an authentic human being. But the following passages have always stuck with me and are particularly relevant here:

> In every so-called primitive society since man became sapient, there has been a period of time during which its young people were subjected to extreme hardship and stress before they could be accepted as an adult. It taught them to expand the limits of themselves. Our culture is sadly deficient in this respect and there is no clear-cut step from childhood to adulthood.
>
> Freedom is misunderstood. Freedom is operating at your greatest capacity. It is pushing the limits imposed by self-doubt or even by outside doubt back. It is the process of reaching for your potential, which is never finished and ends in this dimension only with physical death. Freedom is never conferred by someone else or taken away by someone else. It exists in the operation of your personality.
>
> This life is not a game. Each one of us during his lifetime is charged with the awesome responsibility to explore his potential. You question the concept of blind loyalty to an institution, and it is well that you do. But consider that there will be those who come after you, and mankind is not yet fully evolved. Someone said that a man must participate in the time in which he lives. Blind loyalty is suspect; dedication to the future is a hallmark of greatness. We are all links in a chain which stretches from the fear-filled nights of

huddled man-apes to who knows what. The strength of our personal link will determine it. The future is plastic and shaping in us.

You do not burden me with your questions. The place of leadership can be a lonely one. That is what they are trying to prepare you for. The place where most of humanity is comfortable is in the crowd. You would be unhappy there and you know that in the deepest part of your being. So do I.

So much depends on you. So much depends on each of us. But some turn aside. You have the choice to do that, too. But I think you will not. I think you will continue to push back the obstacles. I think that you will learn to become master of yourself.

After receiving that letter, I reengaged fully and pressed forward. I have read and reread it countless times since graduating from Annapolis. It was a precious gift from a remarkable woman. Not only was her timing perfect, but her message, given with love, was absolutely on point. That letter was a powerful act of leadership from a mother to a son. Rather than criticizing me, ordering me not to quit, or telling me to "follow my heart," my mother provided me with a critical perspective shift that helped me process my experience. This simple act of loving communication continues to be a powerful reminder to me about leadership and the importance of love, trust, and timely words of encouragement.

—Sean

A couple of key points stand out to us as particularly relevant to *your* leadership development. First, a leader's words can impact others in deeply profound ways that often help set a new course for the road ahead. Words from those we respect can serve as a nudge, a jolt, a pull, a push, or simply as a safety net that helps us find the courage to take a chance. Second, a fresh perspective and even a slight change in direction are often all that's needed to help another person move forward.

The first step on a new journey, or in any change of direction, is often the most difficult—and always the most important. That step requires courage and preparation. Before you begin your intentional learning journey in earnest, you need to understand the purpose of your journey, and you should have a sense of how you plan to reach your destination. You can. You must. It's time (and yes, there *is* time) for a comprehensive do-over.

If you are willing to commit to making leadership development an important part of your life's journey, the payoff will far exceed the investment in time and energy. Not everyone is willing to do the hard work it takes to embark on and navigate this intentional journey. We are pleased you are ready to move forward.

THE MIRACLE QUESTION: WHY?

Warren Berger, in his thought-provoking book, *A More Beautiful Question*, suggests that we typically try to address challenges by asking the wrong question: *How?* How might I solve this? Armed with this pragmatic approach, we then roll up our sleeves, reach into a convenient toolbox to grab a familiar tool, and start building or destroying. However, when we begin with *how*, we tend to overlook the underlying source or cause of the challenge. We fail to envision a desired outcome and then neglect to think creatively about innovative solutions to achieve that preferred outcome.

Berger suggests a better way: starting with *Why? Why* is this thing I want seemingly beyond my reach? Another powerful question should then follow, beginning with *what if. What if* those roadblocks did not exist? Only then, after you've addressed *why* and *what if*, should you seek to answer *how*.

Getting clear on your *why* doesn't limit your thinking; it actually unleashes it. The answers you develop will enable you to purge traditional solutions and will serve as a powerful source of self-motivation. This spark will light a torch and allow you to find solutions beyond your previously limited perspective.

This is worth a closer look and is deserving of the following important exercise. Take some time with it over the course of the next several days. Consider your responses. Walk away. Come back to it. Redo it. And then redo it again.

REFLECTION

✓ Clarify your *why*: the question or questions most fundamental and important to *you* regarding leadership and leadership development.

✓ Envision *what if* you achieved your desired end state. If a miracle happened tonight, when you woke up tomorrow, who would be present? What would they say and do? What would happen? What would that look and feel like? What opportunities would present themselves?

✓ Brainstorm (all ideas are valid) *how* you could make that happen—your intention, your commitment, and your actions.

A commitment is a serious thing, not to be taken lightly. Committing to your leadership development is like any other serious commitment you make to transform a significant aspect of your life, whether your health, marriage, or your financial situation. Every real commitment must start with a powerful *why*. Your journey will begin to take shape as you start envisioning what, and who, it might include. Objective goals and a growth mindset will be required. You will need to reprioritize some things in your life so you can allocate the necessary time, attention, and energy. You will need a level of determination, a healthy humility, and resilience. Like every meaningful journey, yours will involve experience, failure, adjustment, learning, innovation, and progress. But first, you need to get clear on your *why*.

A FIXED OR A GROWTH MINDSET?

As an educator, I spend a good deal of my time determining my individual students' learning styles: auditory, visual, kinesthetic, or social. More important than learning style is the student's attitude toward learning. I have found a strong correlation between the attitude one brings to learning and the potential for learning. Of each of my students, I frequently ask myself the following questions:

- Does the student cling to their comfort zone, or are they willing to move into their stretch zone?

- Are they naturally curious?

- Do they want to grow? Are they ambitious?

- What is their locus of control? Do they feel their life's outcomes are primarily self-determined, controlled by others, or a matter of destiny?

continued

- What is their degree of self-efficacy? Do they believe they have what it takes to learn a new skill?

In addition, I often ask my students to reflect and self-identify which of the following categories best describes their willingness and readiness to learn:

THE PRISONER

Prisoners are captives of their situation and exercise no input or control. Passive and compliant, prisoners do not want to be where they are and anticipate the day when someone releases them from their bondage. Prisoners never start the journey and, in fact, often want to avoid it altogether.

THE PASSENGER

Passengers embark on their journey on their own cognizance but expect others to get them to their destination. Passengers do as they are told, no more and no less, and possess little expectation to influence outcomes. Passengers are along for the ride.

THE VACATIONER

Vacationers are competent and look good while performing their tasks. Clearly in their comfort zone, vacationers enjoy a high degree of control over their journey and destination and have little interest in (or tolerance for) change, uncertainty, or hardship. Vacationers believe they have crossed the finish line, are coasting through life, and are basking in their self-perceived glory.

THE EXPLORER

Explorers look under every rock and behind every tree to find out what could be. Explorers take reasonable risks, accept failure as a learning opportunity, and keep moving forward with an indelible expectation of discovery. Explorers find their journey and understand they will never cross the finish line.

—John

Lifelong learners have an insatiable appetite to grow, expand their capabilities and their self-awareness, and improve. They intentionally fill their brains, train their hands, and suck the marrow out of every experience life offers. They habitually ask questions and actively seek answers. They read, listen, observe, and take notice of their environment. They talk to and engage with the people around them. They take reasonable risks, try new things, and aim to succeed even when success isn't guaranteed.

REFLECTION

- ✓ Reflect on your attitude toward learning and personal growth and development.
- ✓ Are you generally satisfied with the status quo of knowing what you know and being who you are? Or do you deliberately and routinely seek to acquire new knowledge and skills?
- ✓ Are you a prisoner, passenger, vacationer, or explorer?
- ✓ Do you have a fixed mindset or a growth mindset?
- ✓ In what ways are you willing to sacrifice who you are for who you wish to become?
- ✓ What clues in your attitude and behaviors lead you to these conclusions?

Commitment and attitude, rather than native talent, most determine your potential in life. It is the same with your leadership development. If you will believe you can become a more authentic leader, commit to the journey, and put in the time and effort, you will create the growth you seek.

MAKING SPAGHETTI: THE LEADERSHIP DEVELOPMENT PROCESS

In one respect, spaghetti is a simple dish. There are three basic ingredients: pasta, sauce, and spices. There are also some tried-and-true methods for preparing, combining, and serving spaghetti. There is, however, no single exclusive list of ingredients, no exclusive preparation sequence, and no single way of cooking and serving the meal. Here's how the making of spaghetti works: You inventory what you have, acquire the ingredients you need, combine them, taste the concoction, adjust the heat, and add spices to achieve the desired effect. Every batch is prepared a bit differently, and every plate has a unique look, texture, and taste. There is bad spaghetti, okay spaghetti, and good spaghetti, but there is never perfect spaghetti. Cooking spaghetti is an art, not a science, and it can be a bit messy.

Leadership development is a similar dish. There are certainly basic ingredients and fundamental concepts. In the final analysis, however, the process of developing as a leader is a creative one, and you are the primary creator. You must inventory who you are and what you have and seek out what you need. You will experiment, learn, adjust, and try again. There is a range of leadership effectiveness between poor and outstanding, but there is no such thing as perfect leadership.

Like preparing spaghetti, developing your leadership capabilities can take place in many ways over the course of many different experiences and can be a bit messy. Whether cooking spaghetti or developing your leadership ability, you need to know the basic ingredients and practice creativity as you move forward.

LEADER FIRST, SPECIALIST SECOND

When I arrived at the Marine Corps' Officer Candidate School, the first step on the path to becoming an officer of Marines, the message I heard went something like this:

"First and foremost, you are expected to become a leader. Technical knowledge and job skills are vitally important, but they are secondary to leading Marines. You may be a physical specimen, a mental genius, or an expert at fixing equipment, planning logistics, or shooting weapons. But if you can't lead, you are of limited value to your unit and of no use to your Marines. You must be a leader first and a specialist second!"

During my initial nine months of officer training, I was assessed in my academics, physical fitness, and leadership skills. Of the three, my leadership performance was weighted much more heavily than the others. So much so that the quickest way to be dropped from the entire program—far quicker than failing an academic or physical fitness test—was to demonstrate a failure to lead (often related to a breach of integrity, self-centeredness, or a failure to communicate effectively with others).

Marine officer school developed my leadership ability in three important ways. First, in the classroom where I learned, beginning with rote memorization, the fundamental leadership traits and leadership principles. I was also given a list of classic leadership books that I was expected to read on my own time. Second, I studied and discussed with my peers historical vignettes and leadership case studies (both good and bad) and participated in mock leadership scenarios on a chalkboard or sand table or out in the field. These were always followed by a thorough debrief led by instructors to draw out leadership lessons learned. Third, as a venue to practice my leadership skills, I was put in multiple leadership roles in my unit and assigned to a real officer or noncommissioned officer (NCO) mentor. Throughout this entire process, my officers, NCOs, and peers gave me continuous verbal and written feedback on my leadership performance.

Only then was I allowed to attend my specialty school, where I learned the technical aspects of my job. Soon after, I was assigned to an operational unit and given the opportunity to lead real Marines on real missions. And that cycle continued. Every time I was promoted, I was sent to another school to learn more about leadership first, provided with an updated book list consistent with my rank, and only after completion of that process sent back to an operational unit—all the while receiving continuous and timely feedback, including annual evaluations of my leadership performance.

—John

Few of us have the time, money, or resources to replicate an intensive leadership growth experience like Marine Corps officer training. Most of our leadership development takes place not in a school or formal training program but rather in the chaotic real world—with real people in real situations that result in real consequences. Is there anything you can gather from the Marines' leadership development process to apply to your own leadership journey? We believe so.

REFLECTION

Consider aspects of the Marines' leadership development model that you could apply to your own life situation:

✓ Expectation and commitment?

✓ Learning about leadership?

✓ Learning how to lead?

✓ Acquiring leadership experience?

✓ Repetition, consistency, feedback?

Effective leadership development is progressive in nature, but there is no set progression. Education, training, and experience—all vitally important—happen concurrently and inform one another. Leadership development is not the result of education *or* training *or* experience, nor is it education *then* training *then* experience. Leadership development is education *and* training *and* experience. Your learning journey may not be structured and sequential, but it can be planned and must be intentional.

REFLECTION

✓ How might you implement such a model in your current situation for you and your teammates?

✓ What resources do you have, right now, to begin this process?

✓ What is keeping you from taking advantage of these resources?

✓ What resources do you need?

Learn About Leadership

Y ou can learn about leadership passively, by simply observing. You can also learn about leadership in a more active and intentional way, by reading books, listening to podcasts, reviewing case studies, and by listening, watching, and paying attention to how real leaders and teammates interact. Learning about leadership as a topic will cause you to wrestle with and refine your own ideas, theories, philosophies, and attitudes about leadership. That is important work you will need to undertake on your learning journey. Let your curiosity and interest drive the journey from time to time.

COLLECTING FIREWOOD

As a junior military officer, I picked up *Killer Angels*, a book about the Battle of Gettysburg. As I read the novel, I realized I needed more context to fully under-stand what moved the characters. I needed to understand what led to each battle and the implications of those battles, so I absorbed myself in America's Civil War history: the politics, strategy, battles, and commanders. The more I learned, the more I recognized what I didn't know and the more eager I became to understand.

continued

Why did the South secede? Why did the Union fight? Why did Lincoln make the choices he did? What were the nineteenth-century economics of the United States? Why and how did the United States adopt the institution of slavery? What did our Constitution say? How and why did we develop our Constitution? Why did the colonies declare independence from Great Britain? Why did Great Britain administer the colonies the way it did? What was Great Britain's history? What was Europe's history? What about the French Revolution? Who was Napoleon? What about the Ottoman Empire, the Crusades, the Roman Empire?

The search for answers illuminated new questions that required a search for new answers. What began as a story about a military engagement in rural Pennsylvania in 1863 became a significant personal quest to understand human nature in the context of world history—power, economics, psychology, politics, and the like. The learning journey was frustrating, in a good way. The more I learned, the more I realized what I didn't know.

Soon after beginning my historical inquiry, one of my mentors, a general in the Marines, gifted me with an appropriate analogy: The amount of wood in a campfire determines the amount of light produced. If you add sticks to the fire, the ring of light grows and illuminates more forest floor and reveals more firewood that can be gathered. You collect those sticks, add them to the fire, and the ring of light grows again. The cycle continues, exponentially.

—John

As you actively and intentionally acquire more knowledge about leadership, you will begin to consider how it applies to how you will lead in your own life. At the same time, you will become increasingly aware of how much more there is to learn. The more you learn, the more enlightened you will become. The more enlightened you become, the greater the wisdom you will gather and be able to apply in your life.

REFLECTION

Think of a few situations in which you learned about something which sparked your curiosity and inspired you to do a deeper dive into the subject:

✓ What learning opportunities resulted from that curiosity?

LEARN ABOUT LEADERSHIP EVERYWHERE

The practicality and usefulness of educational resources vary widely. Some are anecdotal and based on opinion, while others are more thoroughly researched. Some resources are pithy and evoke our emotions, while others feed our intellect. Some are trendy, while others are timeless. They all have tremendous value if you truly open yourself to them.

Your learning style and the resources you seek out will determine what works best in your personal situation. As with most things in life, breadth and depth are best. A wider range of topics and resources is better than a narrow focus. Search the Internet for leadership-related blogs and articles, read leadership and management books, and observe and talk to people with leadership experience in different fields. Get a sense of what is known about leadership, how people are thinking about leadership issues today, and what leadership may look like in the future. Reach beyond your backyard and engage with people from diverse backgrounds and experiences in a variety of environments and venues to understand proven principles, as well as fresh new ideas.

Although there may be significant cultural differences between people and among different professions, effective leadership is effective leadership, regardless of the context. Many apps, websites, blogs, podcasts, videos, magazine articles, and professional journals are devoted to leadership. Seek them out. Movies and videos can be a great resource and are often a wellspring of provocative speeches, quotes, and quips. The evening news, your favorite sitcom, and political elections all contain leadership nuggets and insights into human nature that are ready for the taking.

The people currently in your life are among your greatest resources. Many of the most profound leadership lessons we learned during our life's journey were from family members, professional colleagues, coaches, teachers, and social acquaintances. Your own leadership successes and failures can provide a treasure trove of information. Virtually every human interaction bound by a shared set of interests or a common goal contains lessons on leadership—or the implication of leadership's absence. Look for those lessons.

THE INTERVIEW

I was about to meet with the upperclassman responsible for giving me my first round of formal performance feedback based on my first semester at the Naval Academy. I respected him greatly, but I felt I hadn't lived up to either his high expectations or my own. I reported to his room, and he invited me to take a seat across the desk from him. He asked how my first year at Annapolis was going. I candidly replied, "I am surviving, sir." He then asked me a simple question I was completely unprepared for: "What do you see yourself accomplishing here over the next three and a half years?"

What were my goals for the next three and a half years? Is he serious? I was in survival mode at the time, doing my best to deal with the personal and professional challenges being thrown at me in rapid succession. My focus was literally on getting through this meeting, then preparing my uniform for the next formation, memorizing the 12-item menu for the next meal, then getting through lunch, and on and on. I couldn't see much past the next few hours.

I quickly cobbled together a few thoughts. I told him I thought I could graduate with a B average, and there were a few extracurricular activities I might pursue. He looked me right in the eye, slowly shook his head, and with a firm, quiet voice said, "No. You are setting your sights way too low. This is what I see you accomplishing." He then painted a detailed picture of the accomplishments he envisioned for me. He said, "I see you doing well academically, obtaining at least a 3.4 GPA. You are a good athlete, and I see you playing battalion football and basketball competitively and at a high level. I also see you taking a leadership role with the Brigade Honor Committee." He then said something I will not forget: "I know you are capable of much more, but *you've* got to *believe* that."

I will never forget how his feedback made me feel: energized, empowered, and capable. I had the strong sense he was being honest with me. He had earned my trust, and the potential he saw in me opened my eyes to what might be possible if I put in the work. I came away from that meeting with a renewed sense of what was possible and with a greater conviction in what I could do. As it turned out, I would go on to accomplish virtually everything he'd envisioned and more.

It was a powerful lesson on the impact a leader can have on those they serve.

—Sean

THE DEEP SOAK

We both love to read. Reading a book may seem like an old-fashioned activity, but we are true believers in the educational experience of spending personal time with a book. Most of the outstanding leaders we've known share this appreciation. Books are unique; they provide you with a deep soak in a subject. Since they are rarely read in one session, they give you time for reflection and consideration. In your bookstore's management and self-help sections, there are numerous books on a variety of topics: facing fears, increasing motivation, losing weight, simplifying life, improving your marriage, and—our favorite category—becoming a better leader. (We're not discouraging online book purchases, but there is something special, even exhilarating, about the treasure-hunt experience of browsing the aisles of a brick-and-mortar bookstore.)

During your intentional learning journey, we strongly encourage you to read widely from the many excellent leadership books available. But don't limit yourself to books about leadership. There are valuable, practical leadership nuggets in virtually every genre. For example, history is a great teacher; novels and memoirs can also be excellent resources, as they reveal the complex world of human emotions and relationships. Although nonfiction informs, fiction can stimulate questions, seed ideas, fuel your motivation, and spark emotion. Make reading an important aspect of your leadership education. Someone once said there is very little difference between a person who cannot read and a person who won't read. Expand your understanding and comprehension of humanity and leadership by doing a deep dive into literature.

There are different ways to read a book. You can buy books, read books, listen to books, or study books. Dogeared pages, highlights, and notes in the margin allow you to analyze and reflect on the content and get an intimate understanding of the author's message. This leads to the formulation of a strong opinion of that content and a connection with how you will apply the content to how you engage in your own life.

Read a book from a leader's perspective. While reading or soon afterward, take the time to write in your journal. What leadership concepts did you take away? What additional questions arose? Think about their application to your own situation. Digest the content by making a commitment to take action in your life armed with these new or refined insights. Write down your commitments and hold yourself accountable. Learning about leadership is vitally important to your development. So, too, is learning how to lead.

CHAPTER 11

Learn How to Lead

L eadership training is the process of learning how to lead through a range of experiences: mentorship, participating in apprenticeships, attending formal schools or training programs, engaging in simulations, and conducting face-to-face or online discussions with other students of leadership. Training teaches you how to apply skills in specific situations and provides you with some of the fundamentals. Through leadership training, you can learn what generally works in leadership situations and collect leadership tools of the trade to apply in multiple contexts.

In any field of endeavor, a certain level of subject-matter understanding and competence are required for a leader to earn the attention and respect of the people they intend to influence. While a leader doesn't have to be an "expert," a reasonable level of relevant knowledge and skill will give you some needed credibility. Leaders know they must work hard to develop and maintain a level of competence in their field so they can serve their teammates in maximizing opportunities and overcoming obstacles.

A FEW WORDS ABOUT TRAINING VENUES

There are many formal leadership training programs out there. Most fall under a few broad categories. Soft skill training teaches you to communicate or serve customers effectively, improve language and social graces, embrace diversity, understand sexual harassment, and the like. Team building improves familiarity among teammates and helps you learn interpersonal communication, collaboration, and collective decision-making skills. Professional training helps you gain knowledge and competence in job- or industry-specific skills, workplace ethics, or earn technical certifications. Managerial training is for supervisors, managers, or executives to learn planning and goal setting, motivating, delegating, coaching, or giving feedback.

Although often narrowly focused, each of these types of training addresses some important insights into various aspects of leadership and are important building blocks in learning how to become an effective leader. The level at which you operate—or your position in the chain of command—doesn't discriminate. Imagine a technical expert who doesn't know how to communicate effectively with their teammates, a supervisor who doesn't know the technical aspects of their work, a great team contributor who doesn't understand where their role fits within the larger organization's mission or vision, or a CEO who cannot think strategically. Good leadership training should cover a combination of skills.

Technical skills relate to the knowledge and proficiency in a particular discipline, industry, or profession—business, construction, outdoor recreation, clergy, law, nonprofit, education, and the like. Effective leaders know their craft—the vocabulary, required resources, policies and procedures, customs, and system inputs and outputs. To be an effective leader, you don't have to be the expert, but you need to have some degree of technical competence along with a commitment to continue your active learning.

Conceptual skills relate to your ability to work with ideas and concepts. Effective leaders can wrap their head around abstract ideas and often complicated processes. They can begin to recognize patterns, strategize ways to navigate the course ahead, and with the active involvement of their teammates, work to solve complex problems creatively. To be an effective leader, you need to develop your conceptual capabilities.

People skills are related to your social judgment and your ability to engage with others, and they are critical to your ability to lead. Remember our working definition of leadership: *Leadership is who you are and what you do to* influence others *to commit to and act in alignment with the mission.* Leaders operate with and through other people in a team context to accomplish a shared mission. You don't need to be the best or brightest on the team nor the strongest and fastest, but you must be able to genuinely engage with others in constructive ways by tapping into their motivations, expertise, experience, creativity, and energy so the team can accomplish its mission. To be an effective leader, you need to develop your people skills.

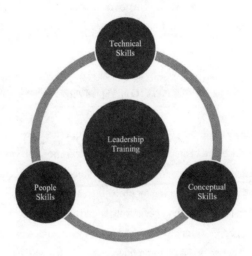

REFLECTION

✓ In your discipline, team, or workplace, rate yourself on a 1–10 scale on your level of the following:

» Technical (professional) skills

» Conceptual (abstract thinking) skills

» People (interpersonal) skills

✓ What type of training or educational experience do you believe would most significantly improve your skills in each area?

To effectively influence others, you need to develop a reasonable degree of competence and confidence in each of these three areas: technical, conceptual, and interpersonal. However, standing alone, technical and professional competence in your area of work or contribution will not make you an effective leader. Becoming a proficient planner or communicator is also important, but even mastering these areas will leave you with a critical gap as you develop as a leader. Since leadership is relational in nature, rather than transactional, people skills are most critical for a leader to master. You may not be a technical expert or a big-idea person, but you must be able to understand, engage with, and influence your teammates. Your ability to constructively engage with others will help advance you from the important role of an individual contributor to the much more impactful role of a leader.

A CAUTIONARY TALE

He was a senior executive in the organization, unquestionably smart and experienced in his field. He had been promoted to a high-level position with responsibility for a large piece of the business. With a history of impressive business results on his resume, he should have been poised for even greater things. Unfortunately, he'd hit a ceiling of his own making. He had never truly understood his personal responsibility to lead with the people around him. Since he had never embraced that responsibility, he had never put effort in learning how to lead. Instead, he fell into a common trap: He tried to control and manage people, often in an authoritarian way. When under stress, as he often was, he could be volatile, sometimes engaging harshly and dismissively with his most important teammates, barking out orders or expressing anger when things didn't turn out as he'd planned.

The impact of his behavior was, well, exactly what you would expect. The people around him did what was necessary to avoid his wrath. In the fear-filled environment he created, his teammates spent great energy and effort to avoid public embarrassment; they focused on surviving the encounter. They hustled about to make sure they stayed out of his way, and they worked hard to comply with his directives. His team was talented and committed, but its performance was focused on mere compliance instead of mission accomplishment. Business opportunities were squandered because potential clients didn't want to deal with his behavior. Morale within the team suffered. Since it wasn't professionally (or personally) safe to take unnecessary risks, acts of initiative and creativity were rare.

He once expressed an interest in a particular leadership book I had recommended to him. I noticed he had a copy sitting on his desk. It soon disappeared. We never discussed it again. I seriously doubt whether he ever read it.

He had become a living, breathing, cautionary tale: the talented professional who failed to make the critical adjustment from individual contributor and manager to authentic leader. The strains on his professional relationships were open and evident. The business results achieved often happened in spite of him, as his teammates stepped up to support one another in carrying out the team's mission. He lost the loyalty and trust of some very good people. He developed no clear successor. Recruiting to his team suffered, as his reputation kept other good people from joining the team. Ultimately, the organization realized it would have to part ways with him, and the end came sooner than he had wished or planned.

—Sean

Look in the mirror. Don't be a cautionary tale. It's never too late to take responsibility for your leadership journey.

WHAT IF I'M NOT PROVIDED LEADERSHIP TRAINING OR AM SELF-EMPLOYED?

You may have had the opportunity to attend some formal leadership training through your employer or from some other source. That's good. We hope it provided you with a deeper understanding and some meaningful resources, but as they say, you can't learn to ride a bike at a seminar. It is even more true with leadership. In general, leadership training is either woefully insufficient or virtually nonexistent in most organizations, and training is typically one of the first things cut when an organization experiences competitive pressure or financial hardships. Some organizations feel they don't have the time or resources to send their employees to formal leadership training. Unfortunately, some organizations are more interested in employee compliance with stilted human resources policies and procedures and not much concerned with developing their employees beyond job-specific technical skills. Self-employed or unemployed people are at an even greater disadvantage. The bottom line is this: It's all on your shoulders. No one will knock on your door and offer to make you a better leader.

Here's some good news. Rich learning resources are readily available for little or no cost. But you must step up, take the initiative, and identify them. These include a wealth of online training programs, webinars, seminars and professional conferences, certification programs, apprenticeships, formal schools, and many quality organizations dedicated to providing leadership training.

In addition to considering cost (from free to very expensive), you should research the quality of these programs and their fit with your personal development needs. Some provide only advice and information; some put you through drills or exercises; others provide follow-up consultation or coaching. Effective training must go well beyond presenting information. Effective training tailored to your unique learning preferences and customized to fit your specific needs can be impactful. Shop with discretion and choose wisely.

Unfortunately, we must alert you to the inherent limitations of any leadership training program. No single program can give you everything you need to develop fully as a leader. First, many can be a bit one dimensional (such as job-specific management competencies or a narrow focus on a particular aspect of leadership) or indiscriminate (generalized to a one-size-fits-all approach to leadership). Rather than teaching a unique human being how to lead in a wide variety of situations, leadership training often addresses only certain types of common issues, solutions, and results. Second, leadership training often attempts to replicate the real world but generally does so in low-risk situations where consequences are minimal. On a positive note, safe learning environments do allow you to take chances where otherwise you might not. However, real development happens best where mistakes and successes yield real consequences. Training—good training—has an important niche in a holistic approach to your leadership development.

SEEK OUT A MENTOR

Since you have made a serious commitment to your leadership development, we strongly encourage you to actively seek out a mentor relationship. We've been mentored by some remarkable leaders and can attest to the incredible value of initiating and sustaining a relationship with a mentor who is willing to guide you. In Greek mythology, Mentor was a tutor, but mentors are much more than teachers. They can provide practical advice, answer your questions, and provide consistent, quality feedback while also modeling exemplary leadership behaviors themselves. A mentor can and should be a powerful resource for your developmental journey.

Mentors have a stake in your success and usually come free of charge. Mentor–mentee relationships are personal and confidential and allow for honesty and transparency. Where can you find such a mentor? Start by looking to those who are successful, respected leaders in your family, workplace, social circle, or community. How do you get a mentor? Ask! Seriously, that's it! Authentic leaders are wired to serve others.

Mentorships sometimes emerge organically, without even a verbal acknowledgment. There is nothing more gratifying to a servant leader than the opportunity to help create new leaders. Over the years, we've been fortunate to mentor dozens of former Marines, professional associates, and students who reached out to us for advice and guidance on leadership challenges they were facing. As servant leaders, we embrace the responsibility to develop leadership in others, accepting we have no higher purpose than to serve them in this way. We will gladly drop what we're doing or reprioritize to do so.

REFLECTION

- ✓ List a few people in your life who you believe would be excellent leadership mentors.

- ✓ For each person, describe a few ways they could help you become a better leader.

- ✓ Do you think they would agree to serve as your mentor? (If you answered "no," you are probably mistaken.)

- ✓ Have you asked them? If not, what are three good reasons for you to do so?

- ✓ Who on your team would benefit from your mentorship? What could you do to become their mentor?

GET A COACH

We strongly encourage you to consider hiring a professional coach to support you on your leadership journey. A coach will engage with you on a scheduled basis to help you achieve your goals. Coaches are different from mentors. A coach's mission is to help you clarify what you want and help you find ways to get there. A coach can help you frame the right questions and find the answers to those questions within yourself. A coach will work with you to develop an action plan and hold you accountable to do what you say you will do. A coach can be your ally, advocate, and champion. Before hiring a coach, have a thorough conversation with several candidates about their coaching credentials, life experiences, and coaching methods. A good coaching relationship should be trustworthy and discrete and should be completely focused on your goals.

GETTING UNSTUCK

When I take clients rock climbing, they often get stuck in one place. While climbing up the rock face, they will come to a difficult spot and say they can't go higher and wish to be lowered back to the ground. "There are no more handholds. There are no more footholds. I can't go higher. I'm stuck."

Sometimes a little coaching can make all the difference. What could happen if you moved left or right or descended six inches? In so doing, they can often see a foothold they didn't know existed. They just needed a different view. What could happen if you tried something you don't think you can do? Often, that handhold they thought was beyond their reach was, in fact, within their reach. They just needed to stretch.

—John

When you are stuck, sometimes you just need some encouragement to adjust your point of view or try something new. Looking at a problem from a different angle or stretching yourself—physically, mentally, and emotionally—is all you needed to get unstuck. A coach doesn't solve your problems but rather helps you find the answers that lie within you.

CHAPTER 12

Practice Leadership

Y ou can gain knowledge from others but not wisdom. Wisdom must be earned through your own experience, from following and leading real people in real situations with real consequences. In your world, through trial, error, and reflection, you will learn what really works and what doesn't really work for you. By experiencing and performing leadership firsthand, you gain insight, wisdom, and a deeper understanding of what you need to do to lead others effectively. It is only by following and leading in your world that you develop your leadership muscle memory.

To gain leadership experience, you need to seek out and take on leadership roles when the opportunity arises. Those opportunities are all around you—at home, at school, at work, and in your community. Virtually every interaction you have with another person in the context of a shared purpose or mission presents you with a leadership opportunity. Authentic leaders listen; develop your listening skills by listening more intently in your daily interactions, focusing on what is being communicated rather than what your response will be. Share lessons learned from your experience. Influence your teammates through the power of your example in the way you conduct yourself and the way you engage with them. Look out for others' interests and put those interests ahead of your own. Find ways to serve your teammates. Encourage and help them to develop a skill set. Help another shoulder a burden.

You don't need a title or position to do any of these things. Leadership opportunities in your life are all around you. Leadership experience comes from your involvement and engagement with other people. By leading others, you gain insights into leadership that you otherwise wouldn't be able to achieve. School is always in session. Your life is your classroom.

LEARN TO LEAD BY ACTIVELY FOLLOWING

You can also learn much about leadership by following the lead of another. Many important insights you must gain about the nature of the leader–follower relationship and who you are as a leader will come from actively following the lead of others. It may seem counterintuitive, but do not ignore this one. You don't have to be "the leader" to learn how to lead. Actively following the lead of another is fertile learning ground.

The military effectively deploys this leadership development method. In the Marines, everyone begins their leadership development in the role of a follower, in basic training or officer training programs. You start at the bottom, not the top. This gives you the benefit of understanding, in no uncertain terms, what leadership looks and feels like from the perspective of a follower in a very real and direct way. Those experiences yield important insights which can't be gained if you begin your learning journey with a leadership title.

We learned a great deal about what it means to lead another human being by actively following and attentively observing others' leadership. In fact, some of the most important leadership insights we've gathered over the years have come from following, even when leadership was ineffective or virtually absent. If you've ever been subjected to an abuse of authority or if you've ever experienced an absence of leadership in situations that called for leadership, you understand in your bones what the implications are. When you have that experience, you realize the choices you have when leadership opportunities appear.

From these experiences, and because of their impact on us and our team-mates, we developed invaluable insights into the things we will never do as leaders, and clarity about the things we will always strive to do. Rather than complaining about ineffective leadership or even marveling at excellence in leadership, we challenge you to observe closely and learn. Take good notes along the way.

These crucial leader–follower experiences, both in training and in real-world scenarios, can give you meaningful insights into what truly moves you and others as they work toward mission accomplishment. In an important sense, you are now in a living and moving human laboratory. Don't wait until you find yourself in a leadership position to begin accruing leadership experience. Start now, while you are in one of the best leadership schools in the world. Pay attention to communication, the quality of relationships, how cultures build, the team environment, the level of attention and care, and so on. Also, this is an important opportunity to learn what it takes to be a good teammate, to build constructive relationships with your teammates, and to serve and support them. Taking direction well, getting on with the task at hand, and delivering on what is expected of you are fundamental responsi-bilities of any team member. By actively engaging in the leadership process from a follower point of view—watching, listening, assessing, and giving and receiving feedback—you can learn valuable lessons and experience firsthand the reciprocity of the leader–follower relationship.

LEARNING HOW *NOT* TO LEAD

I can still picture him standing directly in front of me as I strained to maintain a strict position of attention in the hot sun. I can feel his eyes glaring at me with apparent disgust as he pointed out an obscure flaw with my uniform or commented on my lack of potential as a future officer. He was a first class (senior) squad leader at Annapolis, and I was one of his fourth class (freshman) targets. He attempted to motivate us through fear and intimidation, and we frankly despised him in return.

While his intent may have been to develop us as future leaders by being tough and demanding, he came across as unreasonably harsh, unfair, and inhumane.

continued

There was a level of disrespect in his voice and actions that seemed unjustified and extreme. He was creative in finding public ways to personally embarrass us and highlight our shortcomings. He was reactive and dismissive and volatile. New to the military experience, I remember thinking, *If this is what passes for leadership in the military, then I'm not going to be able to lead.*

Fortunately, most upperclassmen showed us, through the power of their own example and the level of their engagement with us, that there was a more authentic way to lead. They took a higher road by building relationships that centered on responsibility, dignity, humility, and respect. I would quickly learn that there are positional leaders, those who posture, puff, and intimidate, and there are authentic leaders, those who lead by the power of their own example and with dignity by inspiring their teammates while serving their development.

I admit that I am now grateful for my hard experience with this man. He helped me to fully appreciate the limits of fear and manipulation in raising individual and team performance. From him, I learned that while fear can motivate, it does not inspire and is ultimately ineffective. People moved by fear tend to react by engaging in defensive and avoidance behaviors. Fear may get you a specific result, but you will get little beyond mere compliance. I also learned about what is achievable when a person attempts to lead solely from title or rank without engaging as a real human being in an authentic way. Much of his behavior was a pretense, a bizarre performance, although I didn't fully appreciate it at the time.

—Sean

Abusing one's authority has nothing to do with real leadership and only serves to degrade the confidence, capability, and commitment levels of a team. Loathing cannot form the foundation of a solid relationship between a leader and a follower. Mutual respect and trust are the higher road, the only road. As a servant leader, you can be tough and demanding, but you must take a genuine interest in the well-being of the person you seek to influence.

The key to learning about leadership while following is to pay close attention to the experience. Reflect in a thoughtful way and commit to the higher road. When leadership is needed, our habit is often to wait for a person in a position of authority to ride in on their horse to lead. If no one steps up and leads, that call for leadership will go unanswered, individual and team morale will suffer, performance will suffer, and accomplishing the team's mission will become difficult. We've all heard people complain about their boss being a poor leader or bemoaning the lack of leadership on a team, as if those complaining were prisoners with no other recourse than to accept their unhappy fate. That is a tragedy. If you find yourself in a situation calling for leadership, take it upon yourself to fill the void. Step up and lead. Find ways, in the moment, to take the initiative, add value, and serve the people around you.

A VOICE FROM THE BACK OF THE ROOM

I was once a member of a military unit deliberating which course of action to take for a very important mission. The planning team—perhaps fifty people assembled in a large room—included the commanding officer, senior staff members, lower-ranking officers and noncommissioned officers, and junior enlisted Marines and sailors. The situation was complex, the consequences acute, emotions were running high, and the time to execute was quickly approaching. Which course of action should we choose? The fog of war was upon us.

During a rare lull in the tense discussions, a voice from the back of the room asked, "Why don't we just go with the simplest course of action and then spend our time working out the details?" Bingo! Without hesitation and without acknowledging the voice, the commanding officer decided on a course of action, and the staff dutifully went to work refining the plan.

The voice from the back of the room was a Navy Corpsman—a lower ranking sailor who possessed no authority and little insight into the multitude of important issues weighing on the staff. What did he do that day? He stepped forward and influenced others to commit and act toward mission accomplishment. He served. He led.

—John

LIFE IS YOUR CLASSROOM

Do you want leadership experience? Whether you work for an organization, belong to a team, or help an unstructured group of people trying to achieve a common objective, there are unlimited opportunities to lead. Get involved. Volunteer. Engage with others. Share the burden and the consequences, both good and bad. Serve. You can get experience leading everywhere—in your family, social group, civic club, and workplace. Leaders emerge in the checkout line at the grocery store, during a church committee meeting, on the little league baseball diamond, at a job site, and in the corporate board-room. In all these venues, leadership is solely needed, and that void can be filled by you!

REFLECTION

- ✓ What are the venues in your life in which leadership is needed?
- ✓ What will you do to fill that void?
- ✓ In what ways are you learning about leadership?
- ✓ In what ways are you training to become a leader?
- ✓ In what ways are you accruing experience leading?
- ✓ Are you a philosopher: reading about leadership without actively leading?
- ✓ Are you a formulator: planning and preparing to lead but hesitant to accept your leadership responsibilities?
- ✓ Are you a juggler: leading without taking time to seek feedback, reflect, learn from your and others' mistakes, and adjust your behaviors?

PRACTICAL KNOWLEDGE

My high school driver's education teacher trained me how to drive. After getting past the classroom part of the program and having endured watching the horrify-ing videos sponsored by the automobile insurance company, I finally got to take the wheel and hit the road. My teacher took me on a planned route with minimal traffic so as to reduce my real-world exposure to hazardous conditions. He constantly kept his foot hovering over the brake pedal to ensure I wouldn't make a fatal mistake. He advised me on driving techniques and tactics to consider in each situation we encountered, talked me through proper driving strategies, and warned me of the consequences of poor decisions. In short, he provided a controlled, safe environment for me to develop my skills while learning basic driving concepts. That training was vital. I then prepared for and passed the test.

But my learning curve skyrocketed the day I got my license and set out on my own. I was now responsible for making my own decisions while owning the consequences of my actions. The intensity of the learning experience increased dramatically, and the real learning took place as I applied what I had learned in training to the context of the real world.

—John

Practical skills come from exploring the reality of what works and what doesn't. Practical knowledge and skills are those you accrue only from leading and following real people in real situations with real consequences. You cannot learn everything you need to know by reading a book or from any academic curriculum or training program. Education and training are a means, not an end. You can learn about leadership and learn how to lead, but unless you experience following and leading, you will never truly and fully develop as a leader. Your experience is ultimately what will enable you to *become* a leader.

CHAPTER 13

The Learning Process

Learning about leadership, learning how to lead, and gaining leadership experience, are the three fundamental components of your leadership journey. How you learn is also vital to your development as a leader.

We are all capable of undertaking tasks with intensive focus and resilience to achieve our goals. Whether it's a mundane task (shoveling snow) or one more intellectually challenging (creating a team strategy), the harder you work, the more likely you are to accomplish it. Practice involves doing a task over and over and then adjusting to achieve competence—the ability to perform a task more efficiently and effectively. Along the way, you reapply what worked and change or discard what didn't work. Think about learning to drive a car, hitting a golf ball, or giving a presentation; with enough repetition, feedback, and learning, you can become darn good at such things!

Hard work and practice of this sort are often narrowly focused on a single task, with a goal of achieving very specific outcomes. Diligence and repetition don't allow your brain sufficient time to absorb and process information, contemplate the larger meaning of that information, and then envision how the information could apply to other endeavors. Valuable insights can be lost, and opportunities that more broadly apply new knowledge and skills can be

Practice

missed. When you aren't intentional about the process of learning, you are unlikely to receive a good return on investment for your time and effort. When it comes to learning, there are no failures, only opportunities.

Since you are now on an intentional developmental journey, a basic understanding of experiential learning principles will be invaluable. Experiential learning is a process as old as mankind. Its conceptual theory was developed through the research of many psychologists and educational philosophers, including David Kolb[1], whose experiential learning model is widely recognized and used today. In general, the experiential learning process is as follows: doing something, intentionally engaging in focused reflection on that experience, forming abstract concepts and generalizations, and then testing the implications of the new knowledge and skills in new situations. Below is a simple modified model of the process.

Experiential Learning

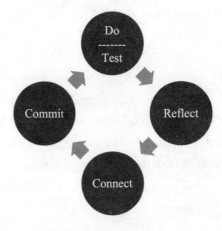

---

1   David Kolb, Experiential Learning: Experience as the Source of Learning and Development
     (Hoboken, NJ: Prentice-Hall, 1984).

Our experience, confirmed by recent scientific studies in human behavior, indicates that this model reflects the most effective way to learn. Quite simply, our brains are wired this way. Here's what the experiential learning process looks like in action:

DO

Engage in a difficult task that requires the work of your brain, your heart, and your hands—something you're not sure you will succeed at, something that leads to real consequences. Do it with people—intellectually, emotionally, socially, soulfully, and physically. Enter new territory, accept some risk, and get out of your comfort zone.

REFLECT

Take time to reflect intensely. Step out of the experience. As soon as possible, walk away and go to your thinking space: unplug, pour a glass of wine, go for a swim, hike to a mountaintop, or cozy up on your couch. Get a pencil and your journal. Write a narrative, make a list, or draw a picture, Venn diagram, or flowchart of the experience. Ask yourself what happened. Objectively recount the details. What did you say, and what did you do? What were others' actions and reactions? What were the outcomes? What worked and what didn't work?

CONNECT

Conceptualize your observations in the bigger picture by taking a 10,000-foot view. What are the key lessons and broad conclusions? What generalizations can you draw from this experience that may apply in different venues—different people, different environments, different missions?

COMMIT

Make a commitment to apply and test your knowledge, insights, and skills in a new environment, with different people, or in a different context.

TEST

Leave faulty assumptions and bad habits behind and test your newfound knowledge and skills. Continue the cycle.

REFLECTION

What distinguishes experiential learning from more arbitrary learning models is the intentional reflection portion. Learning experientially means you reflect upon rather than merely react to events. Instead of jumping to action, experiential learners first take the time to make or discover meaning. Experiential learners are deliberately contemplative in their forward thinking; they don't proceed without first looking back. Learning becomes a process of constructing knowledge with the aim of creating future applications and not just achieving outcomes or becoming more informed, skillful, or proficient at a given task.

DEBRIEFING

Teams learn reflectively through the disciplined practice of debriefing after an action or event. If you've ever been on a high-functioning team, you've likely heard this sequence of questions as the team debriefs after an event or exercise:

- What happened?
- Why did it happen?
- What did we do well?
- What can we improve upon?
- How can we apply these lessons?
- What will we do in the future?

If you are like most busy people and time is limited, understand that you don't need to reflect on every experience moments after it happens. Think in terms of hours or days. Reflect after completion of significant events (e.g., after a successful work project or a painful coworker conflict) or after chunks of productive time (e.g., at the end of the day or a few times per week). Intentional reflection doesn't need to be a time-consuming process. Think purposefully and deeply, but aim to extract a few key takeaways and develop a few important commitments. Write them down or sketch them out in your journal, then revisit them often to hold yourself accountable. Share your learnings with your teammates where possible, and make personal commitments based on those learnings. Reflection is a learned skill, and like any new process, habit breeds proficiency. Through hard work, you accomplish tasks. Through thoughtful practice, your performance improves. Through learning experientially, you expand your capacity to broadly apply knowledge, insights, and skills to future tasks.

Effective leaders commit to moving their team to accomplish their mission. They work hard to bring about those results, a process which produces higher levels of proficiency and confidence. Effective leaders are deliberate learners who make the most of their experiences through reflection, creating meaning, committing to what will be, and acting on those commitments as they press forward. Effective leaders involve their teammates in the learning process. Now on to the essential leadership concepts.

Part 4

Essential Leadership Concepts

CHAPTER 14

Mission: Leadership's Top Line

W e're struck by the many aspiring leaders we work with who either don't know their organization's mission, are too busy to pay it much heed, or—worse—don't believe it is relevant. Perhaps this is because organizational mission statements are often created at the highest level of management and lack the buy-in of those who do the actual work required to accomplish the mission it espouses. Mission statements are often hung in frames on meeting-room walls and are sometimes referred to in one-and-done employee orientation programs. In many cases, the mission statement is poorly constructed, misleading, or simply so broad it is rendered meaningless. Regardless, it is vitally important for every team member to understand and commit to their team's mission. Ensuring every member of the team has mission clarity is a critical responsibility of every leader. It's doubly important for you to know why this is so. The team's mission is so important that we've incorporated it in the very definition of what it means to lead.

UNDERSTAND YOUR MISSION

Your team's mission is, in essence, what your team was created to accomplish. The mission should capture the purpose for which the team was created. Without a clear and compelling mission, there is no good reason for your team to exist.

A clearly defined, compelling mission is a powerful unifying force for the individuals on your team. The team mission pulls people together, drives their level of engagement, inspires them to align their efforts, and fosters an appreciation for their interdependence with one another. A clear mission will help guide the team's planning and decision-making related to organization, training, resources, and support, and will inform your requirement for talent and people. Ultimately, your mission helps define your team's progress, and its accomplishment will determine the team's success. We refer to the mission as a top-line concept because it should be at the top of your conceptual leadership model.

Every member of the team must have a mission orientation, which requires that every individual on the team have a clear understanding of and commitment to the mission. The primary responsibility of each team member is to make that mission come to life.

It's common for there to be multiple team missions within a larger organization. Functional divisions or departments, geographical chapters, or project teams may have their own mission statements that specifically describe what they do in support of the parent organization's mission. Each subordinate unit's mission is then nested within the higher mission.

Your parent organization's mission (if you are on a team within a larger organization) should align all members, including you and your teammates, within the organization. If your team has a distinct mission statement, it is in addition to, not separate from, your parent organization's mission.

If your team hasn't created a clearly defined mission, you've got a great leadership opportunity in front of you. Work with your teammates to create one. If you've inherited a mission statement, you have an opportunity to clarify or refine it. You and your teammates should work together to ensure your mission reflects precisely why your team exists. Doing so is a valuable and rewarding exercise that will yield tangible results.

There are many tutorials available on how to write a suitable mission statement, and you can find many examples of both successful and inadequate mission statements online. Do some research and find a few you believe are both clear and compelling.

Although crafting a meaningful mission statement for your team is beyond the purpose and scope of this book, we want to share a few important points. Your mission statement should do the following:

- Avoid the *too*s: too vague, too detailed, too little, too much, too mundane, too lofty

- Transcend short-term goals and should be resilient enough to endure temporary or circumstantial changes in the environment

- Reflect your team's desire and intent in a clear, succinct statement that includes (in no particular order) what you do, how you do it, why you do it, and who you do it for

- Serve your team, just as your team serves the mission

- Use strong action verbs and avoid phrases such as "to be #1 in our field" or "to be the best in the industry"

REFLECTION

Think of a team with which you identify closely—the one you spend the most time with or that occupies the most important niche in your life.

What is your team's mission? If you don't know your team's mission or can't describe it in clear and simple terms, you've got important work to do. Find or create one ASAP! Involve your teammates. They will need to be aligned. Now, write your mission at the top of a blank journal page, and consider the following questions:

- ✓ How clear and compelling is your mission?

- ✓ How can you improve it?

Your team's mission should be simple, focused, well defined, and fully understood and embraced by every member of your team.

BELIEVE IN AND COMMIT TO YOUR TEAM'S MISSION

In calling a leader "a dealer in hope," Napoleon Bonaparte captured an important aspect of leadership. Hope is a powerful emotion that leaders can tap into and should strive to keep alive. One of the dynamics that enables a team to operate at or near its true potential is what we refer to as *the audacity of belief*. Hope for a positive outcome is good, but mere hope is not enough. Leaders do more than foster hope. Teams infused with authentic leadership exhibit a strong conviction and unalterable belief in their ability to accomplish the mission, even in the face of overwhelming odds.

To lead effectively, you must first be personally convinced that your mission is both meaningful and achievable. When you and your teammates fully commit to that mission, magical things begin to happen. When every member of a team exhibits the audacity of belief, the team can transform what is merely *possible* into what is *likely*. But it starts with the leaders. If you don't fully own your team's mission or for any reason (ethical or otherwise) cannot, you will not be capable of authentically influencing those around you.

Leaders work to maintain and strengthen a shared conviction in mission accomplishment with their teammates. There is no real team without all members embracing the mission. Individuals must have a deep and abiding conviction—an audacity of belief—that they can accomplish the mission regardless of obstacles and conditions that exist or arise.

THE AUDACITY OF BELIEF

A few years ago, my sixteen-year-old daughter was involved in a nearly fatal automobile accident. Her car was struck directly on the driver's side by a fully loaded 18-wheeler traveling at full speed. The accident scene was horrific. The truck had completely collapsed the driver's side of her car, and the force of the impact had pinned her against the passenger door. Her injuries were catastrophic: Her neck was broken at C-1, a lung had collapsed, her jaw was fractured, her ribs and hips were shattered, her legs and feet were broken, and her life was slipping away. By any objective standard, there was no reason to believe she would survive.

I am happy beyond measure to tell you that she did survive, and after a lengthy and difficult recovery, she is now thriving. Her life was saved, in no small part, by the committed teamwork of a team of first responders. After the accident, I sought them out to express my deep gratitude and to hear their story.

I learned some remarkable things. Among those, was this: Despite all the evidence to the contrary, they moved with the conviction that they could save my daughter's life. They worked with an unalterable belief that their individual and team efforts would change the outcome. They were armed with the audacity of belief.

They had confidence in their own capabilities because they were well trained. They believed in their teammates and trusted one another because they had formed as a team. They shared leadership as the situation unfolded—serving each other and serving the mission. And the mission was clear and compelling.

I am convinced that the single most important thing that created this miracle was their absolute conviction they would save my daughter's life. That belief became a self-fulfilling prophecy and determined the outcome. It drove their performance, heightened the level of their collaboration, sharpened the clarity of their communication, and elevated the quality of their leadership and teamwork.

—Sean

Just as you must believe in your mission, you must fully commit to its accomplishment. Leadership's top line is mission accomplishment, and an important measure of a leader's effectiveness is the team's ability to accomplish its mission. Mission accomplishment is a hallmark of effective leadership and is ultimately the direction in which effective leaders move. In a nutshell, your work is to serve, support, and move people, in practical ways, toward accomplishing the mission.

Your teammates' effort and energy must remain aligned with the mission. To do this, you and your teammates must avoid anything that does not support that mission (misaligned effort or off-mission activity). You cannot fake commitment, and you can't demand it of others if you don't have it yourself.

Since leadership involves people committed to and acting in alignment with the mission, your bottom line is your ability to influence others to bring that about.

MISSION FOCUS OR PEOPLE FOCUS?

If you've ever taken a personality-type inventory, you were likely branded "task oriented" (primarily focused on what people do or produce) or "relationship oriented" (primarily focused on how and why people relate to each other). We all have natural inclinations toward one or the other—in some cases, to an extreme. A singular focus on task, with a disregard for the people involved, may alienate the very people needed to accomplish that task. Too much emphasis on relationships and the human dynamics at play may divert attention from the planning and execution of the required task. Regardless of your personal inclinations, this is an area where a more balanced approach will be most constructive.

*Mission is the **what**. People are the **how**.*

MISSION OR PEOPLE: A FALSE DICHOTOMY

I was once asked in a public forum whether mission or people take precedence. I immediately recognized the flaw in this question; it's one of those gotcha questions that presents a false dichotomy. The schoolbook solution in some quarters might be that mission is most important. However, I disagreed with that answer. The reality of leadership is more nuanced than either/or.

"I don't think leadership works that way," I responded. "Although mission is primary, the truth of the matter is you cannot accomplish the mission unless you serve and support your teammates. Your team's mission can only be accomplished by and with people, so the correct answer to the question is mission and people are equally important."

—John

CREATE A CLEAR PICTURE

Leaders operate simultaneously in two different time zones: the present and the future. They serve their team in the present but envision and prepare for the demands of the future. In looking forward, leaders engage with their teammates to flesh out a vision of what the journey ahead will demand of the team. A leader then works alongside and in support of their teammates to bring that vision to life.

Vision is not a complex concept. As with the team's mission, you should keep it simple. Leaders essentially take their teammates on a journey to a future state. To get to that place, every leader and every member of the team must be able to vividly see what that journey will require and clearly envision how that future state will look and feel. Every member of the team must anticipate the look and feel of the conditions, circumstances, and environment they will encounter so they can both prepare for and adapt to the situations they will face.

The ability to create a clear vision of the team's journey isn't a mystical gift granted only to the few. Don't count yourself out if you don't consider yourself a visionary. Spend some focused time and energy imagining what can be and what may lie ahead. Practice some forward thinking and involve your teammates in the process. Visioning is about creating a vivid, detailed picture of the way ahead and then communicating that picture so every one of your teammates can see it.

To create a vibrant, compelling vision, ask some *what if* questions. A vision provides your team with something to aspire to and prepare for. Create a picture of what that journey will entail and where it will end. Envision a successful outcome. Consider scenarios that can oppose your team's forward progress. Communicate the vision to your teammates. Then serve them in your leading to make that outcome a reality.

WHAT ARE WE TRYING TO ACCOMPLISH HERE?

A few years ago, I was instructing an executive leadership development program for general managers of the large business units of an international corporation. They were all smart, professionally competent, and successful in their industry. They had signed up for the program to develop their communication and leadership skills. As you might guess, many had type A personalities.

continued

I was facilitating a scenario-based exercise in which we tasked the group to build a rope bridge across a ravine. It was a complex mission with lots of moving parts—ropes tied around trees with specific knots, carabiners attached to nylon webbing, a multitude of technical requirements and safety protocols to follow, and a set time limit in which to complete the project. We gave each participant an instruction sheet with a diagram of how to complete their individual piece of the system and provided them with the necessary equipment to do their assigned task. However, none of them could imagine how all the pieces would fit together. The challenge for the group was to collaborate and build this bridge with, broadly speaking, teamwork and leadership.

Once the group started, confusion ensued. Some participants were slinging ropes around trees, some were clipping carabiners together, some were tying knots in webbing. Everyone was talking and doing but not with each other. No one had an idea of what the final product should look like; as a result, no one had a clear vision of the path forward.

With haphazard communication, little collaboration, and no progress, things were going nowhere fast. After approximately fifteen minutes, I noticed one of the participants stop what she was doing, move to the side, and stand watching and listening as her teammates flailed. After a few moments, she managed to get their attention, which wasn't easy. Once everyone finally stopped moving and looked at her, she calmly asked, "What are we trying to accomplish here?"

That's all it took. One person spoke, then another, then another. People listened. Questions were asked, and answers were developed. Ideas were raised and expounded upon. People started sharing information with each other. A vision was seeded that quickly disseminated among the team. A plan of action was developed. Progress ensued. The mission was accomplished: A well-constructed rope bridge was completed on time.

The team's problem wasn't a lack of will, intellect, or talent. The problem was one of leadership: a lack of vision and the collaboration this vision would stimulate and support. The vision was born of a fundamental yet critical question: "What are we trying to accomplish here?" In this simple question, this member of the team stepped up and led her teammates. By asking a simple question, she helped create a common vision of the future so that the mission could be accomplished.

—John

MISSION FOCUS

No team operates in a vacuum. Every team operates in support of an overriding mission, the very purpose for the team's existence. Effective leaders create mission alignment by ensuring the mission stays in their line of sight as they shift their focus between their own actions and the actions of those around them. As a leader, you must continuously work to clarify and place everything you and your teammates do within that mission context. Bring the mission to life for your teammates so they can align their individual and collective focus, energy, and effort in that shared direction.

REFLECTION

Frequently ask yourself and your teammates the following:

✓ Are we on mission?

✓ What aren't we doing that would bring us closer to mission accomplishment?

✓ What are we doing that is distracting us from our mission?

✓ What human capabilities or material resources do we need to develop or obtain to succeed in our mission?

CHAPTER 15

People:
Relationships Matter

L eadership is about people. When you consider your impact as a leader, relationships matter. In fact, the quality of your relationships with your teammates is so critical that it is a mission-essential element. This should be obvious to you, since people are central to the focus of every leader and are at the heart of any meaningful definition of leadership.

Leadership centers on a set of responsibilities you have to your teammates. Your ability to lead rests on the quality of your relationship with the members of your team. In that respect, leadership is relational in nature. The depth of your leadership impact will rest on how you relate to and engage with the people on your team. As former Secretary of State Colin Powell once observed, "Leadership is all about people. It is not about organizations. It is not about plans. It is not about strategies. It is all about people—motivating people to get the job done." Keep the following distinction in mind: Leadership is not something you do *to others*; it is a responsibility you carry *with others*.

Your efforts should be dedicated to building meaningful relationships with those you serve through your pursuit of ways to develop and support them in moving forward. Authentic leaders take this reality into account and engage with their teammates in healthy relationships. Develop those connections. Get to know the people around you and let them come to know you.

Since leadership is a relationship in which we serve others in support of a shared mission, our ability to influence another person is founded on the human connections we build. This requires you to exercise empathy, your willingness and ability to understand others' feelings. Empathy requires you to open yourself to another's experience and reality. Without empathy, there is no true relationship, and a person in this situation has a very limited ability to deeply influence another person. In this state, an attempt to lead often dissolves into a mere transactional interaction in which we trade this for that.

Authentic leaders operate at a deeper level of relationship: a level of true engagement. As human beings, we are often prone to making unjustified judgments and unfounded assumptions about the people around us. Leaders seek *authentic* relationships with their teammates. The only way you are going to earn trust is to expend the time and energy to get to know your teammates and give them the opportunity to know you. It's that simple.

Make the effort to appreciate what your teammates have been through— the range of their experiences—to more fully understand their perspectives and the basis for their hopes and ambitions. Do the work to understand and to appreciate their accomplishments, expectations, and fears. Don't make the mistake of placing your teammates in broad categories or restrictive boxes. Get to know them. With knowledge comes appreciation, understanding, and insight. If you wish to move another human being, you've got to show you care and are invested in the relationship. You can then effectively be of service to them.

When you come to know the people you wish to influence, you will develop insights into the following questions:

- Why do they respond or react in this way?
- Why do they take this position or that?
- Why are or aren't they fully engaged in what we are trying to accomplish?

- What are their true intentions?

- What is moving them?

- What do they hope to achieve?

- How do they perceive the environment around them?

- What threats and opportunities do they envision?

- What pressures are they under?

Leaders move beyond what they assume might be going on inside a teammate's mind or heart and work to uncover the answers to such questions. Research, and our own experience, indicates that most of us have poorly developed capabilities when it comes to reading the motivations and intentions of other human beings. We often think we are good at this, but it turns out we are not. Leaders have a responsibility to move beyond this guessing game. You are responsible for filling in the blanks by discovering and developing that information by interacting and sharing experiences with your teammates, so you can properly understand their perspectives and realities—both real and perceived. It is only with this deeper level of understanding that you can build a real relationship that will allow you the opportunity to lead.

This will take a focused effort, and it will require some time. Don't rush it. Get to know your people. You've got to go beyond merely reviewing their resume or past performance evaluations in their employee file. And if you think you've checked this box by Googling their names to scan their social media activities, you are sadly mistaken. Spend meaningful time with them. Understand and experience their reality from their perspective. Be present. Be interested. Listen to their stories. Find out where they came from, discover what shaped them and what drives them, and learn about what they aspire to accomplish. Ask questions. Observe them in good times and when they are under pressure. Celebrate their professional and personal accomplishments and be there when they go through difficult times.

It is important you help them come to know you. Since every relationship is a two-way street, as a leader you must find ways to let your teammates understand who you are. Look again at our leadership model. Notice that the arrows symbolizing your relationship with your teammates go both ways, from you to each of them and from each of them back to you. We aren't suggesting that you share your deepest, darkest feelings with your teammates. But keep it real, keep it simple, and be courageous enough to be human. Clarify your background and experiences (beyond your resume). Help your team members understand where you are from, the experiences that shaped you, and what it is that you value. Help them to see what you hope to accomplish with the team and how you view your role as their teammate. Clarify your own level of commitment to the team and its mission. Be authentic. Don't try to be mysterious or enigmatic or act like a cardboard cutout of some mental image you have of what a leader should be. Show them that you understand your own strengths and weaknesses, just as you wish to understand theirs.

In her meaningful essay, "Briefing for Entry into a More Harsh Environment[2]," Morgan Hite describes the lessons one can incorporate from a wilderness expedition into their everyday life. One of those lessons contrasts the strong bonds developed between expedition teammates who entrust one another with their lives and our propensity to avoid close connection with people in that other world:

> "Your own aliveness is measured by the aliveness of your relationships with others. There are so many more people to choose from in that other world, and yet somehow we get less close. Remember that the dangers are still present; any time that you get in a car with someone, you are entrusting that person with your life. Any reasons that seem to crop up not to get close, examine very carefully."

YOU CANNOT LEAD AUTHENTICALLY WITHOUT LOVE

If you wish to lead in an authentic way, you will need to lead with love. When we refer to love in the context of leadership, we aren't referring to romantic

---

2   Morgan Hite, "Briefing for Entry into a More Harsh Environment," http://www.hesperus-wild. org/writing/essays/briefing.htm

love. The ancient Greeks had a term which captured the highest form of love, characterized as selfless and unconditional—*agape* love. To lead as a servant, you will have to tap into your heart, that place of authentic human connection we often keep buried. Love is a critical element in your ability to lead authentically, as a servant. It creates the emotional space for a real relationship based on responsibility and service, where trust is extended and grace is necessary.

Perhaps love as a basis for leadership is a concept foreign to you. Many of us have been conditioned to keep others at what we perceive to be a safe emotional distance. If you don't "let them in," nobody can disappoint you. Maybe you are just plain uncomfortable with the word. That's fine. You don't even have to say it. You just have to do it. This may help: Think of *love*, like *lead*, as a verb. It is something you *do*. Love those you seek to influence. Love them as you engage with them, build a relationship, and find ways to serve them in your leadership. This will transform your relationship, your level of engagement and service, and your leadership impact. If genuine, people will respond in remarkable ways.

LOVE IS REQUIRED

I recently picked up lunch at a fast-food restaurant. While waiting for my order, a poster caught my eye. In big bold letters, the sign read:

A SANDWICH WITHOUT MEAT *ISN'T*.

Great marketing: very clever! After reflecting on it for a moment, I was inspired to think of the following phrase, which I wrote down in a notebook I always carry with me:

A LEADER WITHOUT LOVE *ISN'T*.

—Sean

Love is an essential element of real leadership. You cannot lead authentically, as a servant, without exhibiting some measure of love. Love enables you to serve, to bring your attention, intention, energy, care, grace, and hope to the relationship you develop with your teammates. When you serve as a leader, you shift your primary focus away from yourself and onto those you serve. With love, you can tap into the deep emotional and intellectual resources you need to be there for your teammates, to fully serve them in accomplishing the team's mission.

For those who seek to lead authentically, there is no way to escape this truth. And you can't fake it. If you attempt to lead without love, you will be revealed as a fraud. If you truly wish to move beyond a weak attempt to manage the people around you, you've got to cross this critical threshold.

We challenge you to take another look at the connection between what is in your heart and how you engage with others. Service, respect, grace, and trust are at the heart of what binds us together as members of a team in pursuit of a shared mission. To love another in the context of leadership, you must be willing to put the other person first and make them primary when it comes to your own intentions and actions. That is the essence of servant leadership.

Leading as a servant is not about being selfless; it is about *serving* others *first*. Healthy, fully integrated servant leaders are not without a healthy ego, but they exercise the discipline to subordinate their ego; self-interest is no longer the primary driver of a servant leader's behavior. Authentic leaders certainly have a strong sense of self-worth, but the value they place in their teammates fuels the way they engage with them and drives the leader's actions. In serving another as a leader, your primary focus must be to engage with your teammates in ways that make them more capable and more committed to accomplishing the shared mission.

Most who fail in their attempt to lead possess sufficient intellect, ambition, and experience. They are simply unwilling to engage with their teammates at the level of the heart. These would-be leaders never succeed at establishing relationships built on mutual trust—the level of authentic trust and interdependence required as a bedrock of team relationships.

Without love, you will be unable to deeply influence the thinking, action, and behavior of your teammates. In love's absence, the would-be leader must resort to manipulation to drive another's performance, using an array of carrots and sticks. That isn't leadership. At best, such a relationship devolves into a mere transaction, trading this performance for that outcome. That is not how authentic leadership operates.

We have been blessed to serve alongside many authentic leaders during our own learning journeys. The leaders who have significantly impacted our leadership journey are an incredibly diverse group in every respect. Some wore military uniforms and held high ranks with impressive titles. Others had no official title whatsoever. Some were civilians and wore no uniform. Some were women, while others were men. These leaders were both old and young. Some were tall, and others were short. Some had impressive academic degrees and were well spoken, while others had little formal education and weren't expert communicators. These leaders worked in a range of professions and held widely different roles in life. What they had in common was this: Without fail, they served us from a place of love.

You are probably familiar with the oft-quoted "love chapter" from Paul's First Letter to the Corinthians. It is spoken in virtually every Christian marriage ceremony and has become so familiar that it has perhaps lost its larger meaning. When you look at it from a leadership perspective, it takes on special meaning. Paul wrote: "Love is patient, love is kind. It does not envy, it does not boast, it is not proud. It is not easily angered, it keeps no record of wrongs. Love does not delight in evil but rejoices with the truth. It always protects, always trusts, always hopes, always perseveres." When we reflected on the leaders in our lives who impacted us so profoundly, we saw these qualities come to life.

These leaders were consistently patient, kind, and humble, and they lacked any sign of envy. They always found ways to honor others without seeking glory for themselves. They were not easily angered and seemed to hold no grudges. They sought out the truth and communicated with candor and respect. They managed themselves in ways that were ethical and moral. They protected others and extended trust to them. They fostered hope, were resilient in the face of adversity, and they persevered through adversity. As further evidence of their love for us, they didn't shy away from pointing out our honest mistakes, and they held us accountable in constructive ways for our decisions, our behavior, and our performance. At times, the feedback stung, but they unfailingly gave it as a gift, in ways that were elevating rather than soul crushing. They held us accountable so that we could understand and extract the lessons from our experiences. They were deeply human and unafraid to share their own humanity. They extended us grace, which we did not feel we always deserved, and they forgave our shortcomings and failings. They gave us the room and guidance and confidence we needed to fail and grow.

These women and men lived lives of strong personal integrity in which they valued truth and commitment. They honored us, and as a result, we became more honorable. They conducted themselves in ways that were worthy of our trust, they consistently did what they said they would do, and they extended trust first, which we worked very hard to earn. These leaders believed in our capabilities and inspired us to explore and develop our potential. Convinced we could accomplish far more than we thought possible, they held us to high standards. In return, we worked hard to apply our talents to surpass those expectations. Everything they did was infused with this kind of love, and from them we learned that love is the most empowering force on Earth.

REFLECTION

Consider what would happen if you were open to extending love to your teammates:

- ✓ How would doing so affect your relationships?
- ✓ What would you start doing?
- ✓ What would you stop doing?
- ✓ What opportunities would present themselves?

BUILDING REAL RELATIONSHIPS WITH YOUR TEAMMATES

We are constantly surprised by how little attention aspiring leaders pay toward building authentic relationships with the people they are privileged to lead. At the same time, many of those who aspire to lead put on a false front or wear a metaphorical suit of armor to protect their true selves from being exposed to their teammates. At best, this results in a superficial relationship, which discourages open dialog and real understanding and often leads to a downward spiral of mistrust, unjustified assumptions, inaccurate interpretations, and irrational conclusions. Whether due to passive ignorance or active avoidance, this failure to build an authentic relationship is leadership negligence of the highest order.

Those who choose not to do the work required to know and understand the pople they serve tend to think along the following lines: If you know little about the people you lead, your relationship with them will be quite tidy and extremely narrow—professional, efficient, and simple. Exposure to your teammates' messy life details—their *baggage*—could complicate your relationship, and it's best to know as little as possible, many believe. So, they choose to stick to the business at hand and ignore the human in front of them; ignorance can be bliss, after all. However, this ignorance can be catastrophic when it comes to leadership, and it surely won't lead to authentic relationships.

If you dig under the surface, you will discover aspects of your teammates that are unrelated to your professional affiliation: You might learn where they grew up and went to school or you might learn more about their background or their family. Knowing who they are, where they live, and what they do outside the office can help you understand their personal and professional motivations. This can give you insight into what they want to accomplish and why. More importantly, you can learn how best to serve them to help make those ambitions come to life. The questions that will help reveal this understanding can spark mutual curiosity and create the opportunity for an ongoing conversation. Consider how much mutual insight and awareness can be gained when you and your teammates have a deeper level of knowledge about one another.

When you understand what they most value and what they aspire to, you'll understand their true strengths, their disappointments, and what makes them unique. Seeking personal knowledge can reveal insights into how the other thinks and why. Doing so will also serve as a shared experience and engender mutual trust and understanding. This familiarity will enable you to build a stronger relationship and allow you to lead and follow one another more effectively and authentically.

As a leader, you have an opportunity and a responsibility to build personal, unique relationships with the people you serve. The topics are not definitive, nor do they come from an existing script; they are simply examples of the level of intimacy required for two human beings to begin to develop a common understanding and bond.

If you feel that your teammates are disengaged from the team or its mission, you should first look in the mirror to determine the level of your engagement with them. Your discussions with your teammates should be genuine and born of a natural curiosity and a desire to serve each other. The driving question you should ask yourself is, "What information would help us move beyond the superficial level and become more connected?" Without understanding who your teammates are, you will lack the necessary foundation to serve them meaningfully and productively.

GRANDMA WISDOM

Throughout my childhood, I was continually bombarded by my maternal grandmother's seemingly endless maxims. She offered them randomly (or so I thought) through a stream of jingles, poems, songs, and simple statements of fact. It wasn't until much later in life that I understood these sayings were strategically offered to equip me to make good choices and ultimately live a good life. I eventually began referring to these maxims as "*Grandma Wisdom*."

One of the greatest nuggets of Grandma Wisdom she gifted me (often sung in perfect key) was "Haste makes waste." Her point, I'm sure, was that the hurried and sloppy approach I was taking to my task would eventually cost me time and often earn me a do-over. Later in life, I relearned the lesson many times over. Imagine the consequences of a hastily tied knot while mountaineering or using a carelessly packed parachute for skydiving!

Grandma Wisdom applies to leadership, specifically to building relationships. Taking the time and making the effort to develop close relationships with your teammates will ultimately save time and reduce bad outcomes.

—John

Building personal relationships may seem inefficient (efficiency is a management consideration, not a leadership consideration) in the short run. It will require your concerted time, effort, and attention. You will have to make it a priority and pursue it. If this is new territory for you, it may initially feel a bit uncomfortable and seem to exceed the boundaries of your professional relationship. That may be true for some people but not for those who wish to lead. Developing a personal relationship with your teammates is not out of bounds; it is center court.

Doing what is necessary to get to know others and to allow them to know you, on a deeper level, is a valuable investment in your time. It gives you the foundation to build a relationship; it enables you to anticipate your teammates' needs and better understand their motivations and behaviors. Knowing your teammates more completely will help you to avoid the messiness and drama that comes from guessing and making wrongheaded assumptions. Take the time to get to know them. Let them come to know you. Start slowly. Lay a foundation, and then build on it with an eye toward the future.

By understanding each teammate's unique background, present circumstances, and future direction, you will better understand who they are and how they think. Only then will trust begin to take root, and your ability to influence another's behavior and perspective will become possible. You will be more capable of appreciating their ambitions and their real potential, and you will gain valuable insight into what motivates and demotivates them. When you understand the people around you on a deeper level, you will understand how to best serve them in accomplishing the team's mission.

KNOW WHEN TO FOLLOW

We had just returned to camp after completing a nighttime training exercise. Operating in Norway in the dead of winter near the Arctic Circle is a physically challenging experience. After we debriefed the mission, we took care of our equipment and began to get a few hours of rest. As I started to settle in, one of the training instructors informed me that I now had a real-world problem on my hands. One of the Swedish soldiers on the team had developed a dangerously high fever and would need to be evacuated as quickly as possible.

We were in a heavily wooded area, far from civilization, and there was no way to bring in either a helicopter or an emergency vehicle. We would have to deliver our teammate to the extract point several miles away by pulling him out on a sled.

I was responsible for organizing and leading the evacuation. We had no GPS, but we did have a map and compass. Although I knew our current location and had the location for the extract, I was unclear about the best route to take. I pulled my team together, explained the situation, and told them everything I knew. I explained that we needed someone to lead us back to the extract point; someone who remembered how to get us through the heavily wooded area we had entered several days prior.

A single person on my twelve-member team raised his hand. He was a quiet, unassuming Navy officer from England. While he had kept up with the rigorous training so far, he wasn't one of those people who really stood out. I'm embarrassed to admit that I hadn't really gotten to know him very well. I also hate to admit I had underestimated his capabilities based on his appearance. I stopped and looked at him and asked him if he was certain he knew the way back to the extract point.

In a confident voice, he said, "Yes."

I paused, looked at my other teammates, and with all the confidence I could muster, said, "Good. You are going to lead us out." Frankly, I had some doubt about his ability, but time was of the essence, and he seemed certain. It was now an act of faith. He would lead, and our team would follow.

We arrived at the drop-off point without incident and put our teammate in the hands of the rescue team. That experience was yet another learning opportunity about the importance of knowing your teammates and their capabilities, rather than relying on appearances or making assumptions. And, again, sometimes your best and highest role is to follow another's lead.

—Sean

TRUST AND TRUSTWORTHINESS

Trust is a firm belief in the integrity and reliability of others. Demonstrating trust in someone is accepting the truth of their word without additional evidence and being confident they will do what they say they will do with benevolent intent. *Trustworthiness* is being deserving of another's trust. Being trustworthy is speaking the truth without fail and honoring your commitments, no matter the cost or consequence. (We'll address trustworthiness in detail later.)

Once built, trust-based relationships foster the connection between people and result in stronger teams; they serve to boost confidence, increase certainty, and make unnecessary the requirement for independent verification. A high-trust relationship means you can focus on what needs to be done—making it unnecessary to look over your shoulder to make sure a teammate will be there when they need to be there. A high-trust relationship also eliminates the need to second-guess a teammate's true intentions and reduces the handwringing that comes with a teammate taking responsibility and ownership of a task or function. In short, when the trust level is high, teams can operate with efficiency and heightened effectiveness in interdependent ways.

Efficiency and effectiveness, however, are secondary in importance to the way people *feel* and respond when they are in a trusting relationship. High-trust relationships foster and strengthen morale within a highly functioning team. A high level of morale yields higher energy and greater creativity and resourcefulness, and, ultimately, a higher level of performance within the team.

REFLECTION

- ✓ How do you feel when another person places their trust in you?
- ✓ How do you feel when you can trust another person?
- ✓ How does a relationship built on mutual trust contribute to the health of your relationship?
- ✓ In what ways do you feel a kinship and connection to those who are trustworthy and who trust you?

ASSUME GOOD FAITH

During my doctoral research, I interviewed small-business entrepreneurs and found they had wide-ranging perceptions about their employees. On one end of the spectrum were those who felt their employees wanted only to do what was necessary (or less) to earn a paycheck and avoid getting fired. They doubted their employees' motives, felt the need to watch them like a hawk, and therefore felt the need to control them. These relationships were transactional, anchored in suspicion and distrust. Their workers performed accordingly, doing only what they were told to do—no more, no less.

On the other end of the spectrum were those entrepreneurs who believed their employees acted with benevolence and wanted the enterprise to succeed; these employees bought into the process and would do their utmost to uphold their responsibilities. These entrepreneurs trusted their employees overtly and unequivocally, treated them as such, and set high expectations that their employees would remain trustworthy. The employees acted accordingly by performing at a high level and taking initiative and by always doing what they believed was best for the company, not out of fear but out of loyalty to their mission and a desire to maintain the trust they had earned. They believed in the team and behaved as integrated players on the team.

—John

Certainly, there is a degree of risk that comes with trusting people. There may be a bad apple in the bunch: someone who abuses the trust extended to them or who takes advantage of a trusting leader. Those will be rare exceptions. When one of your teammates proves not to be trustworthy, you may be able to help them learn from that experience, or you might find it necessary to move them along to their next journey. Most people are trustworthy and deserve to be trusted, and everyone deserves the opportunity to earn your trust.

REFLECTION

- ✓ What is the greater risk to a healthy relationship—mutual trust or mutual distrust?
- ✓ Why do you believe this to be true?

YOU WON'T ALWAYS BE RIGHT

As a young Marine officer, I was responsible for a team of Marines. I had extended trust to them, and they had come to trust me. One day, the results of a drug test came across my desk, indicating that one of my young Marines had tested positive. I was surprised. He was a fine young man who worked hard and took his military

continued

service seriously. When I shared the test results with him, he looked me right in the eye and told me it couldn't be true. He explained he had never used illegal drugs and was at a loss to explain how the test could have come back positive. I told him he needed to be honest with me because I was going to speak with the commanding officer on his behalf and demand a retest. He assured me he was being honest and thanked me for my trust and support.

I went to see the battalion commander, a wise, seasoned combat veteran. I told him about the results of the drug test and explained that I trusted this young Marine. I told him I thought there must have been some mistake with the test results or the chain of custody. He looked at the report and then smiled at me. He asked me why I trusted this Marine. I told him that he had looked me in the eye and denied using any illegal drugs; he had a solid record of performance, and he was a steady member of our team. The battalion commander asked me if I was sure we wanted to challenge the test. I replied affirmatively and said that I trusted this young man. The colonel said, "Well, I will go along with you. If you are right, we will know soon enough. And if you are wrong, you will learn from this."

Unfortunately, I was wrong. My Marine failed his second drug test and was discharged from the service. I had misplaced my trust in him. Here's what I learned: Trust must be earned, but your default approach will be to extend your teammates the opportunity to earn your trust. Another thing I found extraordinary in this experience is that the commanding officer didn't chastise me for being wrong. He didn't call me out or chide me for being mistaken. He appreciated my *trust first* default setting and trusted me, in turn, to learn from my mistake.

—Sean

MOTIVATION AND COMMITMENT

Leadership is all about people. A basic understanding of human nature, then, is crucial to your leadership development and effectiveness. Any attempt to develop as a leader without a basic understanding of how people (in general) and your teammates (in particular) function will ultimately fail. You cannot build a relationship or influence a person you don't know.

More importantly, get to know your teammates, so you can more fully appreciate what drives and moves them and what may be holding them back.

Spend time with them; share in experiences with them and share learnings from your experiences. Communicate with them thoughtfully and with candor, and don't forget that the most important part of communication is active listening. Share your stories and understandings and seek out a deeper understanding of where they've been and where they are going. Move well beyond their resume or personnel file. Dig deep and go beyond your first or second impressions. Find out how they view the world around them.

What is it that moves a person to *commit* their time, energy, effort, and skill to a team's mission and then to *act* in support of that mission? That is an important question for you to consider. What is your theory about what moves people in general? More specifically, what moves each of your teammates? Keep in mind that not every person is motivated by the same things. Answering the following questions from your own perspective is a great place to start.

REFLECTION

Review the following list of generally accepted motivators, and add your own to the list:

- ✓ Success
- ✓ Opportunity for growth
- ✓ Challenging work
- ✓ Rewards
- ✓ Money
- ✓ Recognition
- ✓ Reputation
- ✓ Respect
- ✓ Clear mission
- ✓ Socialization
- ✓ Being part of a team
- ✓ Learning and growth
- ✓ Pride
- ✓ Promotion or a title
- ✓ Serving others
- ✓ Accomplishment
- ✓ Love
- ✓ Belief in mission
- ✓ Other motivators

Identify the three items on this list you personally consider most motivating. Then identify the three that motivate each of the individual members of your team. Which of these compel people to act in the short-term in exchange for something tangible? Which of these compel people to act over a sustained period because of how it makes them feel?

Some people will perform reasonably well in exchange for a short-term benefit (pay and benefits), while others require a deeper form of motivation to bring out their best efforts and highest level of commitment (such as service to others or pursuing a meaningful mission). Leaders understand if they intend to tap into a deeper level of commitment for the long haul, they must engage their teammates' need to feel they are a part of something worthwhile. Similarly, when people know they are respected, their voices are heard, their contributions are valued, and their efforts are supported, they naturally tend to feel inspired and committed. These emotions generally cause people to put their heart and soul into a task. In addition, people who are moved deeply tend to take initiative, seek out ways to support their teammates, and undertake a mission with dogged determination. These are the conditions authentic leaders strive to establish.

When it comes to motivation—and demotivation, for that matter—one size does not fit all. We are not all moved in equal measure by obtaining or pursuing the same things; some sources of motivation have a greater impact on a particular person than they do on others. Sources of motivation can be deeply personal and vary widely from person to person.

Make the effort to learn what motivates each of your teammates, and why. Take the time and find opportunities to truly understand them. Watch them, speak with them, and seek to discover their inspirations, aspirations, fears, and anxieties. What do they think about you, their teammates, and the work they do? What do they need from you to foster their deeper commitment to act in alignment with your team's mission?

REFLECTION

- ✓ What will you do this week to understand what moves your teammates to act and commit to the team's mission?

- ✓ What will you do this week to motivate your teammates to act and commit to your team's mission at a deeper level?

Leaders must also understand the other side of the coin: the things that *demotivate* people. Jim Collins, in his book *Great by Choice*, observed that "the best leaders don't worry about motivating people; they are careful to not demotivate them." Collins makes an interesting point. If you are fortunate enough to surround yourself with a group of teammates who are internally aligned with the team's mission and are fueled by a healthy level of self-motivation, your primary responsibility as a leader is to continue to fuel that fire through your service while ensuring the environment you create doesn't undermine that effort.

REFLECTION

Review the following list of conditions that typically demotivate people, and add your own to the list:

✓ Public humiliation

✓ Failure to receive credit when due

✓ Disrespectful behavior

✓ Poor performance

✓ Unclear mission

✓ Unclear or low expectations

✓ Lack of commitment

✓ Insufficient remuneration

✓ Insufficient resources

✓ Insufficient support

✓ Favoritism

✓ Absence of teamwork

✓ Unfairness

✓ Lack of training and preparation

✓ Fear

✓ Lack of trust

✓ Lack of opportunity

✓ Other demotivators

Identify the three that demotivate you the most. Identify three that you believe serve to demotivate your teammates. Which of these exist in your team? How do they affect commitment and performance? Why? What can you do to remove them?

Engage closely with your teammates to determine what moves them. There is absolutely no reason to guess. Instead, observe and ask. By understanding what motivates and demotivates the individual members of your team, you and your teammates can build and maintain commitment and inspire action toward mission accomplishment.

CHAPTER 16

Self: The Leader's Heart and Soul

How you lead rests largely on who you are as a human being. Your values, beliefs, attitudes, motives, and ethical principles directly impact how you behave toward and engage with others. An intimate knowledge of the man or woman in the mirror is integral to your leadership journey. This part of your leadership development journey is critical; it requires work no one else can do for you. You will need to dig deep and do some focused reflection to establish a firm personal foundation. You must do this internal work; there is no way around it. The bedrock of wisdom is to know yourself.

Among the questions you will need to answer during your learning journey are the following:

- What do you truly value?
- What are your beliefs and assumptions about other people in general, and how did you arrive at those?
- Do your behaviors accurately express your values and ethics?

- What is your motive for leading? What motivates you in a team setting?

- What ethical standards do you hold for yourself and others?

- What leadership traits do you embody? Would your teammates agree?

- How well do you acknowledge and control your emotions?

- Are you humble? Do your words and actions express your humility?

- Do your behaviors reflect respect for your teammates? Are your behaviors consistent with how you aspire to lead?

For good reason, self-knowledge is considered the cornerstone of true wisdom. Who you are and what you believe impact your conscious and unconscious responses to the people, events, and environment in all aspects of your life. They form the foundation from which you engage with the people around you. Your level of self-knowledge is an important key in your authenticity as a human being and your effectiveness as a leader.

BE, LEARN, and DO—in that order. Your leadership effectiveness starts with who you are (BE). A narrow focus on how leaders should act—how they "should" walk and talk—is the wrong approach to your leadership development. Focusing on leadership styles also comes with the same limitations. You are a distinct human being with unique experiences, values, beliefs, and qualities, and you will naturally lead in ways that are different from any other leader. While your actions and behavior, the way you engage with the people and events around you, are ultimately of great consequence, they organically flow from who you are. What you know and what you are learning (LEARN) will then shape how you act (DO). We are not interested in helping you to act *like* a leader; we are interested in helping you *become* a unique and authentic servant leader.

CHARACTER

Your character is critical; it is revealed in the way you conduct yourself and in the way you engage with people. Character is of particular importance to leaders, as leaders are continually tested by people and events. Without a solid moral and ethical foundation, you will be tossed about like a ship without an anchor. There is no more powerful influencer than your exhibiting a strength of character. A strong character is magnetic and compelling; it's just the way we are wired as human beings. You may not be the smartest, most talented, or best-looking member of the team, but if you are a person of strong moral character, people will follow you.

WHAT IS CHARACTER?

As I was growing up, my church elders, Boy Scout leaders, coaches, and teachers seemed unanimous in their opinion that all good boys must have a high dose of character. I was reminded of this often, and I believed them. However, I didn't understand the meaning of the word; character was an ambiguous and elusive concept for an average kid struggling to understand vocabulary.

When I was fifteen, that ambiguity ended abruptly when my paternal grandmother said of her husband, "There is not a man on this Earth with more character than your grandfather." At that moment, I understood exactly what character meant. I admired my grandfather greatly and wanted to please him and be like him. I certainly couldn't list all the adjectives to describe his qualities and traits, but I knew he was a good man—the type of man I aspired to become.

To this day, I'm not certain I can accurately and definitively describe what character means. In one sense, it's too broad to define. But in another sense—as the saying goes—you know it when you see it.

—John

VALUES

What you truly value in your life influences your priorities. Your values serve as a foundation, the pillars that shape the ways you interact with others and engage with the world at large. You are much more likely to find fulfillment and happiness when you act consistently with those values. It is also true that you will experience disappointment, emptiness, or guilt when you act in ways that are inconsistent with your real values. The degree to which you are acting in alignment with your values is a good test for whether your life is moving in the direction you want it to.

Values are deeply personal, and it would be unrealistic for us to create a definitive list of leadership values. Nevertheless, leaders must have a strong grip on their values, and we encourage you to work your way through the following brief values-clarification exercise. Identifying your core values will help you identify what matters to you most. Your values can change over the course of time, so even if you've clarified your values in the past, completing this exercise again may offer you some surprises.

REFLECTION

Read through the following list of values, and add your own (nouns, adjectives, concepts, feelings—anything you value greatly):

✓ My country   ✓ Truth or integrity

✓ Fun   ✓ Wealth

✓ Freedom   ✓ Loyalty

✓ Knowledge and wisdom   ✓ Security

✓ My friends   ✓ My family

✓ Status or recognition   ✓ Love

✓ Harmony   ✓ Success

✓ Authenticity   ✓ Service to others

✓ Power   ✓ Adventure

✓ God or faith   ✓ Health

✓ Fairness   ✓ Happiness

Consider and prioritize. In your journal, list the five values most important to you. From those five, circle your top three. This is personal, so be honest with yourself. These are your core values. Add some narrative explanation if you wish, describing why you value these the most. Which of your behaviors best express your core values to your teammates? What are you not doing that would better express your values? What are you doing that is misaligned with your values? What is it that you want to do more (or less) of to better align yourself with your core values?

BELIEFS

Your beliefs are important. They serve as the lens through which you judge, interpret, and interact with people and events. Others may perceive your beliefs as unfounded or irrational, but your beliefs are yours.

Authentic leaders embrace certain key beliefs and attitudes about themselves, their leadership role, and their teammates. Authentic leaders believe they must own and carry out their leadership responsibility; and they view themselves as a steward of their relationships with their teammates. They also believe in the deep potential of human beings; they believe people inherently want to do meaningful work in support of a worthwhile mission and wish to be a part of a supportive team that will inspire and bring out the best in themselves and in each of their teammates. Authentic leaders believe every human being deserves dignity and respect; they believe they have an obligation to interact with their teammates responsibly, thoughtfully, and with benevolent intent. Authentic leaders believe every teammate deserves to be extended trust, and they believe they must earn their teammates' trust every day by following through on their commitments; they strive to do what they say they will do. Authentic leaders regard their own knowledge, skills, and talents with a sense of gratitude and humility and consider them a team asset; at the same time, they humbly recognize, acknowledge, and appreciate both their limitations and their gifts.

ATTITUDES

Your attitudes color your perspectives on life, inform your perceptions, and shape your expectations of others. Is the glass half-empty or half-full? Are

people's intentions suspect or are they honorable? Are people generally trustworthy or are they not to be trusted? Are others in your life there to serve you,
or are you there to serve others?

Servant leaders embrace a unique perspective on their role and relationship with the people and the world around them. Their identity centers on a
personal mission, which is a powerful motivator, to serve and support others
in the direction of mission accomplishment. As you internalize your responsibility to lead, you must clarify the attitudes you hold about yourself, your
teammates, and your leadership role.

MOTIVES

Everyone has a motive or motives that underlie their behavior. You may
be internally motivated (by love, safety, fun, challenge, serving others) or
externally motivated (by money, recognition, rewards, promotion, material
things).

Servant leaders are motivated, first and foremost, by a desire to serve
others in pursuit of a worthy cause. Your individual gifts and talents, fueled
by a healthy level of ambition, can serve as an important source of strength
as you lead. However, servant leaders remain humble and recognize that
their importance to the team is measured, primarily, by how well they serve
their teammates in pursuit of the team's mission. Serving in how you lead
then becomes its own source of motivation.

Each time you engage with a teammate, check your primary motive. If
you find it is something other than to serve, support, elevate, empower, or
develop, you should reconsider your intentions!

PRINCIPLES

Your principles represent a moral reasoning that arises from and is consistent
with your values, beliefs, attitudes, and motives. Principles begin with "I will
always" or "I will never" do something.

YOUR GUIDE TO LIVING A GOOD LIFE

One of my mentors, a Marine Corps general, modeled for me how to use principles to help ensure behaviors are consistent with values. He used, as he called it, his FFCC rule—faith, family, country, and corps—as a mental model to prioritize his values and guide his actions. His faith was primary, his family was second, his country was third, and the corps (his profession) was last. The general told me he would do nothing for his profession that would compromise his faith, family, or country; he would do nothing for his country that would compromise his faith and family; and he would do nothing for his family that would compromise his relationship with God. The general's deeds certainly matched his words.

His straightforward approach resonated deeply with me. At that stage of my life, I was completely absorbed in my career and engaged in raising a family—work, husband, father, sleep, repeat. I was so busy doing that I was not taking the time to consider whether my actions were consistent with my values. I was not consistently walking my talk.

Soon after this conversation with the general, I sat down and wrote out a set of principles I felt strongly about. I titled them "My guide for living a good life." These simple *I will always* and *I will never* statements have since served me well as a litmus test for evaluating my decisions and have guided my behaviors. I have altered these principles a bit over the years, based on what I most needed to pay attention to at various stages of my life, but, to this day, the original copy lives in the top drawer of my desk, and I read and reflect often on what it contains.

—John

REFLECTION

Revisit your three core values, and perform the following exercise:

✓ For each value, write one, two, or three principles that would guide your behaviors in a way that others would understand what you value most.

Authentic leaders have a firm grasp on their values, beliefs, attitudes, motives, and principles and use them to guide their behaviors.

Character is the embodiment of your combined values, beliefs, attitudes, motives, and principles. It is intrinsic and renders you unique. Character lives in your head and your heart and is inextricably linked to your behaviors.

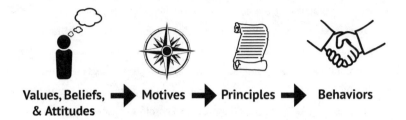

Values, Beliefs, ➡ Motives ➡ Principles ➡ Behaviors
& Attitudes

Effective leaders are authentic and genuine; they say and do what they believe, and they believe in what they say and do. Leaders understand that people will neither follow nor respond constructively to a person whose behavior is not aligned with their values. One cannot lead others when their conduct betrays their principles. For example, a person who says they have others' best intentions in mind while acting in ways that put their own interests first is merely creating a facade. This is not authenticity. Such a person's true nature will be revealed; their teammates will see right through that smokescreen. If a leader's behaviors conflict with their values, it can be concluded either that the person's stated values are not operational, that the person lacks principles or a real commitment to those principles, or that they are simply misbehaving.

WHEN BEHAVIORS ARE NOT CONSISTENT WITH VALUES

A few years ago, I was leading an executive leadership development program and facilitating a discussion about significant life experiences that make us who we are. One participant recounted an experience in which his company offered him a promotion and transfer to a new location across the country. Excited for the opportunity, he accepted the job immediately, without consulting his family. He bought a house in the new location, moved his wife and kids, and went to work. On the day the movers arrived at the new home, the man's wife asked him to come home and watch the kids while she went to the store. Although he was frustrated to be asking for time off in his first few days at work, he relented and came home.

As soon as his wife left, he sent the kids to the backyard and called his office to engage with his new colleagues. With his phone glued to his ear, he was laser-focused on the conversation; time passed. Approximately forty-five minutes later, his wife returned and he heard a scream from the backyard. She had found their youngest child face-down in the swimming pool. (Happy ending—the child survived!)

This executive recounted to our group how this traumatic event fundamentally changed him. He had always stated, and believed, that he primarily valued his family and considered work to be secondary. But after this event, he realized his behaviors were not aligned with those values. He related that while he remained committed to his work, he refused to place it above what he valued most.

—John

Morality is about right and wrong; the degree of "goodness" or "badness" of one's intentions, decisions, and actions. Individuals, groups, and societies explicitly or implicitly establish acceptable codes of conduct. Conduct that is good or right is considered moral; conduct that is bad or wrong is regarded as immoral.

People of strong moral character—those who are righteous and honorable—think, say, and do things that are right and good. Virtue, behavior that expresses moral standards, is a habit for people who possess high moral character. Such people do the right things in the right way for the right reasons every time, no matter the cost or consequence.

REFLECTION

✓ Name a few people in your life who have strong moral character.

✓ What is it about their behaviors that led you to this conclusion?

✓ Think about a time when you had to make a difficult moral decision. What was the outcome? How might it have turned out if you had decided otherwise?

People often avoid issues of "right and wrong" at their place of work, as if morality is a remote theological concept suited only for church or some vague philosophical notion that has no place in the pragmatic, quantitative professional environment. Situational ethics seem to be the order of the day, and immoral acts are frequently justified as "just business." These people conduct themselves as if the workplace is no place to pass moral judgments, when nothing could be further from the truth.

What aspect of human interaction—personal or professional—could possibly be exempt from moral reasoning? There is no "work self," "home self," and "play self"; there is only one you—physically, mentally, *and morally*.

The bottom line with respect to morality is this: Authentic leadership has a moral element. Leadership requires you to be principled in your thinking, clear in your intentions, and consistent in your actions.

DIFFICULT CONVERSATIONS

Morality serves as a foundation for every human interaction. When two people differ on important issues, the first place to start when exploring their conflict is in the values, beliefs, attitudes, and ethical principles that underpin their thinking. Rather than diagnosing a disagreement by evaluating behaviors (what was said or done), you should first take the time to look deeper for differing value systems and perceptions of morality (what is right and what is wrong).

Unfortunately, moral issues are often not clear-cut and finding solutions to moral dilemmas can be elusive. Conversations about morality can be difficult, awkward, and emotionally exhaustive; if not handled in a constructive spirit, they can create more resistance than growth. At the same time, conversations about morality and ethics are fruitful and serve to purge wrongheaded assumptions while helping you, as leader, *understand* why others think the way they think and do the things they do.

ON LEADERSHIP TRAITS

No discussion about leadership or leadership development is complete without a consideration of leadership traits: those human qualities that engender the respect and confidence of others and contribute to effective leadership. The traits typically exhibited by effective leaders have been well researched and thoroughly documented; innumerable lists of admirable leadership traits have been created and compiled, and we encourage you to explore them. Our own experience confirms the belief that authentic leaders consistently exhibit certain personality traits. We will do a deeper dive into those shortly, but first we want you to understand a few important points.

One's personality traits are a product of both nature and nurture. We are born with some traits and develop others along the way. These traits don't confine or fully define you. At no point in time are you stuck with the traits that others may ascribe to you. We have seen people grow and develop when properly moved to do so. With the right level of self-discipline and awareness, you can develop new habits and consistently exhibit a new combination of traits. In this sense, traits can also be aspirational and represent who you wish to be.

Understanding generally desirable leadership traits can serve as a valuable guidepost for your personal leadership development journey. Understanding which behavioral leadership traits are valued in your profession or your team's culture will serve you and your teammates well. A clear understanding of the specific traits valued in the Marine Corps' culture (in alignment with its unique mission) was very important to us both as we worked to refine and develop our own leadership capabilities.

The Marine Corps takes its accepted leadership traits very seriously. Rather than merely publishing a list of the desired leadership traits and hoping this list would somehow work to instill those traits in its leaders (and the behaviors that would naturally flow from them), the Marine Corps took it to another level. As officers with clearly defined leadership responsibilities, we were formally evaluated on the degree to which we consistently exhibited each of the desired traits. They included justice, judgment, dependability, initiative, decisiveness, tact, integrity, endurance, bearing, unselfishness, courage, knowledge, loyalty, and enthusiasm. Along with supportive education and training, as well as the power of example and ongoing mentoring, this evaluation process helped to ingrain a mere list of aspirational traits into the very fiber of our being; they became a part of who we were and how we operated. Exhibiting these traits on a consistent basis became a personal responsibility, a daily reality for us, and remains so for every Marine. Incorporating these traits required our continuous exercise of self-discipline and reflection, bringing a strong developmental aspect to the learning process.

REFLECTION

- ✓ List the five attributes you believe best capture the essence of who you are as a leader.

- ✓ List five attributes your teammates commonly use to describe you. Don't make assumptions; ask a few people who will be honest with you.

- ✓ List five traits you believe are hallmarks of a good leader. Think of effective leaders in your life.

- ✓ What qualities do you most admire and tend to experience as having the greatest influence on you?

While identifying desirable leadership traits is a good start, it is only a beginning. You must then do the hard work of incorporating them in how you live, engage, and interact with others, through your consistent behavior. Traits describe behaviors; they don't make them happen. To incorporate a certain trait, you must consistently exhibit behaviors aligned with that trait. For example, to conduct yourself with integrity, you must determine how you can exhibit integrity in every interaction you have with those around you. You can't simply walk around and proclaim, "I am a person of integrity." Instead, your actions will speak to your integrity.

As we have asked you to do, we have also identified the foundational traits we believe authentic leaders consistently exhibit: integrity, a service orientation, commitment, resilience, and competence. With each trait, we have suggested corresponding behaviors.

INTEGRITY

Display your true values. Don't pretend to be something you are not. Say what you believe and believe what you say—always and without exception. Think and say the truth, and behave responsibly, respectfully, and with honor and courage, regardless of the cost or consequence. Clarify right from wrong in your own mind, and act accordingly. Help others do the same.

SERVICE ORIENTATION

Serve others first, before you seek to serve yourself. Subordinate your personal needs and interests to the needs and interests of your teammates in accomplishing the mission.

COMMITMENT

Believe in your team's mission and commit your attention and effort to taking action in support of that mission. Faithfully serve your teammates as they work in pursuit of its accomplishment. Be loyal and dedicated to your teammates, and back them up when they need you.

RESILIENCE

Face adversity and endure hardships, so that you can learn to overcome obstacles through hard work and perseverance. Don't complain about your personal plight, and don't blame others or make excuses. Attend to your well-being by taking care of your physical fitness, mental dexterity, and spiritual health.

COMPETENCE

Work to know your stuff, and continue to develop the knowledge and skills needed to effectively carry out your responsibilities. Be an active student of the enterprise; continue to challenge yourself to learn and grow. Maintain situational awareness with respect to your teammates and your dynamic environment. Maintain awareness of your abilities and limitations, and manage both your energy and emotions.

EMOTIONS MATTER

We are all social beings, to one degree or another. The desire to be with others is in our physical and psychological makeup. As such, your emotions—and your interpretation of others' emotions—influence how you and those around you behave. As you interact with others, you will find yourself interpreting the emotional cues you receive.

Your capacity to effectively manage your own emotions while accurately reading and thoughtfully responding to the emotions of those around you is critical to your leadership effectiveness. As a leader, you need to fully appreciate how you influence others through your emotions, and you need to understand how emotions impact your relationships. While your words can impact a person's commitment or behavior, your emotions are often much more powerful.

If your emotions don't align with your words or actions, you can create an emotional disconnect. That disconnect can cause others to question the true meaning behind a message or question your real motives, which not only serves to undercut the clarity of your message but can also undermine your leadership effectiveness.

Emotions are highly contagious. As we've learned from experience, fear breeds fear, calm evokes calm, and confidence can spread like wildfire when you and your teammates do the work required to earn it. If you choose (and it *is* a choice) not to exercise a reasonable level of self-discipline in managing your emotions as you lead, you will undermine your ability to effectively influence those around you. Your unwillingness to manage your emotions will also seriously damage the relationships you've sought to build. Likewise, if you have a difficult time accurately interpreting others' emotions, or you simply choose to disregard them, your response may prove to be counterproductive or downright destructive. This may cause you to come across as either uncaring or adversarial, which may not be your intent. Your ability to lead, to deeply influence and connect with your teammates, depends in no small part on your emotional intelligence.

REFLECTION

✓ Take a few moments to reflect on an experience from your past in which a leader exhibited a strong emotion such as anger or delight, indifference or engagement, courage or fear.

✓ How did the leader's emotion affect you?

✓ How did the emotion affect other members of the team?

Because emotions are so powerful, as a leader you need to understand and manage your emotions with care. If you are unclear about how you come across, ask for feedback from those you trust. Check your tone of voice, body language, facial expressions, and level of energy. While we strongly advocate authenticity in how you engage with your teammates, always keep in mind that the emotions you exhibit can either support or undermine your intentions. Maintain awareness in how you come across and manage your emotions thoughtfully.

DROPPING A CALM BOMB

Wilderness expeditions are wrought with uncertainty and challenging circumstances. Weather turns ugly, gear breaks, equipment malfunctions, injuries and illnesses occur, interpersonal conflicts arise, and plans change. When these eventualities occur, negative emotions can derail clear-headed thinking, cloud objectivity, and make situations appear worse than they are.

I once worked with an expedition coleader who, despite the severity or nature of any crisis, was always able to manage her own emotions. This afforded her the ability to choose the most effective response, rather than merely reacting to circumstances. Emotions are powerful in human relations, and her ability to manage her emotions enabled her to stay constructively engaged with her team and bring

continued

her teammates with her. She always exhibited a good dose of coolness—what our team referred to as "dropping a calm bomb on us." As an experienced professional, she recognized and accepted the seriousness and potential consequences of bad situations, but she didn't allow those thoughts to drive her emotions. The effect of her composure on her teammates' emotions and their responses to adversity was consistently remarkable. Calmness begets calmness. Rather than assuming the worst and rushing to make rash decisions, her teammates approached challenges with a measured, rational perspective.

—John

SOCIAL AWARENESS

While a certain degree of native intelligence is required of any person who hopes to lead, your intellect will only get you so far when it comes to influencing and moving others. The world is crowded with those who are smart and knowledgeable yet fail to connect authentically with others. This inability to relate in human terms often comes from a lack of social awareness: the unwillingness or inability to interpret the emotions of others. You might call it a lack of people sense or a low level of emotional intelligence. Without a reasonable level of self-awareness or awareness of others' emotions, your relationships will suffer. That's a major problem for someone who seeks to move others as a servant leader since relationship skills are critical to your ability to lead. You cannot lead effectively if you cannot connect constructively.

If a person is emotionally tone deaf, they will often act in ways that are entirely misaligned with the emotions of others. Your ability to accurately read a person's emotions will directly impact your own ability to communicate. If you read emotions with some degree of accuracy and compassion while reasonably managing your own, you have a far greater chance of connecting with and influencing the people you wish to lead.

As a leader, be intentional in managing the emotional signals you send. You also must develop the ability to effectively read the emotional state of the people around you. If you can't or won't manage your own emotions or develop the ability to read those of others, you will have a devil of a time figuring out how to constructively engage as a leader in support of your team.

MEET THEM WHERE THEY ARE

I've had two faculty colleagues whose ability to read others' emotions were at opposite ends of the spectrum. One consistently failed to detect her students' disinterest, confusion, or negative reaction toward her lesson. Unable or unwilling to notice social cues, she would drone on and on while following her script, even as her students were left behind, disengaged, or perplexed. When given feedback, her default response was, "The students should be interested in my lesson." The other colleague focused on learning rather than on teaching. He used his social radar to sense his students' engagement with the lesson and was willing to make immediate adjustments, including a complete change to his lesson plan, to ensure the students engaged with the information. His default approach was, "What must I do to improve student engagement?" The latter colleague was clearly displaying servant leadership.

—John

When we advise you to exercise self-discipline and awareness in managing your emotions and in reading the emotions of your teammates, we aren't suggesting you become something inhuman, or that you change your intrinsic personality. In fact, your individual personality grounds you in authenticity and makes you interesting—even compelling—to others. If we all had the same personality characteristics, this would be a boring world! Even in strong, mission-focused cultures, the authentic leaders we've observed were unique individuals possessing unique sets of strengths and weaknesses, shaped by their own backgrounds and experiences. Be real. Be authentic. Be yourself, but be a work in progress.

ON HUMILITY

Consider the brilliant quote attributed to C.S. Lewis: "Humility is not thinking less of yourself, but thinking of yourself less." Humility is an essential trait of authentic leaders because it allows you to be authentic and build real relationships with your teammates. Since the concept itself is often misunderstood, let's take a closer look at what it really means. This is one you've got to get right.

Humility doesn't require you to denigrate yourself, downplay your gifts, or minimize your ability to contribute. Humility doesn't require you to consider yourself less capable, less talented, less *anything* than you really are. Humility naturally arises when you shift the primary focus of your attention and effort away from yourself and your own interests to your teammates and their interests. Humility also requires you to accept the reality that you are no more important to the team than any other member of your team (or any other person in the room, for that matter).

True humility allows you to own your gifts, your unique talents, and your hard-won capabilities. These are among the things that make you special and allow you to contribute to the team. Humility also allows you to recognize and embrace your growth opportunities, your flaws, your shortcomings and your mistakes. A strong sense of humility helps you to serve with an understanding that you are no more important than the people around you. Having humility simply means you've got a solid grasp on reality and an accurate picture of the truth. As a leader, you know you will never be strong enough, smart enough, creative enough, or skilled enough to accomplish the mission on your own. A team's mission can only be accomplished through the collaborative and cooperative effort of a highly functioning team.

HEALTHY PERSONAL AMBITION

While serving others with humility in how you lead, aligned with your team's shared mission, must be primary in your mind and heart, there is still room for a *healthy* level of self-interest and personal ambition. But exercise caution. Personal ambition operates on a sliding scale from healthy to unhealthy and must always be kept in check when you serve those you lead. There are few things more unforgiving than a leader who uses other human beings for the primary purpose of fulfilling their personal ambitions.

A healthy level of personal ambition can be a very good thing. It can serve as a powerful motivator to help you prepare and perform at your highest levels. It can move you to achieve more than you otherwise thought possible. A healthy level of ambition can also serve as a source of inspiration to your teammates. However, when your ambition shifts to serving yourself first, driving you to obtain personal benefit or recognition at the expense of your teammates or at the expense of the mission, it becomes unhealthy. Unhealthy ambition will quickly erode your teammates' trust and confidence in you as a leader, and will erode your ability to influence them.

When you shift your primary focus from yourself to others, as you must when you lead as a servant, you need not forfeit your personal ambition. Instead, your personal ambition expands to include your serving your teammates' success. This shift helps you to maintain a healthy sense of ego and humility. When you expand who you are to include serving your teammates in accomplishing the team's mission, your personal and professional aspirations become even more obtainable. Authentic leaders understand this reality: When the team wins, you will win.

LEADER BEHAVIORS

Leadership traits alone don't prescribe good leadership. We can't construct an authentic leader by consulting a list of favorable traits. It doesn't work that way. Becoming an authentic leader requires much more than attempting to adopt a collection of generally accepted leadership traits. To become an authentic leader, you must both internalize and consistently exhibit those traits through your behavior. Your teammates are paying attention, so let them consistently observe the traits in you. What you say and don't say matters, and what you do and don't do matters. Act accordingly.

Whether you are worthy of a person's trust, and whether you are someone worth following, will depend largely on your consistent words and deeds. When your words and deeds truly reflect your values, when you actually walk your talk, you become worthy of another's trust and worthy of being followed. You can't force anyone to permit you to influence them. That is not how authentic leadership works. While you may be able to make people react through fear or intimidation, you will never be able to inspire them to follow your lead.

In this book, we've tried to avoid dogma, and we recognize the unique nature of each leader's relationship with the people they strive to influence. Having said that, we have identified some common constructive and destructive leadership behaviors we believe may serve as a resource for you on your leadership development journey:

Authentic leaders DO...	Authentic leaders DON'T...
Lead people	Manage people
Inspire and influence	Demand compliance
Assume good faith	Assume bad faith
Put their teammates first	Put themselves first
Respect others	Disrespect others
Earn respect	Demand respect
Earn loyalty	Demand loyalty
Seek and take responsibility	Avoid responsibility
Fix problems	Fix blame
Hold themselves accountable	Avoid accountability
Hold others accountable	Criticize others
Accept blame	Deflect blame
Embrace reality	Avoid or ignore reality
Give credit	Take credit
Delegate authority	Hoard authority
Share information	Hoard information
Obtain and provide resources	Hoard or deny resources
Dominate the listening	Dominate the speaking
Protect their teammates	Endanger their teammates
Create safety	Create fear
Perform as part of an interdependent team	Perform as an independent individual
Learn from mistakes	Ignore mistakes
Remain humble	Exhibit arrogance
Elevate others	Demean others
Earn trust	Demand trust
Do what they say they will do	Fail to follow through
Lead by example	Lead by decree
Focus on mission and team	Focus on self

HOW SHALL I BEHAVE AS A LEADER?

Deep inside, you already know the answer to this important question. You very likely have a clear image of leadership behaviors that tend to inspire, move, and elevate you. You probably gained that understanding through experience, especially if you had the good fortune to follow the lead of a person who led authentically, as a servant. Likewise, you probably have a vivid picture of what kind of leadership behaviors are demotivating, debilitating, and dispiriting. We've all been subjected to these conditions. They are not easily forgotten, as they tend to leave scars.

Here's a great exercise, one we have been using for years in our coaching and speaking, to help you get a solid grasp on which leadership behaviors to adopt and exhibit as you lead. This exercise was developed by Dee Hock, the founder and former CEO of VISA. We appreciate it for its simplicity and wisdom. There are two parts:

- Make a careful list of all things done to you that you abhorred. Don't do them to others—ever.

- Make another careful list of things done for you that you loved. Do them for others—always.

REFLECTION

- ✓ Carefully create your own list of those things done to you that you hated and found destructive, demeaning, disrespectful, or disempowering.

- ✓ Carefully create your own list of the things done for you that you loved and that inspired, energized, and empowered you.

- ✓ Use this list as a handy guide for what never to do to others and what to always do for others, as a tool to help diagnose your leadership effectiveness, and as a resource to develop the leadership potential of your teammates.

Leaders act in the context of a team and appreciate the dynamic forces surrounding a team's effort to accomplish its mission. They recognize that high-level team execution requires a committed, collaborative effort of inter-dependent individuals who are focused on accomplishing the mission. In a team, individuals bring their individual efforts, skills, resources, and energy together to accomplish a shared purpose. Teams are formed to accomplish what individuals, working independently, cannot. Leaders appreciate the tremendous power of teamwork. A team makes possible a genuine collaboration of talent, energy, and effort focused on a shared mission. A real team is significantly more effective, more resilient, and more capable than a mere collection of individuals. Leaders have a strong team bias and an unalterable team perspective, a perspective that shapes and informs everything they do. Effective leaders build, support, and operate within the context of a team.

Let's now press on to consider the context in which you will be leading: the team.

Part 5

The Context for Your Leadership

CHAPTER 17

The Team: Where Leaders Operate

U p to this point, we have focused on the leadership essentials of mission clarity and alignment, your relationship with your teammates, and self-awareness. The strength of your relationship with your teammates is one of the most important factors in your ability to lead effectively, so it's time to unpack what a team is and how teamwork operates.

Some of the most important questions surrounding leadership are tied into the concept of a team, and they are basic ones. What is a team? How are teams created? At what point does a collection or group of people become a team? What happens within a team? How do teams operate? What does a team need in order to operate at its highest level? Who (if anyone) are the formal or informal team leaders? How can you tell? What are the leaders' (assuming there is more than one) roles and responsibilities? How do you build and sustain teamwork? What are the important team leadership competencies?

Leadership is best understood in a team context. Whether your team consists of two or more; you and a family member, you and a project team, or you and the leadership group of a multi-national corporation, the fundamentals are the same. For example, we have created our own team—On Mission Leadership, LLC—to serve our mission of developing authentic leaders. You may be curious about who is *the* leader of On Mission Leadership. That's an easy one: We both are. It is a dance. There are situations in which John leads, inspires, and influences; there are also those in which Sean leads, inspires, and influences. And without fail, we lead and serve one another in the context of our shared mission.

Our team's logo, shown above, depicts a knot known as the Flemish bend. The knot's purpose is to join two ropes of similar size. It is often used in mountaineering or nautical applications, where strength and reliability are paramount. Each rope leads and follows the path of the other; when dressed properly, the strands don't cross each other. The knot takes some time and effort to tie, but if done properly, it doesn't need a backup or safety knot; even if one rope comes partially undone, it will hold securely. The Flemish bend knot serves as a powerful symbol of a healthy team built on strong leader–follower relationships driven by purpose, interdependence, mutual support, equality, and resilience.

Leadership comes to life in the context of a team with a mission, so it is important that you understand what leaders *do* within a team—how they orient and sustain the team's focus and performance while serving their teammates in executing the mission.

WORKING TOGETHER VERSUS TEAMWORK

At the conclusion of every team training I facilitate, I lead a debrief to help my clients identify and reflect on what went well and what could be improved in the future. When I ask my clients to identify the single factor that contributed most to their success (or lack of success), responses typically include "Teamwork!" or "A lack of teamwork!" But when I ask, "What does teamwork *mean*?" there is inevitably a long pause followed by some vague reference to people working together, cooperation, communication, and the like. People rarely have a clear explanation of what teamwork entails, let alone how it is created or sustained.

—John

Consider a group of people pushing a car out of a ditch or pulling a rope in a tug-of-war contest. Typically (although not always), they are working together. They do have a clear common goal and appear to be cooperating to achieve that goal. But whether that group is a real team is a very different question. Teamwork involves much more than merely working together. And team leadership involves much more than simply yelling "Push!" or "Pull!" A real team requires a clear mission, a supportive culture, defined shared values, and authentic relationships with trust and commitment among the team's members.

Members of a real team are interdependent, rather than independent. Interdependence means that while each member of the team carries a primary responsibility for this or that, they also have team responsibilities; they are not truly independent; they very much depend on their teammates to provide support in some important way. In a very real sense, teammates are joined by overlapping responsibilities to and for one another. No member stands entirely alone. Safety, performance, survival, and success depend on the strength of the relationship among members of the team. On real teams, members do the following: They share leadership, establish structure, norms, and expectations, communicate openly, collaborate to decide important issues, give and receive feedback, and deal with conflict openly and constructively.

WHAT IS A TEAM?

A team is made up of interdependent individuals aligned with a shared mission. One of the key aspects of a team is that its members are literally interdependent; they not only work alongside their teammates to accomplish their shared mission, they are mutually dependent on one another. Being a teammate is a relationship of consequence, and on highly functioning teams, behavior is driven by a deep sense of responsibility to and for one another. As a member of a team, everyone's performance contributes directly to and is bound together with the performance of their teammates. The ownership of responsibilities, while they may overlap in some cases, must cover the spectrum of what needs to be accomplished to carry out the team's mission.

Teams come in many forms: formal or informal, permanent or temporary, new or long standing. A team may be formed around a particular set of responsibilities. There are teams that plan and organize; teams that manage and run functions; teams that analyze and develop recommendations; and teams that build, create, and produce. In your life, you are likely a member of more than one team. Whether you are an executive, manager, supervisor, technical specialist, laborer, mother or father, neighbor or volunteer, you spend the lion's share of your time and energy operating in a team environment.

Once you get a handle on what authentic leadership at the team level requires and once you start to understand who you are as a team leader, you can begin to appreciate how leadership operates in more complex organizations. If you happen to lead within a larger organization, we implore you not to skip the core team leadership fundamentals. Even the CEO of a global corporation with tens of thousands of employees has team leadership responsibilities. They lead the larger organization through their engagement with a team of executives, who then lead their own teams. The CEO generally has a group of direct reports, is accountable to a board of directors, has an executive support staff, serves directly on numerous committees and work teams, is likely a member of an industry group, and probably has their own family within a community in which they live. All of those roles and relationships require their leadership.

Virtually everything leaders accomplish is done by, with, and through individuals and teams who then engage and execute with other individuals, leaders, and their teams. Organizational success depends on the quality and depth of leadership within each team. Individual and collective performance rests on the nature and quality of that team leadership, and this ultimately determines whether the mission will be accomplished. The chain of causation is direct and tight. This is precisely why we focus on leadership in a team context. Leadership is best understood and has its most profound impact at the level closest to the work that must be done to carry out the mission.

REFLECTION

- ✓ Locate that journal page with your team's mission written at the top.
- ✓ Below it, draw a circle and inside of that circle write the names of every member of your team—the people you work most closely with toward accomplishing your team's mission.

Don't worry about their titles, specific roles, or responsibilities. Just list your teammates' names. If you don't yet know every one of your teammates' names, find out ASAP! Introduce yourself and learn about them!

WHAT HAPPENS WITHIN A TEAM?

Dynamic forces impact a team and its performance. Collaboration and conflict, innovation and maintaining the status quo, joy and disappointment, production and destruction, profit and loss, the extraordinary and the mundane, success and failure—all of these experiences take place within a team. Additional forces, such as rapidly changing conditions and a highly competitive environment, require—demand—effective leadership. Virtually every meaningful accomplishment in our lives is the result of a team effort. Leaders at every level pay special attention to what, how, and why things happen, and look out for the welfare of their teammates throughout the team's journey.

LEADERS REVEL IN THEIR TEAMMATES' CONTRIBUTIONS

I recently attended a Tony Bennett concert. Yes, *that* Tony Bennett, the legendary crooner of "I Left My Heart in San Francisco." Although he was over ninety years old at the time, he performed at a remarkably high level. On this night,

continued

he appeared with a band of four skilled musicians. While I certainly enjoyed the music, what really struck me was how beautifully Mr. Bennet *led his team*. I was deeply impressed by the way he engaged with each member of his band. During the evening, he recognized each of them by name on numerous occasions. Every time a song featured an extended solo performance by one of his colleagues, Mr. Bennet would shout out their name as they began to play. Every single time.

But he didn't just share the spotlight with his teammates, he made sure the spotlight shone on them. During each teammate's solo, he would literally turn his back on the audience to face his bandmate, focusing his full attention and admiration on his fellow musician. He would snap his fingers to the beat while joyfully taking in their performance, and you could see he was smiling the entire time. He would frequently turn and motion to the audience to applaud during these solos, and we willingly followed his lead.

—Sean

Authentic leaders bring their best individual performance to the table, and they find ways to serve their teammates. As they serve, they show their respect and appreciation by expressing genuine joy in their teammates' performance. Leaders foster that elevating environment, one which recognizes and supports the individual and collaborative effort of the entire team. Leaders don't seek the spotlight; they look for ways to shine the light on their teammates' contributions. When the team's performance is best served by stepping back and following another's lead, authentic leaders follow wholeheartedly, creating the space for others to lead.

Thank you for the leadership lessons, Mr. Bennett!

WHO IS THE "TEAM LEADER"?

Don't strive to be *the leader*. That's about a title or position. Instead, strive to become *a leader*, a person who is prepared for and capable of leading in an authentic way. There is a world of difference between the two, and it is important you understand the distinction. As you know, *the leader* is frequently used as shorthand to identify a person in a position of authority. Most teams have designated an individual, based on either merit or seniority, as *the* team leader. This person is typically granted a level of authority with respect to the people who work on their team and is generally responsible and accountable for the team's performance. If asked, most would say this person is "in charge" of the team. In other situations, the team leader may have been selected by their teammates for one reason or another, such as their talent, performance, expertise, or popularity. Regardless of how or why the "leader" designation was made, if that person lacks the real capability to lead, they will rarely succeed over the long haul, when adversity raises its gnarly head. Teams without true leadership tend to either disband or find ways to elevate those from within who can provide that leadership.

Our broad range of military and civilian work experiences have shown us that a formally designated team leader can serve some important management functions. Although it can be an important role, carrying the title is not the same as *leading*. Lead is a verb. The person holding the position of team leader (captain, supervisor, foreman, chair, president) can use their authority to provide a degree of structure and stability, can help clarify lines of primary responsibility and can administer accountability for the team, and, *if they are capable of leading*, can provide an important level of leadership to support the team and its work.

But here is the critical point where *the* team leader may not, in fact, be *a* team leader. The central question is whether a person is, in fact, leading. Although it is reasonable to expect that a person with a title or position of authority will exhibit leadership behaviors, this is not always the case. Many people in positions of authority do not, in fact, lead.

On a wilderness expedition, for example, every task must be accomplished collaboratively: Preparations must be completed, maps must be read, gear must be obtained, organized, and carried, firewood must be gathered, food must be cooked, and tents must be struck. Every individual on the team has a set of both individual and team responsibilities. Many times, people will find and fill a niche, but everyone works together to make it all happen. Tasks, then, are both independent and interdependent. So, too, with leadership. Team members serve their fellow team members by both following and leading.

When leading, you must maintain a focus on your behavior: on the positive action you must take to serve the needs and interests of your teammates.

Leadership is essentially a principled vocation of service requiring your deep personal commitment. Leadership becomes an important aspect of who you are and how you identify yourself: as a person capable of leading. Leadership does not arise from a title or a designation.

While designating *the* team leader is important to clarify organizational lines of responsibility, leadership is a shared set of responsibilities, and every member of the team can and should be *a* team leader.

WHAT IS A LEADER'S BEST AND HIGHEST ROLE?

When determining your best and highest role as a leader, you will choose from a range of roles in service to your teammates. To help explain what we mean, consider a parent–child relationship. Think of the multiple roles a parent holds between spoon-feeding an infant and sharing wisdom with a self-reliant teenager. Consciously or not, good parents continuously ask themselves what their child needs at a particular point in time, knowing that there is no one-size-fits-all answer; they adjust their role accordingly. For a parent, these roles may include provider, teacher, disciplinarian, coach, supporter, or advisor. Sports also serve as a useful analogy for leaders, since sports teams operate in a dynamic, fast-paced environment. Consider a basketball team captain. There will be circumstances when their best and highest role is to step up and take a last-minute shot, or pass the ball to another teammate, or encourage their team from the bench. In all cases, leaders seek to fulfill their best and highest role while considering the needs of their teammates in line with the team's mission.

Prepare to lead your teammates from the front when that is your best and highest role, and step up to follow another teammate's lead when that is called for.

Rarely are you simply a "leader" with no other responsibilities. You may have a primary role in your organization to provide a technical or professional service. You certainly have an obligation to carry out your responsibilities in that role. But because you personally define yourself as a leader, you will also look beyond the limited scope of that role to determine whether and how you might lead in support of the team's mission. You may need to be a driver (organizing and directing teammates), a teacher (coaching and encouraging teammates), a follower (participating and supporting teammates), or an enabler (delegating and empowering teammates). In every situation, ask yourself, *What is my best and highest role?* and prepare to assume that role to help your team accomplish its mission.

REFLECTION

Analyze collaboration on your team:

- ✓ What are some situations in which you lead your teammates?
- ✓ What are the situations in which you follow your teammates?
- ✓ What roles do you share with your teammates?
- ✓ What roles do your teammates share with each other?

We have all approached a road construction project where it appears very little is being accomplished. Several supervisors are standing around holding clipboards and cups of coffee while a single laborer is busy shoveling dirt. While some degree of supervision is undoubtedly required to ensure engineering standards are being met in a safe and productive way, it may appear that human effort is being mismanaged. What would happen if those supervisors dropped their clipboards, set down their coffee cups, and picked up some shovels?

Sometimes a leader serves best when they organize and supervise their teammates in accomplishing a task. In other situations, a leader's best role in serving their teammates may be to help shoulder the burden.

CHAPTER 18

Orient Your Team

T hink back to a time when you first joined an existing team, such as your first day at a new job or the first practice of the sports season. You likely went through a somewhat awkward orientation period, with questions like the following: *Why am I here? Who is in charge? What is expected of me? What are the boundaries? Who is he? Who is she? What kind of team is this? Are we competing or collaborating? What can I expect of my team-mates? How will I be treated? Am I safe? How long and hard will we work? Is this just for fun, or are we in it to win it? What are the boundaries? When is lunch? Where is the bathroom?*

These questions are perfectly natural and understandable. The answers will certainly be revealed over time, but before individuals can focus and truly become productive members of a team, they need to have some basic questions addressed. When leadership is lacking, these foundational questions often go unanswered or, worse, unasked. Those who are tentative team members will perform poorly right out of the gate. So, first things first. To get off to a strong start, team members must wrap their heads and hearts around their individual and shared expectations. These expectations cover a range of matters, including the nature of the experience, the team's purpose, what the team will do to achieve its purpose, and how individuals are expected to contribute. Effective leaders are intentional about helping every team member get these questions answered promptly and clearly. Leaders help orient their team by doing the following:

- Setting the tone
- Formulating a common purpose
- Establishing team norms
- Creating team structure

WHAT KIND OF TEAM AM I ON?

Authentic human interactions are at the heart of leadership behavior. Before diving into the task at hand, build your relationship with your teammates. Take the time to communicate on a human level. Engage with them. Connect with them. Make eye contact, shake hands, pat a back, or give a hug, when appropriate. Learn their names and come to understand their background and ambitions. Start the intentional and ongoing process of learning about them. Acknowledge and appreciate their contributions, and express your trust and confidence in them.

Through your words and deeds, this discipline will speak volumes to them about who you are as a human being and a leader (two things which are inseparable) and will help them understand what kind of team they have joined. Your genuine engagement will help put your teammates at ease; they will know they are safe, valued, and appreciated and not just another cog in the wheel. People want to be a valued part of a team, not a replaceable component in a bureaucratic machine.

Promote and nurture mutual trust and respect among your teammates by setting the tone from the beginning, when your team is formed. Do it again each time a new member joins the team. Strengthen it along the way in every interaction and every engagement with a teammate. The tone you set by how you relate to others and how you clarify what teammates can expect from one another will not only serve as a powerful example for others to follow but will strengthen the team's defining culture. Every interaction matters. Be aware, be intentional, and set the tone. Never forget this truth: Culture is created not only through what a leader refuses to tolerate but also through the behavior, conduct, performance, and ethics they do tolerate.

Authentic leaders work to create a mission-focused, servant-led environment in which every human being is respected and elevated. They seek to meet the needs and the expectations of their teammates. Ask your teammates this question: "What do you want from your team experience?" The list will probably include some universal desires and needs, such as these:

- To be a part of a meaningful mission
- To discover, develop, and contribute my strengths and talents
- To earn trust and respect, to trust and respect my teammates, and to be treated with fairness and dignity
- To be involved and consulted in matters that affect me
- To share in the fruits of the team's labor and to be recognized and compensated fairly
- To earn sufficient authority and have access to the resources needed to carry out my responsibilities
- To be supported by a culture that reflects our important core values

This list will also help you to more fully understand what you, as a leader, must provide. You will be working to ensure that these needs are met. Leading as a servant is hard work!

THE FIRST ORDER OF BUSINESS

I frequently experience situations in which leaders and followers engage with one another right out of the blocks in full task mode by addressing an issue—telling or asking—without so much as a simple greeting. While this is certainly appropriate in time-critical or life-threatening situations (the building is on fire), it is a wrong-headed approach in most day-to-day interactions. Making business the first order of business reduces the relationship between teammates to a this for that transaction.

When a teammate engages with me in task mode, I first give an appropriate personal greeting and, time permitting, take a moment to find out how they are doing. This typically results in a smile and effectively resets the table, humanizing the teamwork we are about to engage in. Here's an important point: *How are you?* should not be an obligatory greeting for the sole purpose of exhibiting your good manners. While civility is important, asking a teammate how they are doing should be a real question offered to stimulate a real answer and fueled by your authentic curiosity. By making our relationships the first order of business, we gain context, understand where each other is coming from, and further build our relationship. Putting the human being first puts task and relationship squarely where they need to be—on equal footing.

—John

WHY DOES OUR TEAM EXIST?

Leaders clarify a common purpose and ensure unity of effort by helping to define the team's mission and supporting goals. Leaders look at the big picture to understand the higher purpose of the team and its broader context to get clear in their own mind why the team exists. They communicate a clear understanding of the team's purpose and, when necessary, refine the team's mission in collaboration with other team members. They question, clarify, explain, and emphasize the nature of that mission until every team member understands and embraces it.

Work hard to ensure that your teammates understand why the team exists, what the team's mission is, and how their primary responsibility aligns with the team's mission. Your teammates must be clear on the connection between their role and responsibility and the team's mission. You can then serve by working with your teammates to clarify performance expectations and develop supporting goals. Remember, that is all about the *why* and the *what*, not the *how*. How the responsibility is to be carried out or the task is to be accomplished is best determined through team member collaboration and planning. Often, the *how* is best left to those who bear the responsibility of carrying those responsibilities. Involve them in the *how*. Let them propose and create the *how*. Let them surprise you with the *how*.

Clarifying the *why* behind the *what* is a critical leadership responsibility. Clarifying why is a powerful way to align and connect the efforts of your teammates not only with your team's mission but also with the mission of your parent organization and your peer teams. Make that mission connection a habit in how you lead and everyone will win.

CLARIFY THE *WHY*

As a young officer, I was once given the relatively simple task of pulling together mission-critical equipment for a Marine unit operating from a ship deployed at sea. Time was of the essence, as real-world events had transformed the deployed team's mission into something not contemplated in the initial planning process. We had very limited time to obtain and organize the requested equipment; we needed to move fast.

I asked one of the Marines on my team to step up and take on this task. Rather than simply handing him the list and ordering him to comply, which I easily could have done, I chose to give him a sense of the *why* behind the *what*. I took a few moments to explain the nature of the deployed team's mission, and I clarified how that mission had evolved. I wanted him to understand *why* the order had been issued by helping him understand the unit's request for support and the reason it was now urgent. I explained how the equipment might be used by the team and what the real-world implications could be. Once he was clear on the mission context and the urgency of the matter, he took the list and moved with enthusiasm and a clear mission focus. He now understood this was not some poorly planned, last-minute order from his lieutenant; he was carrying out an important responsibility in support of a critical mission on behalf of his fellow Marines.

In giving this young Marine a clear line of sight between his responsibility and the mission capabilities of the deployed unit, along with a clear understanding about their changing mission and a sense of its urgency, he literally became an integral part of that team's evolving mission. Communicating the context, the nature of the mission and its urgency, also provided this Marine with the full understanding he needed to carry out his responsibility at the highest level. At the same time, I fulfilled another important leadership responsibility: I exhibited my respect for him as a teammate.

It took me only a few moments to do this. You always have time to clarify the *why* behind the *what*. In a practical sense, providing context strengthens mission alignment, increases the likelihood of better performance, and strengthens relationships.

—Sean

HOW ARE WE TO BEHAVE TOWARD ONE ANOTHER?

This one is simple. Always, and without fail, treat your teammates with dignity and respect, and require your teammates to do the same. Tolerate nothing less. If you have ever been on a team where a member of the team treats another poorly, you know how disruptive it can be. If language, attire, work ethic, performance standards, and the like are not aligned with the team's standards or are inconsistent among teammates, the quality of execution often suffers. Typically, this happens when people are unclear about behavioral expectations. Don't make them guess. Ensure standards and expectations are clearly defined and well understood by every member of the team and are fully embraced. Strive for excellence. Make sure you are leading by example and that accountability among your team members is real. If a teammate uses foul language, comes to work in a dirty T-shirt, produces low-quality work, or clocks out before the work is done without reason, conflict will arise, and a festering resentment among teammates can build and become debilitating.

Establish clear team norms by working with your teammates to set acceptable standards of individual and team behavior, early and often. Ask your teammates what behaviors are expected and what behaviors should be rejected. What is appropriate and what is inappropriate? What is acceptable and what is unacceptable? How do we dress? How do we speak to one another? When do we work, and when do we play? What customs and courtesies will help drive our performance and lead to mission accomplishment? What behaviors do we leave behind, and what behaviors do we take forward? Once those norms are established, you must consistently set the example and model them, or they will become meaningless.

ESTABLISH TEAM NORMS

Establishing team norms is one of the first and most critical steps I take before embarking on a wilderness expedition. Experience has taught me the failure to do so is a recipe for disaster. Soon after teammates create and agree on our team's purpose and goals, we have a thoughtful and thorough discussion of team norms—the behaviors we will accept and those we will reject. The discussion is collaborative, with a healthy dose of give and take. Each team member articulates their commitments and expectations and listens to others' commitments and expectations. We record them, edit them, and work together to create a comprehensive list. Ceremoniously, we individually sign the document to express our buy-in and preserve it for future reference.

During the expedition, if an individual team member feels the norms are not being upheld or that an adjustment is needed, they are expected to bring it to the team's attention for resolution. This collaborative approach leads to team self-regulation and ensures that all team members, not just the person of authority, has the responsibility to enforce our expectations.

—John

REFLECTION

✓ Write down a few of your most important team norms—the behaviors that are expected and the behaviors that are unacceptable.

✓ Are these your norms alone, or do the rest of your teammates accept these as the team's norms?

✓ Have you and your teammates discussed and clarified these team norms? If not, what can you do to induce this conversation?

WHAT IS EXPECTED OF ME?

One of the common sources of team dysfunction is people not understanding what is expected of them or when it is expected. You've probably experienced this, and you may even have been its cause. Unfortunately, leaders and followers are often forced to make too many assumptions when it comes to expectations of performance, behavior, and commitment. We tend to operate from a belief that people should know what is expected of them in their role, or they should be able to figure it out by reading their job description or considering their role in light of the team's mission. While they may eventually figure it out, that clarity often comes only after an extended, stressful period of trial-and-error. Bypass all of that. Respect them. Be clear. Clarify your expectations of your teammates up front. Make sure everyone understands what and why. At the same time, help them clarify what they should expect of you when leading. Avoid the trial-and-error approach to discovering expectations.

Create a supportive team structure, and build a strong sense of team awareness by clarifying individual responsibilities and performance expectations. Work hard to discover your teammates' personal goals, strengths, and growth areas, and assign primary responsibilities and tasks accordingly. Establish time constraints and clear performance standards, so your teammates know what is expected of them, when it is expected, and why. Be deliberate in setting a positive example of the behavior you expect. Work with your teammates to develop clear priorities and clarify short-term goals. Ensure that no team member is uninformed or even remotely unclear of what is expected of them.

As soon as a team forms and every time new a member joins or leaves, or when significant changes occur to the team's mission or structure, you have a leadership responsibility to orient your teammates. Getting people aligned early and often helps build trust and confidence among your teammates, clarifies the team's purpose and mission, and illuminates individuals' expectations. When you orient your team, you are building a sense of community among your teammates, which is the foundation of your team's culture.

CHAPTER 19

Sustain Your Team

A team's performance will be measured, in no small part, by how effectively it advances toward its mission. To support this, leaders must attend to many diverse operational issues—tasks, budgets, schedules, resources, and environmental pressures, to name just a few. A team is not an inert object but rather a dynamic, living organism made of individual human beings. Although they are bound by commitment to a shared mission, these people must find ways to work together to maximize effort, generate ideas, create value, understand changing conditions, and solve problems. For a team to sustain itself, its members must have solid social and interpersonal skills.

Leaders help team members develop the social and interpersonal skills necessary to sustain their team by modeling these critical skills and by consistently seeking and clarifying answers to the following questions:

- How do we communicate?

- How do we decide?

- How do we exchange feedback?

- How do we deal with conflict?

- How do we improve?

- How do we deal with changes within the team?

HOW DO WE COMMUNICATE?

When leading, it is important to both set the example and clarify communication expectations and standards. For example, you could begin by establishing these core communication standards: *We will communicate clearly, completely, and frequently with one another, with respect and with care.* Effective interpersonal communication is a vital skill for leaders and their teammates. Leaders must first model effective communication. Without fail, leaders must treat the messenger with dignity and respect, especially when the news is bad. Always remember that communication is a two-way street; it is much more than merely transmitting information. Authentic leaders dominate the listening; they discipline themselves to listen actively in every interaction with their teammates. Listen to understand, not to respond. Put your electronic gadgets away, sit up, make eye contact, and listen intently. Pay attention to your teammates' nonverbal cues and body language. Ask clarifying questions to understand both the message and the messenger. Listen more than you speak. And when you do speak, do so thoughtfully and with respect, purpose, clarity, and conviction.

Missing or incomplete information impedes both decision-making and team performance. Critical information essential to the team's performance often already resides somewhere within the team, but, for many reasons, it may not be known to those who need it the most. Establish an environment in which it is safe to share information in a robust way, both the good and the bad. Don't allow relevant information to be hoarded. Make sharing information the team's default mode.

While information can be a source of power and knowing what others may not know can feed one's ego, authentic leaders never hoard information or seek to manipulate others based on their ignorance. Authentic leaders default to sharing information to ensure that all team members have what they need to fully address the realities at play. When in doubt, err on the side of sharing more information rather than less. Ensure that this practice becomes a cornerstone in your team's culture. Your teammates can operate at much higher levels and can take initiative more effectively when they have a clearer picture of the present reality. Facts must be shared with your teammates, even when the truth may not be the version they would prefer.

Ensure that your team maintains a healthy balance of respect for advocacy (individuals speaking on their own behalf) and inquiry (individuals seeking to understand what others think). Leaders must make it safe to do so. At the same time, you need to find ways to embolden some of your teammates to express themselves when they find communication difficult; you may also find it necessary to encourage others to listen when they do not want to hear.

HOW DO WE DECIDE?

Nothing can destroy team morale or effectiveness more thoroughly than a pattern of slow, rash, or low-quality decisions. Leaders serve well by ensuring team members collaborate at high levels by understanding how team decisions are made. Different decision-making strategies are more appropriate for different situations, depending on the complexity and consequences of the decision and considering the speed decisions must be made.

Autocratic decision making is when one person decides. Although quick and efficient, autocratic decision making has its limitations, namely that other teammates' perspectives aren't considered. When autocratic decision making is the norm, team members tend to do exactly as told, no more and no less.

Democratic decision making is majority rule. Voting is quick and efficient, and all teammates have a voice in the matter. But with a vote, minority opinions don't count, so the quality of the decision may be less than ideal.

A consensus happens when all team members have the time to deeply consider the issue, advocate for what they believe, and agree on the best course of action. If the process is carried out with discipline, this strategy can create buy-in from all team members and often results in high-quality decisions. Although time consuming, a consensus may be the most appropriate strategy for important decisions with significant consequences.

You will find many decisions are made through a combination of all three strategies—a little discussion, a survey of where the majority opinions lie, the person with rank or authority being the final arbitrator and decision-maker. Regardless of the method used in a particular situation, ensure that team decisions are made with intention. The way a team decides is often as important—or more important—than the decision itself.

Never forget that timeliness is a key consideration in decision-making. Don't strive for "perfect" decisions; there is no such thing. Make the best decision you can based on the information and in the time available. Adjust as you move forward and as events unfold. Ensure that your team members collaborate, understand, and agree on the methods of decision-making.

HOW DO WE EXCHANGE FEEDBACK?

Performance feedback can be a gift when it is provided and received constructively, in a timely fashion, in the right manner, and in the right spirit. Unfortunately, that is not always the case. If team members don't have the right mindset and haven't developed basic skills in giving and receiving feedback, the consequences can be negative; good performance can go unacknowledged, small mistakes can become big problems, and big problems can put the team's mission in danger.

Help your team develop a culture of healthy feedback by modeling proper methods. Give timely, consistent, quality feedback to others, with the clear intention of helping them learn and become more effective. Actively request and value feedback from others. Listen with humility, and then act upon the feedback. Here's a powerful habit to develop: After receiving feedback from another, first say, "Thank you!" Feedback is a gift. Treat it accordingly.

FEEDBACK IS A GIFT!

Team members on extended wilderness expeditions have no choice but to work with and alongside one another. Intimate, interdependent relationships demand

continued

that they deal with their teammates' behavior—both good and bad—for the long haul. Teammates, then, must have a healthy attitude toward feedback, with the necessary tools to give and receive it. Before we begin an expedition, I gather my teammates together and facilitate a discussion about feedback—what feedback is and how it should be perceived, given, and received.

—John

Feedback can be a developmental, constructive form of communication intended to acknowledge and encourage good behavior (affirmative), suggest improvements to counterproductive behaviors (adjustive), and correct unacceptable behavior (corrective.) Feedback should never be given as a reprimand for poor performance. Feedback is not a punitive measure intended to scold, demean, rebuke, admonish, or dress down a fellow teammate. Make your feedback constructive, meaningful, and practical. Craft your feedback so that your teammate can build and grow with it.

Avoid adjectives as a stand-alone form of feedback. Adjectives in and of themselves ("You made a stupid decision" or "You did an awesome job") can evoke strong feelings but fail to inform in a constructive way. Recipients of this type of feedback may feel good or bad about their performance, but they have nothing specific or actionable to improve their performance.

Feedback should be provided in a timely manner, after you have had time to reflect but soon enough after the event that memories are intact and lucid. It should also be provided in a forum that is private or, if appropriate, in a small group setting. Invite the recipient to receive the feedback by asking, "May I give you some feedback?"

Don't feed without asking for it back. With sincerity, ask the recipient of your feedback whether they agree with your point of view. Then ask them to provide feedback in return. Keep an open mind and a welcoming posture for them to do so. Make it safe. Listen intently. Say, "Thank you." Once their feedback is provided and received, shake your teammate's hand or exchange a smile to show you appreciate their willingness to listen and speak. Leave the door wide open for more mutual feedback in the future.

HOW DO WE DEAL WITH CONFLICT?

Conflict can be as uncomfortable as it is inevitable. Opinions may differ, personalities and egos can clash, and, as a result, humans will act in human ways. Sometimes people will go on the offense to win the conflict—speaking without listening, raising their voice, posturing, and doing what it takes to get their way. More commonly, people withdraw from the conflict and head to the sidelines to avoid it—denying, hiding, ducking, and dodging or agreeing, conceding, or complying against their best judgment.

Help your teammates understand the difference between healthy and unhealthy conflict. Intellectual conflict—the struggle of ideas—is healthy for your team. Intellectual conflict inspires thought, broadens minds, and creates knowledge and wisdom. Remind your teammates that the purpose of an argument is to discover the truth, not score a personal victory. Also remind them that when the challenge of ideas becomes personal, conflict becomes unhealthy. Interpersonal conflict, if unattended and left to fester, turns a team into an emotional mess of wounded people hurting wounded people. When dealing with conflict, model the behavior you wish to see in your teammates.

DEALING WITH THE PEBBLE

A colleague of mine uses a hiking analogy for dealing with interpersonal conflict: "When you feel a pebble in your shoe, if you don't stop, take off your shoe, and remove the pebble, the pain doesn't go away. It just worsens until you're unable to focus on anything else. Eventually, you develop a blister and lose your ability to move forward."

—John

Avoiding conflict merely defers the pain and usually makes it worse. Failure to acknowledge and effectively deal with conflict is a recipe for disaster in any relationship. The problem isn't usually how to deal with conflict (there are abundant conflict-management strategies out there, and you likely have your own); the problem is, most often, avoidance.

Recognizing and dealing with interpersonal conflict is productive. It enables your team to self-correct and move forward. Don't avoid conflict; rather, face it squarely, and help your teammates learn to manage through it. Serve your teammates by encouraging them to be transparent with their feelings, empower them to address their concerns with others, and help your team develop the tools and strategies to effectively address conflict when it arises.

Of course, the best way to reduce (not avoid) interpersonal conflict is to establish a healthy feedback system within your team. When a feedback system exists, issues are nipped in the bud before they take on a life of their own and become problems.

HOW DO WE IMPROVE?

Your teammates are busy. There are widgets to produce, information to collect, analyze, and report, targets to reach, tasks to complete, and deadlines to meet. Typically, the members of your team are heavily engaged in carrying out their own duties while upholding responsibilities to the team and its mission. What needs to get done always seems to outpace the limited time and resources available. No matter how efficient and effectively a team works together, there rarely seems to be enough time to accomplish it all.

In the daily grind, team members can become habituated to doing the same things over and over with little consideration of the changing external realities and shifting circumstances. It is easy to lose a mission perspective: that clear line of sight between a person's primary responsibilities or the immediate task at hand and the team's mission. Why are we digging this hole or building this bridge in the first place? This is one of the critical reasons a team needs to debrief regularly. Periodically pause, step away from the fire, take a breath, gain perspective, make an assessment, and adjust.

Structure time for debriefing daily, weekly, at the end of every important event, and when significant change occurs. Set the expectation among your teammates that debriefing is a fundamental team function, as important as any other daily task. Debriefs should be free from distractions and convened soon enough after an occurrence for the details to be fresh in people's minds. Debriefs should be anticipated and valued, not dreaded and avoided. During a productive debrief, leaders ask these questions:

- To what degree are we moving toward mission accomplishment?
- What are we doing well? What is working? Why?
- What are we not doing well? What is not working? Why?
- What do we need to change?
- What do individuals need?

HOW DO WE DEAL WITH CHANGES WITHIN THE TEAM?

We sometimes think of our teams as fixed entities. On any given day, we engage with the same people in the same way. Based on our past experiences, we often create an expectation of our teammates' performance, regardless of their true potential or capability.

Teams are anything but static. They operate in dynamic conditions and change over time, sometimes subtly and often profoundly. New members join, and old members leave. People learn and develop competence and confidence or lose their nerve. Relationships are born, strengthened, tested, and stressed. Procedures are developed, refined, and discarded. Old tasks are completed, and new tasks emerge. Commitment waxes and wanes, and morale rises and falls. Add to these internal dynamics the incessant change of outside circumstances, and you begin to understand why your team operates in a constant state of evolution.

We've seen this evolution play out again and again. Although the stages are rarely predictable and certainly not inevitable, you need to recognize and appreciate them when they occur during your team's life cycle. Your awareness can guide you and your teammates regarding what the team needs at any given stage. As a leader, it can also help you determine your best and highest leadership role in support of your teammates.

You may be familiar with psychological researcher Bruce Tuckman's five stages of group development.[3] We've confirmed the veracity of this model in our own experience countless times and consider it worth emphasizing for you. Tuckman observed teams develop through five stages: forming, storming, norming, performing, and adjourning. Teams typically progress from one stage to the next, unless an event such as a loss or addition of a team member causes it to reset to an earlier stage. Based on the dynamics at play, some stages take longer, while others pass more quickly. They can also take place out of sequence, be skipped, or recur.

FORMING

When your team is newly formed, when a new member joins the team, or when your intact team undertakes a new mission, your teammates will have to orient themselves to the new dynamics, people, processes and patterns, and tasks. Regardless of the maturity or strength of a team before the change, some degree of uncertainty and inefficiency will understandably result. Your teammates will grapple with their primary responsibilities as they adjust to personnel or mission changes. Serve your team during the forming stage by exhibiting patience. Take a hands-on approach by teaching and providing specific direction for your teammates when they need it.

STORMING

Once your team is formed, challenges brought on by change emerge. Your teammates begin to feel comfortable expressing discontent and challenging each other's opinions, which can be contentious and may be considered unpleasant or painful to teammates who are averse to conflict. Serve your teammates during this stage by facilitating effective feedback and helping them manage conflict. Help them recognize that conflict is natural and acceptable and show them that dealing with it will ultimately strengthen

---

3   Bruce W. Tuckman. "Developmental sequence in small groups," *Psychological Bulletin*, 63, no. 6 (1965): 384–399.

your team. In time, your teammates will discover one another's strengths and weaknesses and begin sorting out roles and responsibilities. Their collective accountability and motivation to achieve the team's goals increase.

NORMING

Teammates begin to adopt and implement practices, establish clear performance expectations, and implement constructive feedback. Step back into a coaching role during this stage by providing broad guidance and ensuring mission alignment while allowing your teammates to discover and develop their own paths to success. Help your team refine their culture.

PERFORMING

Ultimately, your teammates begin to function as a team. They find ways to get the job done smoothly and effectively and without unhealthy conflict or the need for extensive supervision. By this time, they are knowledgeable, competent, autonomous, and able to effectively make decisions. Dissent is expected and accepted, if it is channeled through means acceptable to the team. Take a supporting role; delegate responsibility to empower your teammates to perform at their highest level.

ADJOURNING

Once the mission has been accomplished or the team faces being disbanded, its members can become disengaged, and residual interpersonal conflict may reemerge. If a new mission is assigned, the team's performance may drop as the new roles and norms are established. It may be difficult for your teammates to remain in the present as their thoughts drift toward future endeavors. Help your teammates process and express their anxieties and concerns, along with celebrating their accomplishments. Help the team remain engaged during this stage until the mission is accomplished.

Explain to your teammates that changing group dynamics are necessary for the team to grow. Leaders do this by setting the tone, formulating a common purpose, establishing team norms and structure, and facilitating effective communication, decision-making, and feedback, while helping manage conflict which may arise. In doing this important leadership work, you can help the team navigate through changing group dynamics.

CHAPTER 20

Team Operations

Just as there are some individuals who don't work well as members of a team, there are also highly functioning teams that ultimately fail to accomplish the mission. Despite working together harmoniously, some key factors may be missing. To accomplish the mission, a team's members must attend to numerous and diverse operational issues, such as planning and budgeting, obtaining physical and human resources, marketing, and serving customers and clients. Your team's unique mission will dictate the nature of these operational issues.

Your level of expertise will likely improve your ability to plan, solve problems, and to teach, coach, and mentor your teammates. But, as we've stated before, a high level of technical expertise is not a leadership requirement.

MANAGING TEAM EXECUTION

Earlier, we distinguished leadership responsibilities from management responsibilities. Although management is not the focus of this book, a few words about it should be said. Regardless of the nature or complexity of your team's mission, you must serve your teammates by taking the following actions:

- Helping them identify and obtain the resources they need
- Assisting them in planning the effort and setting supporting goals
- Developing solutions to problems and resolving issues
- Supervising performance in appropriate ways to ensure results

PROVIDE MISSION-ESSENTIAL NEEDS

Every team needs sufficient resources to operate at its optimal level. These can include facilities and equipment, information and software, training and expertise, the necessary talent, and the like. When sufficient resources are available, your teammates can focus their attention fully on execution. In an environment where resources are scarce and your team's energy is diffused, accomplishing the mission becomes much more difficult. If they have insufficient resources, your teammates will probably feel demoralized and will be unable to even envision a path forward.

While your teammates may never feel they have all the resources they need, they must have access to those essential for the mission. Leaders are responsible for ensuring their team has what it needs. Work with your teammates to identify, acquire, and share mission-essential resources. Involve them in the process. Determining mission-essential needs can be as simple as asking your team what they need. Then get to work assisting them with acquiring those resources. You will frequently find that a struggling teammate only needs a certain tool, an improvement in workspace ergonomics, a particular resource, a piece of information, some context, a technology upgrade, or additional training to overcome a stifling obstacle.

MAINTAINING SITUATIONAL AWARENESS

Expedition sea kayaking is one of the most technically demanding activities for an outdoor leader. First, they must personally master and know how to teach the technical aspects of paddling a craft—body position, paddle strokes, boat edging and maneuvers—and be able to rescue themselves or others in a variety of environmental conditions. Navigation requires the ability to read a chart, use a compass, plan a route, and keep track of their location, day and night. They must know how much food to bring and how to cook it, how much gear to bring and how to use it, and how to pack everything efficiently. Numerous environmental factors must be attended to—wind, weather, waves, tides, currents, bugs, sand, and sun. Add self-awareness, self-management, and group dynamics—leading, teaching, communicating, conflict management—and it can be quite a complex undertaking. How does a leader stay on top of it all?

When training sea kayak leaders, I encourage a multidimensional approach to maintaining situational awareness:

- Look up and look down. What is the weather doing? What are the seas doing?

- Look left and look right. Where is the nearest safe landing? What hazards should be avoided?

- Look back and look forward. Reflect on what happened. What lessons were learned and can be applied in the future? Where are you in relation to your goal or mission? What's next and after that?

- Look outside and look inside. How is your team doing? What do they need from you? How are you doing? What do you need?

—John

REMOVE OBSTACLES

Challenge, change, adversity, and loss are realities for any team, just as they are our constant companions in life. The resulting sense of disappointment, although understandable, should not lead to thoughts of failure and should never hamper the team's ability to move forward. Your responsibility as a servant leader is to help your teammates constructively process setbacks and use them as stepping stones to advance the mission.

Recognize obstacles for what they are: complications that need solutions, opposing forces that need to be overcome. We are not suggesting that you should simply wish them away. Instead, do what authentic leaders consistently do: Call out the problem, and face it head-on. Develop the habit of exercising the discipline of calmly taking stock of the unpleasant realities at play. As you do so, you can also exhibit an important leadership trait: resilience. When obstacles appear, as they often will, a good dose of realistic optimism will fuel a spirit of opportunism, which will serve you and your team well. Energy wasted by wringing your hands is better spent clasping your teammates' hands to learn lessons and seek solutions.

WHAT IS THE REAL OBSTACLE HERE?

I was on an extended wilderness expedition my team had been planning for months. A few weeks into the trip, as we were preparing to hike into a pristine wilderness gorge, white ash began floating in the sky, accompanied by the faint smell of smoke. Our situation had changed abruptly and dramatically. Somewhere in the vicinity, a wildfire was raging. How far away, in what direction, and how fast it was moving were all unknowns. After a quick brainstorming session, we determined we had no recourse other than to cancel our trip through the gorge and quickly evacuate the area.

Once we were in a safe place, we reflected on what had happened to find meaning in the situation. We considered our lost opportunity to experience the gorge and grieved our immense wasted planning effort. How could we overcome this major obstacle to mission accomplishment?

One of our teammates suggested that the change was not an obstacle to our mission but, rather, an opportunity to accomplish our mission in a different way. The trek through the gorge was only a means to accomplish our mission, not the mission itself. Rather than lament our loss, we decided to continue our expedition by river, in canoes. We achieved our trip objectives; the method was unexpected but nevertheless effective.

As it turned out, the wildfire wasn't the obstacle to mission accomplishment; the real obstacle was the limited way we thought about our team's mission. It took an act of leadership by one of our teammates to help us recognize the nature of the real obstacle.

–John

SUPERVISE TEAM PERFORMANCE

A proper level of supervision is required for team members to reach high levels of individual and team performance. "Proper level" is a key phrase to note when it comes to supervision. It shouldn't surprise you to know that we don't tolerate those who feel compelled to over-supervise or micromanage.

The Marine Corps teaches six troop leading steps, which clarify the fundamental actions required of a leader in support of a mission. Supervision is the final and perhaps most important troop-leading step. It requires a leader to properly oversee execution to ensure mission success. Supervising involves aligning and steering individual and collective effort, distributing information and resources, monitoring performance and providing constructive and timely feedback, teaching and coaching, and ensuring individual and team performance meets expectations.

If your image of supervising involves sipping a cold drink while sitting back in an overstuffed chair with your feet up, you are mistaken. Supervising properly requires you to look for patterns in performance and outcomes, identify disruptions and obstacles, monitor progress, and help solve problems, all while keeping a laser focus on the prize: mission accomplishment.

WHERE ARE THE GREEN BEANS?

When I was eight years old, I was busy trying to stay out of trouble one summer day. My mother decided to give me a task to keep me occupied. With little guidance or preparation, she told me to go out into the garden and pull all the weeds. *Sounds easy enough*, I thought. I ran out the door and opened the gate that led to a large garden she had carefully planted that spring.

With no training and little prior experience, but armed with a great deal of energy and enthusiasm, I quickly scanned the entire garden. To my untrained eye, it appeared to be absolutely overrun with weeds, which probably explained why I, rather than any of my brothers, was given this important responsibility. Certain areas contained nicely aligned rows of plants, so I identified them as vegetables which must not be touched. Other areas of the garden were populated with

continued

randomly placed plants, so I quickly identified them as "weeds" which must be destroyed. I reviewed my clear orders in my mind: "Pull up all the weeds." So I went at it.

I took only one break during the next several hours, and that was to enlist the help of my little brother. This was a much bigger job than my mother had apparently contemplated, so backup was needed. He was only seven, but he was even closer to the ground than I was, and he could pull weeds fast. A few hours later, once we'd cleared the entire garden of all offending weeds in accordance with the highest standards I could muster, I ran back into the house. I proudly reported that I had completed my mission and I was ready for her inspection.

As we approached the garden, my pride swelled as I surveyed my extremely thorough work. I pointed to the rather substantial pile of weeds my brother and I had captured. I can still hear my mother's shocked question:

"Where are the green beans?"

"The what?" I asked.

She said, "The green beans! You've pulled all the green beans from the garden!"

Mission failure. I felt terrible, of course, but the damage had been done. There would be no green beans on the table that year.

In my defense, a reasonable level of training and preparation, along with an appropriate level of supervision, would have made a great difference in my ability to execute this clear mission. This is a lesson I've never forgotten.

—Sean

Proper supervision is a key leadership responsibility when aligning effort. Each of your teammates brings a different level of motivation, talent, and skills to their work. Observe intently to learn the value your teammates bring to the table. Play to their strengths. Help each member find an appropriate niche in the team effort. You don't have to be in a position of authority or responsibility to supervise properly. Every team member is accountable to every other team member; proper supervision is a *shared* responsibility.

A proper level of supervision is also one of the ways a leader maintains individual and collective accountability for performance. Holding yourself and your teammates accountable for meeting expectations is critical to your team's success. Constructive accountability is an act of leadership, not a form of judgment. As with providing constructive and timely performance feedback, supervising constructively and properly is a powerful way to serve and develop others.

Conversely, micromanaging stifles performance, initiative, and collaboration—all of which are obstacles to great teamwork. Telling people how to do their job denies them the opportunity to figure things out themselves and to learn and grow from the process. Not only is micromanaging ineffective, it is inefficient and communicates a very clear message that you do not trust your teammate's ability to carry out their responsibilities. Whether you are aware of it or not, when you micromanage another person, you express your belief that they lack the capabilities to accomplish the task.

While there will be times when close supervision is required, especially when a member of the team is first learning how to carry out a task or shoulder a responsibility, a leader must be mindful of the *degree* of supervision required. Few things in this world must be completed in a "my way or the highway" fashion. We are often astounded by the level of creativity and insightful thinking others can bring to resolving an issue, resulting in solutions we hadn't even imagined. You may find your teammates carrying out a responsibility in a way that is far better than the method you would have directed. Clear the obstacles and provide support so that your teammates can bring their full value to the mission.

Leaders serve well when they create an environment where a teammate is given the grace and provided the space to fail and learn. This makes it much more likely a teammate will develop a personal sense of confidence and gain a deeper level of competence. There will often be times when a lighter leadership touch is best. Create that space for your teammates, extend grace, make real-world learning safe, and give them room to grow, learn, and discover. Hold your teammates constructively accountable for results, but do not micromanage their decisions and execution.

Teams perform best when they take full ownership of their mission. This ownership requires mutual accountability among teammates and a level of sufficient, not suffocating supervision.

CHAPTER 21

Team Culture

C ulture is a powerful element of every team. It plays a significant role in guiding behavior, shaping relationships, and supporting how the team accomplishes its work. It is important for you to understand and appreciate what makes up your team's culture; as you lead, you will expend time and energy in shaping and strengthening it. Culture is the team's social DNA, an aggregate of the team's values, conventions, and beliefs. Culture incorporates the often unwritten rules that guide people on a team in how to operate, execute, and engage with their teammates and with the outside world. Clarifying the team's culture is a key element in transforming a mere collection of individual contributors into a real team with a shared purpose.

In the Marine Corps, the core identity and perspective of every Marine is as a rifleman—the Marine on the ground, with a weapon in hand, who does the dirty work required in combat. Even in modern warfare, with its high-tech weaponry and multidimensional battlefield, it is the rifleman who ultimately bears the responsibility to face the enemy.

The Marines' famous axiom, "Every Marine a rifleman," has important operational and cultural implications. Every Marine, regardless of rank or job specialty, is first trained in basic infantry skills and is required to maintain their marksmanship skills throughout their career. This holds true even for Marine lawyers! Marines are always prepared to drop what they are doing, pick up a rifle, and fight.

The cultural implications are even more profound. Marines take great pride in identifying themselves as riflemen first. This term of endearment serves as a powerful bond between generals and privates, pilots and truck drivers, infantrymen and computer programmers, and artillerymen and administrative clerks. It connects approximately 180,000 human beings with a single identity, a shared purpose, and a common understanding. In the Marines, every Marine a rifleman is the cultural and operational reality.

Every team has a culture, whether it was intentionally created or not. It may be constructive or destructive, weak or strong, and we can assure you it has a significant impact on how your teammates perform and how the team executes. Regardless of whether it was created intentionally or arose piecemeal from an aggregation of personalities, policies, situations, and decisions, your team's culture impacts everything the team does and everything it is. Culture incorporates what is truly valued in the team: It informs how people communicate and share information. It sets expectations for how people will be treated. It determines the degree of innovation and establishes the level of risk that is acceptable. Culture also captures the way a team responds to adversity and change and how its members carry out their responsibilities.

Leaders understand the importance of culture, so they become culture warriors, in a sense—vigilant in their effort to clarify, embody, protect, and strengthen their team's culture. Leaders fulfill this responsibility in many ways: through the power of their example, through what they pay attention to and what they disregard, and through which behaviors are applauded or corrected.

The culture you as a leader help to create, shape, and nurture through your actions serves to guide individual and team performance. A team's culture directly impacts virtually every aspect of the team. Culture clarifies what is important and what is not, it sets boundaries and provides guardrails for behavior, and it drives expected performance. At the end of the day, a team culture will either materially support or dramatically undermine its members' performance, and it will ultimately determine whether the team accomplishes its mission. Don't take it for granted.

DEFINE AND CLARIFY YOUR TEAM'S CULTURE

Composing a carefully crafted culture statement can be a worthwhile task, but keep in mind that this statement must truly reflect your team's realities. Culture embodies the realities of how teammates engage with one another and how the team operates to get things done.

As you and your teammates create clarity around your team culture, ask yourselves the tough questions:

- Who are we, now, in reality?

- Who do we aspire to be?

- Do our policies, priorities, decisions, and actions support our team's mission?

- Do we have clearly stated values, beliefs, and expectations?

  » Are they operational?

  » Do they really guide our behaviors?

  » Do they truly represent the reality of the way we do things around here?

  » Are they regularly communicated, discussed, contemplated, relied on, encouraged, embraced, and celebrated, or are they simply paid lip service?

Leaders value clarity. At the same time, there is no specified content or set format for defining your culture in a culture statement. It should be as long as it needs to be, but shorter is better, so strive to limit it to a paragraph or two. Here are some options for you and your teammates to consider for inclusion in your team's culture statement:

- Your core values

- Your beliefs

- Your mission, goals, and priorities

- Your behavioral traits and attitudes about your teammates, those you serve, and the work you do

- What it's like to be part of your team

Your culture statement should define your team's culture; it should describe who you are, but it can also describe who you aspire to be. If it is aspirational, get to work right away on making it real. You and your teammates have a responsibility to make your culture statement come to life.

MAKE YOUR ASPIRATIONS MATCH YOUR REALITIES

Virtually every corporation in America has created a culture statement. Unfortunately, many don't reflect reality when you pull back the curtain and look at the real values that guide the priorities, decision-making, and relationships in that company. When the culture you claim bears little resemblance to the cultural realities at play, a fancy culture statement becomes a meaningless decorative piece, suitable only to adorn a conference room wall.

In large, complex organizations, many distinct subcultures can develop within smaller teams. That can be a problem if those cultures don't align with the organization's mission. Energy and attention must be invested in aligning each team's culture with that of the parent organization. Cultural disconnects are disruptive. Here's one that really raises our hackles: cultures claiming to value their people as their number-one asset, when all other evidence speaks to the contrary. Here's another one: claiming your culture is ethical when the reality is that your team incentivizes unethical or immoral behavior or turns a blind eye to such conduct.

A clear, inspiring, and supportive culture will powerfully influence a team's performance. It can materially impact the way teammates relate to one another and the way they respond to what is happening around them. Leaders must understand, honor, and be intentional about culture, because that commitment impacts the way its people engage and operate.

Consider for a moment what contributes to the creation and maintenance of a team's culture. You may not have thought about it in these terms, but every family, every team, and every organization has a culture, its "social DNA." It is often unstated and builds over the course of time in frequently unintentional ways. Leaders have the primary responsibility to determine whether the team's culture will be shaped in an intentional or haphazard way. If not fostered deliberately and thoughtfully, a team's culture can easily develop in less than constructive ways. Culture builds over the course of time, layer upon layer, event by event, and interaction by interaction. A team's culture may be a force-multiplier, or it may work against a team's purpose, weighing it down and creating and bureaucracy where flexibility, innovation, and speed are required. Unfortunately, most cultures are created in unintentional ways. Leaders must step up and take responsibility to intentionally shape and nurture a supportive, adaptive culture.

WE DON'T DO THAT HERE

I was once second in command of a Marine Corps unit. On one occasion I expressed my discontent with behaviors of a few of my junior officers by simply stating, "We don't do that here." Although it was an offhand remark made without much intention, it immediately gained traction with the officers and became somewhat of a standard quip among many of the Marines in our unit. Whenever a Marine exhibited behaviors clearly incongruent with our common values, one would only need to say, "We don't do that here," to remind ourselves of the culture we had developed and our pride and commitment to uphold it.

When asked why we accepted or rejected certain behaviors, most of us would refer to our team's cultural norms rather than military regulations or protocols. The social influence of this simple phrase became much more powerful and profound than the legal limitations set by rules and regulations designed to control our behaviors.

–John

REFLECTION

Consider the ways do the following questions reflect the reality of your team's culture:

- ✓ Our team's mission and vision are supported by our culture
- ✓ Our behaviors are congruent (or not) with our shared values
- ✓ Our titles and team structure align with our mission

✓ How we recognize, acknowledge, and reward performance

✓ How we hold ourselves accountable

✓ How we share and handle voice, and how we include and exclude ideas

✓ The words and terms we use

✓ The stories we tell about ourselves and our place in the world

✓ What we revere and what we despise

✓ What behaviors and results we tolerate and what we won't

✓ Who we hire, promote, discipline, and terminate

✓ How we engage with external stakeholders

✓ How we define and deal with success, uncertainty, and failure

✓ How we share the fruits of our labor

How do you describe your team's culture? What do your teammates do that reflects your team's culture? What steps can you take to help better define, shape, and nurture your team's culture?

LEADERS ESTABLISH THE CULTURE . . . EVEN WHEN THE LEADER IS ABSENT

Over the years, I've had the opportunity to speak with retail store managers about the direct connection between the quality of their leadership and the culture developed in each store. My intent was to emphasize the importance of their role in shaping and strengthening that culture, not only from the perspective of legal and policy compliance, but from the perspective of operational effectiveness, team morale, and performance. I stressed the connection between how they lead and the culture they create.

I reminded them that a healthy culture drives performance and the quality of the experience. At the corporate headquarters, we can lay the groundwork for culture building through official communications, policies, decisions, organization, and processes. But the most important builder and protector of each team's

continued

culture is the responsible leader's impact on the social reality within that team. While the company can set them up for success, the reality on the ground at each store creates the conditions for performance and the standards for treatment of every human being who works there.

To illustrate the point, I would tell them that I could visit any one of their stores and, with fifteen minutes of close observation, I'd know a great deal about the quality of their own leadership. I explained I didn't have some type of super-power; I've simply learned that the behavior and performance of a team reflects a team leader's capabilities. If you pay close attention to a range of things, you can learn a lot about the leader.

During one training session, a manager raised his hand. Somewhat concerned, he said, "Um . . . I don't think that is fair. What if I'm not there when you visit our store?"

I smiled and said, "That is precisely the point." I explained, "You see, as a leader, you have the responsibility to establish a culture in your team. You get to hire the right people, onboard them, see to their training and development, look out for their welfare, and then lead them by example, as a servant leader. You have the responsibility to set the example of the behavior and conduct you seek from them. You are responsible for developing their ability to lead. You establish the store's "social DNA." You clarify what matters and what the real standards and expectations are. They will generally act in accordance with that culture, whether you're there or not."

—Sean

Culture is strengthened, or weakened, with every interaction you have with your teammates and with those you serve. Reality is the only thing that counts when it comes to culture; it's not about what you claim is true about what matters; it is the reality that is of greatest consequence. Culture has been defined as the "social DNA" of a team, and it helps shape virtually every aspect of how human beings engage with one another, carry out the mission, and perform. As a leader, you must understand that everything you do or say, and what you don't do and don't say, counts. Every interaction and example you set, on every day and in every way, is an opportunity to strengthen or weaken your team's culture. Be aware and be intentional.

TEAM LEADERSHIP

There is hazard in any attempt to reduce team leadership to a formula. Leading human beings is anything but formulistic. We offer here a summary of the team leadership principles we've presented to help you create a picture of what you can do to lead your team with confidence and competence.

First, ground your leading with the perspective of a servant leader; it is the heart of authentic leadership. Understand, believe in, and commit to your team's mission. Build authentic relationships with your teammates and share leadership responsibilities. And know yourself and manage your behavior, and emotions. Let this servant leadership perspective inform your engagement with the people around you as you determine your best and highest role, in alignment with your team's mission.

Next, take action. We've described tenets that, if acted upon, will materially assist you and your teammates to work together more collaboratively and perform at a higher level. You need to understand your team's mission, cultural expectations, and structure. You need to exhibit excellent interpersonal skills. You need to attend to operational issues that both inhibit and contribute to mission accomplishment. Share these team challenges and opportunities with your teammates and serve them in shouldering the burden.

Finally, work to build a resilient team culture, one that can weather adversity. Help your teammates create, shape, and nurture your team's culture so it becomes living expression of who you are and who you aspire to be.

Leadership principles help guide *what* you need to do as a team leader, but they do not explain *how* you will do it. We've provided insights on each principle in this chapter and throughout the book, but ultimately the *how* is learned and developed through training and experience. Review the principles often, put them into practice consistently, learn from your mistakes, engage with your teammates and adjust. Over time, you will develop the skills needed to master them.

We created the following diagram to assist you as you build, shape, and strengthen a resilient team culture:

Build a Resilient Team Culture

MISSION

- ✓ Set the tone
- ✓ Formulate a common purpose
- ✓ Establish team norms
- ✓ Create team structure
- ✓ Facilitate effective communications
- ✓ Ensure collaborative decision-making
- ✓ Develop a healthy feedback system
- ✓ Manage conflict
- ✓ Conduct timely debriefs
- ✓ Deal with change
- ✓ Obtain mission-essential needs
- ✓ Remove obstacles
- ✓ Supervise performance

Part 6

The Way Ahead

CHAPTER 22

What Now?

W e encourage you to view your personal growth as an adventure. The rate you progress on your leadership development journey will be based on the quality of your interactions with other people. Your ultimate impact and effectiveness as a leader will depend on their response to you. While your leadership goals and intentions may be clear, outcomes are sometimes uncertain and are often difficult to quantify. You may not fully comprehend your influence on those around you until years later, if ever.

A plan, by its very nature, is aspirational. It is a forward-looking, how-to roadmap that connects the dots between your current reality and your destination. But plans are sequential steps that are often difficult to track. They may not stand the test of time and can derail when setbacks occur, or conditions change. Since your journey to authentic leadership has no end, developing a plan to get there can feel like an exercise in futility.

A mindset, on the other hand, is inspirational. A mindset is a strategic how-to-be approach to move toward a worthy goal. A mindset is anchored by commitments and habits of thought and behavior and is biased toward action. A mindset is highly resilient and can withstand changing circumstances. Develop a mindset to move forward, not a detailed plan to get there.

MEASURING SUCCESS

You may wonder how you will know whether your leadership is having a positive impact on your team. Walking on a treadmill is great exercise. But a treadmill only records effort; it does not measure progress. Just because you're walking doesn't mean you're getting anywhere worthwhile. The same is true of your leadership journey. We hope you will consider, embrace, and apply the principles we have offered in this book. But doing so only reflects the degree to which you follow our guidance; it does not measure your progress toward becoming a better leader. You need to first determine your criteria for success.

Measuring Success

 **MISSION**   **Progress Toward Mission Accomplishment**

Team Commitment and Behaviors

Leader Character and Behaviors

You will determine the metrics you'll use to measure your leadership success. It is difficult to quantify the level of influence you can have on your teammates' behavior and their degree of commitment to the team's mission. However, human behavior and business results are observable and measurable. Focus, then, on you and your teammates' actions and your team's progress toward accomplishing your mission: *What are we saying and what are we doing? To what degree are we making progress toward accomplishing the mission?*

REFLECTION

Ask yourself the following questions regarding your character and behaviors as a leader, including what ways and to what degree:

- ✓ Are you being the person you wish to be?
- ✓ Are you expressing your values through your words and deeds?
- ✓ Are your words and deeds serving your teammates?

Ask yourself the following questions regarding your teammates' behavior, including what ways and to what degree:

- ✓ Are your teammates' words and deeds serving one another positively?
- ✓ Are your teammates sharing power and holding one another accountable?
- ✓ Are your teammates' words and deeds aligned with the mission?

Ask yourself the following questions regarding your team's missions and accomplishments, including what ways and to what degree:

- ✓ Are mission-essential needs being met?
- ✓ Are teammates overcoming challenges and finding new opportunities?
- ✓ Is your team accomplishing its mission?

How will you define success? Will you use terms like *change*, *improvement*, or *achievement*? There are subtle but important differences between altering something, enhancing something, and accomplishing something. Create specific, measurable, and achievable objectives, and word them precisely. Write them down and discuss them with your team; ask to be held accountable and hold your teammates accountable as well. Together, celebrate your achievements, and make changes where you fall short.

DEFINE YOUR LEADERSHIP INTENTIONS

CREATE YOUR PERSONAL LEADERSHIP PHILOSOPHY

I once took part in a leadership development program requiring each participant to create a brief leadership philosophy. At first, I thought the exercise was unnecessary. After a few decades leading teams in the Marines and in the private sector, I thought I knew who I was as a leader. But refining that philosophy and capturing its essence on a single sheet of paper for my teammates to read was a different matter entirely. It required me to look deep, to clarify exactly who I was as a leader and capture what I truly believed. I understood the importance of the assignment. How can my teammates be clear about me as a leader if I'm not clear in my own mind?

It was to be a living document, subject to change as time went on. It had to be written in the simplest language possible. Crafting it was a challenge because I had to drill down to get to the essence of what I truly believed about who I was as a leader, about what my teammates could expect of me, and about what I expected of them. I had to clarify the behavior I would tolerate and what I would *not* tolerate. After several drafts and a couple of late nights, I ended up with a document that I felt accurately captured my core leadership beliefs.

When I returned to work, I shared my leadership philosophy with each member of my team, in one-on-one meetings. I wanted to ensure I was being clear with them. I also shared it with some of my colleagues and my own CEO. I have used it in many ways over the years, including interviews with candidates so that I could determine whether it resonated with them and whether they felt they would be a fit with our team.

Here is what I created:

MY LEADERSHIP PHILOSOPHY

Serving as a leader is a privilege. I take this responsibility very seriously and view it as a sacred trust. I will lead with humility and by example, as a servant, through my actions and words. I am not your "boss." I will challenge, inspire, teach, and coach, but I will never "boss" you.

You and I no longer act solely as individuals. We now operate as members of a team and are accountable to our teammates. Always keep that in mind. I will engage with you as an individual, but I will always consider your performance in the team context.

I will be trustworthy and will trust you until proven wrong. Truth, integrity, character, and commitment are key to our success. I will give you my best effort, with energy and passion. I will ask the same of you.

We were retained to do far more than just get the job done. We are here to help this company navigate through uncertainty. We will be initiators, problem solvers, opportunity creators, and both students and teachers.

You are critical to this team's success. I will support your growth and your ability to succeed. I intend this to be the best job you and I ever have, and I will engage with you to hit that goal. Remember: Every day is training day. Teachable moments are all around us. We will take full advantage of these.

Take ownership of your area of responsibility. I will be by your side as a resource.

Take thoughtful action and make timely decisions. Do not fear honest mistakes, as they are the source of important lessons. Act ... Learn ... Act ... Learn.

Everyone you and I encounter will be treated with respect. A critical part of our job is to serve the needs of our associates so that they can serve the customer. Always say "please" and "thank you."

I will ask a lot of you. If I am unclear or unreasonable, or if I appear to be wasting time, energy, or resources, I want you to push back. If I make a mistake or fail to follow through, please tell me. Feedback is critical to us all. My door is always open.

I am tolerant, but I will not tolerate excuses, blame, a lack of integrity, failure to operate as part of the team, failure to prepare, or a refusal to take ownership.

Our success will also depend on shared leadership and on your ability to lead. I will support you in your leadership development and will help you define your role and your opportunities to lead.

—Sean

Your personal leadership philosophy must not be a summary of your thoughts on leadership or an essay *about* leadership, nor should it be a policy document that dictates organizational procedures. Instead, it should be an authentic, intimate, and pragmatic account of how you view your leadership responsibilities, your role as a leader, and your commitments to and expectations of your teammates. Writing your leadership philosophy will compel you to clarify your beliefs for your own benefit and, once completed, will serve to communicate those beliefs to your teammates so they can understand your expectations more clearly and hold you accountable to do what you say you will do. The people you serve are trying to figure out who you are and what you bring to the team, as well as what you expect of them. Avoid the uncertainty; give them a clear picture.

Start from the heart. Draw from your experience and tap into your aspirations for your team. Keep it simple and direct. Write your leadership philosophy in the first and second person—from you to your teammates. Whether you type it or audio or video record it, your leadership philosophy should ultimately be communicated face to face with your teammates.

REFLECTION

- ✓ Compose your leadership philosophy. Take ample time to do this; multiple drafts and revisions are encouraged.

- ✓ Share it with someone you respect and ask for feedback. Adjust accordingly but make sure it accurately reflects an authentic version of you.

- ✓ In what ways has writing your leadership philosophy clarified your beliefs about your leadership responsibilities, your role as a leader, and your commitments to and expectations of your teammates?

- ✓ How will your teammates benefit from understanding your leadership philosophy?

- ✓ How will you benefit from sharing your leadership philosophy with your teammates?

WHAT YOU CAN DO RIGHT NOW TO BECOME A MORE AUTHENTIC LEADER

Throughout this book, we have emphasized the importance of committing fully to your intentional learning journey. This is a key starting place in your leadership development; without commitment, there can be no accountability, and no real forward progress. While a commitment to become a more authentic leader is a good start, it's admittedly too vague to be particularly useful. So, to help you better define what your commitment requires, we offer nine foundational leader commitments that begin with the affirmative words, "I will . . ." We crafted these commitments with care, to challenge you and to shape your perspective as you move toward becoming a more authentic and effective leader. But while commitments are essential, they don't sufficiently inform behaviors; for that reason, we have included a few disciplines under each for you to consider. These disciplines are intentionally broad, requiring you to refine them so that they can be applied in the context of your life.

As you read each leader commitment and the associated disciplines, take some time to reflect. Envision how each would impact you in your world (in your personal, community, and work life) and those of your teammates. Don't simply accept them at face value. Turn them over in your mind. Question them. Test them. Does each commitment and discipline make sense to you? Do you agree with them? To what degree are you willing to make each commitment? Can you do so authentically? If it helps, restate the commitments and disciplines in your own words, so they fit you like a glove, so they fit your team and your realities. We are humble enough to know that we haven't cornered the market on leadership wisdom, so have at it.

These commitments and disciplines are not intended to be restrictive or limiting. On the contrary, as you apply them in your life, you will find them to be expansive, supportive, and liberating. They will serve as your north star as you lead, providing direction and focus as you do the work of an authentic leader: Serve your teammates in alignment with the team's shared mission.

LEADER COMMITMENTS

Leader Commitment #1
I WILL OWN MY LEADERSHIP RESPONSIBILITY

Define yourself as a leader

Carry out your responsibility to lead

Leader Commitment #2
I WILL OWN MY LEADERSHIP DEVELOPMENT

Commit to become a better leader

Learn experientially

Leader Commitment #3
I WILL LEAD AS A SERVANT

Adopt a servant leader perspective

Assume your best and highest role

Lead authentically

Share leadership

Share power

Share the burden

Leader Commitment # 4
I WILL COMMIT TO OUR MISSION

Know and believe in your mission

Commit to accomplishing your mission

Understand your mission in its broader context

Leader Commitment #5

I WILL MASTER MYSELF

Know yourself

Be virtuous

Set a positive example

Maintain your health and well-being

Manage your emotions

Be humble

Leader Commitment #6

I WILL BE RESPONSIBLE AND ACCOUNTABLE

Take full responsibility

Be accountable

Leader Commitment #7

I WILL BE AUTHENTIC WITH MY TEAMMATES

Know your teammates

Stay grounded in the present

Trust and be trustworthy

Treat everyone with dignity and respect

Praise your teammates in public

Correct your teammates in private

Leader Commitment #8

I WILL ALIGN MY TEAMMATES' EFFORTS

Orient your team

Facilitate communications

Facilitate decision-making

Exchange feedback

Manage conflict

Conduct debriefs

Meet your team's mission-essential needs

Identify and remove obstacles

Supervise performance

Leader Commitment #9

I WILL BUILD A RESILIENT TEAM CULTURE

Create, shape, and nurture your team's culture

Uphold your team's standards

Here are a few practical tips to help you apply the related disciplines in your life:

- Replace the words *your teammates* with the actual names of your teammates.

- Give context to each discipline by associating it with real-world events. What is happening with your team today?

- Include tasks you are working on, challenges and opportunities you face, and the environment in which you operate.

Continually assess the degree to which you are putting your commitments to work. Are you truly walking your talk? Open your journal often and list the various ways you express the disciplines—words and deeds that lead others to believe you are following through on the commitment. List the ways your actions could better bring each commitment to life.

Prioritize the disciplines. Which ones are you already doing? Which ones could you do better? Which ones are you not yet doing? Which should you focus on first? As you experience, reflect, and discover along your journey, you may wish to adjust the disciplines. If they are not specific enough or appear to be too difficult or disruptive, simply break them down into small action steps. Walk before you run.

BRING THE LEADER COMMITMENTS TO LIFE

A consistent and thoughtful application of these leader commitments will allow you to engage more fully as an authentic leader in your unique circumstances toward your team's mission.

If you feel the commitments are inspirational, great! Use them as a source of inspiration on your journey. If you believe they are aspirational, that's fine, too! Continue to reach for them, and by so doing, bring them within your grasp. Most important is for you to make them *operational* in your life. Read them. Reflect on them. Prepare to act on them. Then do them—today! Consistent application is required. Perfection in their execution is not required, but you must devote yourself fully and faithfully.

Finally, hold yourself accountable, and enlist someone you trust to provide supportive accountability. Plant a stake in the ground. What leadership commitments will you carry out today, tomorrow, and next week? Ask for feedback and seek assistance from your teammates, a mentor, or a coach. These commitments have no life span; you will never achieve perfection, so continue to dust them off and revisit them. Oh, one more thing: Enjoy the journey! Make this a joyful learning experience.

YOUR CALL TO ACTION

The process of becoming an authentic leader may seem daunting at first. Stick with it. Leadership fundamentals are not particularly difficult to understand, but grasping them is only a preliminary step. The real work that will make a positive difference in your life and in the lives of the people you lead and follow is how you express that understanding in the way you lead with your heart, your head, and your hands.

BE: WHO ARE YOU?

Commit to Becoming an Authentic Leader

We can't overemphasize the importance of *intentionality* in your leadership development. Becoming a more authentic leader must be in the forefront of your mind. Define yourself as a person with leadership responsibilities, adopt a servant leader mindset, embrace the opportunity to lead, lead with love, and challenge yourself to grow.

Clarify Your Core Values and Attend to Your Heart

Clarify your values, beliefs, attitudes, and ethics. Since these directly shape your thoughts and behavior, they matter greatly. Your teammates need to know what you stand for and what you won't stand for. They need to know whether you are a person who deserves to be trusted and whether your motives are ethical and honorable. They care about what you know and what you do, but they need assurance and evidence of your moral character. Think deeply about your values. Understand your beliefs and attitudes about others. Ensure that your ethical principles and the behaviors you exhibit are integrated and consistent with your values. Be a man or woman of character.

Adopt an Explorer's Attitude

Move beyond your comfort zone with a growth mindset. Be courageous and naturally curious so you can discover what behaviors work and don't work. Take reasonable risks, try new approaches, and appreciate that there are no failures—only learning opportunities. You cannot fail.

LEARN: WHAT DO YOU KNOW AND WHAT ARE YOU LEARNING?

Become an Active Student of Leadership

Study leadership broadly. Read about leaders and leadership. Observe those who call themselves leaders and those who are leading. Find opportunities to meet with and talk to leaders. Get a leadership coach; take part in leadership training. As the adage goes, "If you want to be a cowboy, you need to know about cows." So, too, with being a leader—you need to reach a deeper understanding about leadership.

Learn from Your Experiences

Reflect deeply, frequently, and with intention. Whether you are leading or following another's lead, pay attention to what is happening. Consider the "what, so what, now what?" approach. Here's how it works: First, intensely observe (*what* happened?). Next, contemplate its meaning in a broader context (*so what* does it mean?). Then, commit to making changes in your perspective, responses, and behaviors (*now what* will I do?). Finally, create specific, measurable, and achievable goals, and seek the support of a mentor, friend, or teammate to provide timely, constructive feedback and to help hold you accountable.

DO: HOW DO YOU CONDUCT YOURSELF?

Exhibit Leadership Behaviors

Ultimately, your actions are what count when it comes to leading. While your intentions matter in shaping your actions, your actions speak loudest. What your teammates hear you say and see you do (and what you don't say and don't do) have the greatest impact on whether and to what degree they will permit you to influence them. Pay close attention to what works and what doesn't. Abandon behaviors that are not congruent with your values and that don't serve your teammates in furtherance of the team's mission. Adopt behaviors consistent with your values. Work to ensure your words and deeds are authentic and consistent.

Lead and Follow

Seek opportunities to both lead and follow real people in real situations with real consequences. Accept challenging assignments, take the initiative on issues that need to be addressed, and seek out developmental opportunities. Leadership does not require you to be in a position of authority. You can lead anytime and anywhere—in your family, your social group, your community, your workplace. Every relationship that involves people with a shared mission presents leadership opportunities. Never pass up the opportunity to serve others through your leadership. If following, do so with your eyes, ears, and heart open, and drink up the experience.

NO GREATER ACT OF SERVICE

Authentic leaders have a tremendous impact on individual and team performance, as well as on the team's ability to accomplish its mission. Motivation, cooperation, influence, and team culture, are positively impacted through leadership. If you wish to make your life, your family, your workplace, or your community better, engage as an authentic leader. At its core, leadership is about service to others, and there is no greater act of service, no higher calling, than serving others. Every instance in which you engage authentically with another human—whether by listening intently, exhibiting trust and trustworthiness, or putting their needs before yours—seeds in them a desire to do the same for others.

WHAT NOW, LIEUTENANT?

My initial military training seemed to last an eternity: boot camp, officer candidate school, officer candidate school, college, officer basic school, and infantry officer training. Throughout the years, my instructors told me leading Marines in the "real Marine Corps" would be much more difficult than leading peers in a training environment. Their words of warning caused some apprehension to be sure, but I knew I had all the tools necessary to practice my leadership craft. I had honed my technical skills, read dozens of books about leadership, spent countless hours participating in rigorous leadership training exercises, and had even gained experience leading my peers. I was capable and confident, and I relished the thought of the day I would finally get to step in front of the Marines I was expected to lead.

When I arrived at my first duty station, as a newly minted lieutenant, I was assigned a platoon of Marines. This was the day I had prepared for; I had rehearsed in my mind a thousand times what I would say and what I would do.

My initial meeting with my platoon was uneventful. I addressed them as a group, telling them a little about myself and laying out my expectations of them, just as I was taught to do in officer training. The Marines seemed fit and attentive. The day went according to plan.

During the weeks that followed, the idealistic image I had painted in my mind began to unravel. I met with each of my Marines individually to make a personal connection and learn a little about them. Although most were doing well, I learned some were experiencing personal challenges ranging from benign human-resource issues to serious family or substance-abuse problems. I quickly learned some of our training resources were scarce and necessary equipment needed repair. The training plan I had meticulously devised became untenable due to a schedule change directed from higher headquarters. My platoon sergeant—my second in command— didn't measure up to the idealistic version of a sergeant I had created in my mind. Worse yet, I learned that, prior to my arrival, my Marines had been training at an extremely high tempo for months with little time off, and morale was low.

The problems seemed complex and overwhelming. The scenarios I had experienced in training didn't seem to offer the right solutions. I decided to go to my company commander (my immediate supervisor) for some advice. He listened intently as I described the troublesome issues and laid out my concerns. He thought for a moment, smiled broadly, and asked, "What now, lieutenant?"

continued

The question hit me like a ton of bricks. Wasn't it the company commander's responsibility to provide counsel? As I stumbled for an answer, his point became crystal clear. The captain was not shirking his responsibility to be a resource; he was upholding his responsibility to be a mentor. He was helping me learn that leadership is not an academic exercise. There are no schoolbook solutions in the real world. My education, training, and experience had prepared me to succeed, but they would not guarantee success. What happened now was on me.

—John

Leaders have a sacred responsibility to develop leadership in others. When you empower your teammates with real responsibility, trust them to act, and support their efforts, you provide them the opportunity to find their voice as a leader. As you move forward on your leadership journey, take every opportunity to help others develop their own leadership capacity. The payoff is profound, for what you keep to yourself disappears, and what you give to others multiplies.

During your leadership journey, as you intentionally learn and lead from a place of authenticity and service, you will find yourself moving *with* your teammates toward mission accomplishment. Your journey will become the destination, and you will find yourself experiencing a deeper sense of joy as you serve. As you consistently apply your leadership skills in all aspects of your life, you will find yourself serving rather than being served, giving rather than taking, and leading rather than standing on the sidelines.

Your journey of discovery can be a marvelous, inspiring adventure. That is our wish for you. We urge you to approach both your learning journey and your service as a leader with a big heart, open mind, and steady hands. Make *service* the driving force behind your leading as you seek to fulfill your "best and highest role" in support of your teammates and in alignment with your team's mission.

Serve your teammates in your leading. Love them. *Leaders eat last.* Remember?

Our families, teams, organizations, and communities need authentic leaders. You have committed to becoming an authentic leader. Go forth. Serve others. Lead well—and enjoy your journey.

Acknowledgments

During our years of military and civilian leadership, we have been deeply blessed to work alongside and learn from many remarkable and truly authentic leaders. They have influenced us powerfully through their example, and we have been enriched by their wisdom and guidance. In no small measure, these people have shaped who we have become as human beings and leaders by showing us the clear link between who we are and how we lead. This book is dedicated to those leaders. We walk forward with them at our side, and we continue to draw inspiration from their example while striving to conduct ourselves in accordance with their wisdom.

We are deeply grateful to you all. This book is our humble attempt to carry on with the critical personal mission you placed before us: to lead authentically as servants, in accomplishing a worthwhile mission to support others in their own leadership development.

What follows is a sampling of the individuals who impacted us as leaders in powerful ways and the leadership lessons we learned from them.

JOHN

Sergeant Jesse Vadari, USMC: *Know your job and hold your team members accountable to know theirs.*

Sergeant Major Royce Coffee, USMC: *Balance personal ambition with a strong dose of humility.*

Lieutenant General Paul Van Riper, USMC: *Remain true to your values and never compromise your principles.*

Colonel Joe Crookston, USMC: *An educator's role is not to inform students but rather to instill a thirst for knowledge.*

General John Paxton, USMC: *It's not about the leader; it's about the team. Love your followers, and lead as a servant.*

Dr. Jennifer Kafsky: *What you keep to yourself disappears; what you give to others multiplies. Make selflessness your default perspective.*

SEAN

Judith Wilson Munds, my mother: *Choose to make life an adventure. Take personal responsibility to develop your potential. Seek out experiences and learn to overcome adversity to exceed your perceived limits. Don't judge others, but work to understand where they've been and why they act as they do.*

Admiral Leon Edney, USN: *Seek greater challenges to grow and stretch yourself as an individual contributor and as a leader.*

Vice Admiral William Lawrence, USN: *Humility is powerful and compelling. Quiet, unshakeable confidence is earned through adversity. Servant leadership is not a leadership style; it is the very essence of leadership.*

Rear Admiral Tilghman Payne, USN: *Lead by example in all you do. Don't underestimate your capabilities. Believe in and develop your potential and the potential of those around you. Thoughtful performance feedback is a gift and a powerful motivator.*

Brigadier General Richard Walls, USMC: *Get out from behind your desk. Seek the input of those you serve and share your thought process with them. Build relationships and maintain them. Actively raise your next level of leaders.*

About the Authors

JOHN'S JOURNEY

 My grandfather's funeral at Arlington National Cemetery was a pivotal moment for me. As a fatherless teenager who had just lost one of his two "greatest generation" grandfathers—both World War II veterans—the ceremony honoring his service was profound and emotional. When the honor guard's final rifle volley cracked, I looked at the Marine to my left clearing his M-1 Garand rifle and thought, *I want to be that guy.* His bearing, his being, everything he stood for was what I wanted for myself.

From the first day of basic training, which happened to fall on my eighteenth birthday, until I took off the uniform more than two decades later, my service as a Marine was more fulfilling than I could have imagined. I traveled the world, saw the best and worst of humanity, clarified my values, and learned how to be a professional. I learned how to lead and how not to lead.

After twenty-four years as a Marine, I began a new journey as an outdoor educator for the North Carolina Outward Bound School. In one respect, this was a plausible career move, for there are many similarities between the Marine Corps and Outward Bound. Both are mission-driven, values-based organizations steeped in history, culture, and tradition. Both organizations

train people to lead others in challenging circumstances with unknown outcomes, and both place great value on leadership development.

The Marine Corps and Outward Bound are also quite different. The Marine
Corps is a governmental, publicly funded, uniformed military service designed
to win battles; Outward Bound is a private, nonprofit education organization
designed to change lives through challenge and discovery. The image of an
infantry sergeant leading Marines in an attack on an enemy position stands in
stark contrast to an outdoor educator teaching students how to pitch a tent.

During my initial training to become an Outward Bound instructor,
I began to recognize the differences between my and my peer instructors'
backgrounds. Most were in their early twenties, fresh out of college, and just
beginning to find their place in the world. As a married, middle-aged father
of two with a mortgage and a full career behind me, I was somewhat of an
anomaly. My peers frequently asked me about my life experiences—where I
served, what I did, and how I viewed various social, political, and military
issues. I felt quite worldly responding to their questions with confidence and
insight . . . until I was asked: "What's the difference between Marine Corps
leadership and Outward Bound leadership?"

I should have been uniquely qualified to answer this question. After all,
the Marine Corps had provided me with a quarter century of leadership
education, training, and experience. I was taught about leadership, studied
leadership, and practiced leadership. I taught leadership at officer training
schools and did my best to mentor leaders in every unit I served. I was pretty
sure I knew a thing or two about leading and developing leaders.

Here was my challenge: identifying the distinction between Marine Corps
leadership and Outward Bound leadership gave me pause. I had never before
considered where they diverged, and I found myself somewhat perplexed
as I sought to clarify it for myself. Not one to be tongue-tied, I offhand-
edly responded with the first quip that came to mind: "Good leadership is
good leadership"—and then I immediately realized that my flippant response
expressed similarity and not difference.

In my struggle to answer the question, a deeper reflective process began.

How does leadership in the military compare with leadership in outdoor
education? For that matter, how does leadership compare between different

venues or disciplines? Are there fundamental truths? Universal principles? What is "good leadership"?

Throughout the next fifteen years, I found myself in an ideal laboratory to wrestle with these questions. I completed my doctorate in education, specializing in human performance improvement, then spent eleven years teaching outdoor leadership at a small liberal arts college. I moonlighted as an instructor of wilderness medicine, whitewater canoe, whitewater kayak and sea kayak, and I continued to lead wilderness expeditions for Outward Bound. I facilitated corporate team building and executive leadership development programs, engaged in community service as a board member of several nonprofit organizations, became a certified leadership coach, and helped raise two sons. These experiences allowed me to practice and observe leadership from multiple perspectives.

Perhaps my greatest asset in my quest for understanding leadership, however, is the decades-long conversation with a lifelong friend, Sean Georges, who grapples with the same questions.

SEAN'S JOURNEY

My grandfather was a trial lawyer and kept an item in his law office that drew my attention at an early age. It was a bust of Abraham Lincoln, and it triggered my imagination and my curiosity about leadership. My grandfather frequently shared stories about Lincoln's life, and I would learn that Lincoln possessed a mysterious (to me) quality my grandfather called "leadership." Although I didn't understand the concept, I did have a strong sense that it was something special, rare, and extremely valuable. I would later come to appreciate that Lincoln's personality, intelligence, and personal drive, shaped by a great deal of adversity, transformed his life into a remarkable leadership journey. Lincoln's bust now sits on a shelf in my home and continues to inspire me in my lifelong personal journey to explore and develop a deeper understanding of what it means to lead.

In high school, I began to read biographies and histories to gain a greater understanding, and I took part in sports and extracurricular activities. I quickly learned that being given a leadership title did not bring either understanding or wisdom and being named co-captain of the high school football team or president of the student council did not transform me into a leader. Fueled by a strong desire to serve my country, my leadership journey kicked into high gear when I entered the Naval Academy at the age of eighteen. I wanted to gain more than a mere academic understanding; I wanted to know, in my bones, who I was as a leader. I knew this understanding could only come from an immersive experience based on a solid foundation which combined both following and leading.

The Naval Academy proved to be an intensive leadership "learning laboratory" in the broadest sense. Annapolis offered a range of direct leadership experiences and a foundational education that would materially shape how I would think about leadership and how I would ultimately lead. Through close observation and direct experience, I began to understand what leadership is and what it isn't. During those four challenging years, I served alongside and observed some of the most remarkable people I would ever encounter. Together, we learned from military veteran instructors and faculty with extensive combat service, including some who had endured the Vietnam prisoner-of-war experience.

I learned much from watching closely those who led well and those who led poorly. Along the way, I learned how leadership works; what leadership looks and feels like from the perspective of both a follower and a leader. I learned that one's ability to lead is not related to rank or personal accomplishments. I confirmed that a leader's character is revealed in their consistent behavior, and character is what ultimately determines the depth of a leader's impact on their teammates and on the team's mission. I identified the leadership behaviors that most moved and inspired me. I also identified those behaviors and conduct that did not inspire or elevate. In short, I began to clarify what I considered *authentic* in leaders and in leadership.

After accepting a commission in the Marine Corps, and during my thirteen years on active duty, I continued to experience both leading and following, and tried to pay close attention along the way. My military experiences cemented the core leadership fundamentals of *responsibility* and *service*, and the opportunity to lead Marines was an honor and privilege I will always treasure. The importance of team and organizational culture, and the responsibility to lead from a servant's perspective, became a core part of who I am and how I engage with others.

When I made the challenging transition from the Marines to the "civilian world," I faced intensely personal questions about who I was as a leader in this new context. How do I lead without rank, uniform, or a clear position of authority? How would I lead in this very different culture, with different missions, values, and culture? What is the essence of leading people? What are the universal principles surrounding leadership, regardless of culture and mission?

Finding those answers, through experience and study, has been the latest chapter in my ongoing, ever-unfolding, leadership journey. For the past twenty years, since leaving the Marines, I have been fortunate to serve as a member of the executive leadership team of a publicly traded national retailer, primarily as its legal and human resources advisor. In alignment with my personal mission to serve in all aspects of life, I have continued to seek out ways to serve my community through nonprofit work. These experiences have continued to stretch and deepen my understanding of who I am as a leader and what it takes to lead, regardless of the nature of the team's mission. I now have a deeper understanding of the individual learning journey each of us must undertake to shoulder our personal leadership responsibilities and to develop our leadership competence and confidence. My intentional learning journey continues.